ACTIVITY-BASED COSTING AND MANAGEMENT

Activity-based costing and management

Ernest Glad

BSc (Hons) MCom CA(SA) ACMA
Management consultant, Auckland, New Zealand

Hugh Becker

DCompt CA(SA)
Professor in Department of Applied Accountancy, University of South Africa

British edition edited by Mike Partridge, MBA, FCMA, University of Brighton
and Lew Perren, DMS, MBA, MBCS, University of Brighton

JOHN WILEY & SONS
Chichester · New York · Brisbane · Toronto · Singapore

© Juta & Company Limited 1995

Published by arrangement with JUTA & COMPANY LIMITED
PO Box 14373
KENWYN
7790
Cape Town
REPUBLIC OF SOUTH AFRICA

This revised edition published 1996 by John Wiley & Sons Ltd,
Baffins Lane, Chichester,
West Sussex PO19 1UD, England

National   01243 779777
International (+44) 1243 779777

e-mail (for orders and customer service enquiries): cs-books@wiley.co.uk
Visit our Home Page on http://www.wiley.co.uk
           or http://www.wiley.com

Other Wiley Editorial Offices

John Wiley & Sons, Inc., 605 Third Avenue,
New York, NY 10158-0012, USA

Jacaranda Wiley Ltd, 33 Park Road, Milton,
Queensland 4064, Australia

John Wiley & Sons (Canada) Ltd, 22 Worcester Road,
Rexdale, Ontario M9W 1L1, Canada

John Wiley & Sons (Asia) Pte Ltd, 2 Clementi Loop #02-01,
Jin Xing Distripark, Singapore 129809

British Library Cataloguing in Publication Data

A catalogue record for this book is available from the British Library

ISBN 0-471-96331-3

Printed and bound in Great Britain by Bookcraft (Bath) Ltd
This book is printed on acid-free paper responsibly manufactured from sustainable forestation,
for which at least two trees are planted for each one used for paper production.

Preface

ABC may be used in common parlance to indicate a degree of simplicity, but as an acronym for Activity-based Costing, it introduces some of the most revolutionary and fundamental changes in management accounting theory and practice.

What originally appeared to be simply a new method of tracing costs to products has led to the development of an entirely new philosophy referred to as Activity-based Costing and Management (ABC & M). In this text a holistic approach is proposed to fundamental issues such as the management of cost, time, quality, funds and constraints through the use of ABC & M. ABC & M is therefore not just a new way of computing business figures but requires a fundamental understanding of all management issues. It is about understanding and not about calculations.

Throughout this book it is accepted that accounting, as is the case in marketing and other organisational efforts, should focus primarily on the *raison d'être* of the organisation — the customer. The realisation that everything the organisation does is aimed at meeting the customer's requirements, is of paramount importance in the design and development of accounting systems.

ABC & M not only exposes the shortcomings of traditional accounting systems but proposes to:

- More accurately determine product costs and the costs of a multitude of other cost objects such as customers, processes, market segments or distribution channels.
- Engender a better understanding and greater transparency of operational processes, activities and cost structures, mainly owing to the particular analytical methodology involved.
- Focus on the outputs of the organisation rather than on the mere measurement of the consumption of resources.
- Expose the shortcomings of functionally structured organisational reporting and replace it with process-oriented, boundary-free structures which have the objective of delivering what the customer wants.
- Incorporate the wealth of non-financial information which is usually an earlier, and often more accurate, indicator of changes in organisational performance.
- Produce timely, relevant and readily understandable management accounts to support decision making.
- Link strategic direction and planning to operational reporting and develop a strategic support methodology by interpreting, measuring and reporting on critical success factors.

- Foster an improved cost management philosophy, *inter alia* through the elimination of all forms of wastage in the organisation and the identification of value-adding and non-value-adding activities in the organisation.
- Move the emphasis away from mere cost measurement and rather focus on the understanding and interpretation of cost structures. This enables organisations to better predict and control future costs.

The approach of ABC & M is not a theoretical one but a practical one which has been tried, tested and shaped by numerous installations. This is particularly apt when ABC is applied to value chain principles and the use of residual income theory, as explained in Chapter 5. We believe that this approach may have far-reaching effects on accounting systems in the future as it provides answers to many perplexing problems.

This book is not merely a collection of new cost measurement techniques but emphasises the philosophies the modern accountant must adopt to help the organisation add value to its shares. It is clear that organisations which do not adapt to the new methodologies will, in future, experience substantial difficulties in being competitive and remaining in business.

It must be realised that management accounting is not subservient to financial accounting but is a subject in its own right — albeit serving a different audience, namely management.

Acknowledgements

Many people deserve thanks for inspiring, motivating, contributing and influencing us in the writing of this text. In addition, we thank our families, the publishers and the editor. Special recognition must be given to Kevin Dilton-Hill for his contribution over the past few years in helping to clarify and crystallise our thoughts and concepts and for revising and constructively criticising parts of this text.

Finally, we would greatly appreciate comments and suggestions from readers.

THE AUTHORS

Contents

1

Shortcomings of traditional cost accounting

INTRODUCTION

Accounting systems, and particularly management accounting systems, have shown relatively little change in the last century or two. However, several important events occurred during the last decade which are dramatically changing the face of management accounting. Researchers and practitioners of management accounting all over the world are seeking improved methods and philosophies to measure and influence the financial behaviour of organisations.

This book deals predominantly with one of these developments, namely Activity-based Costing and Management (ABC & M) and its place among the many new techniques and methods which management could use to influence organisational fortunes. The use of ABC & M should not be seen as a panacea for all organisational problems, but as one of the critical tools in a holism of approaches which management may require in order to manage organisational affairs.

This chapter gives a synopsis of the historical developments which led to the traditional systems which could be found in most organisations in the mid 1980s. It also explains why the traditional approach is untenable in a modern world-class company. The requirements of a modern cost and management accounting system are identified and then explained in the rest of the book.

HISTORICAL DEVELOPMENT OF COST ACCOUNTING: A SYNOPSIS

Origins of accounting

Financial and numerical record-keeping of transactions, obligations and assets has been taking place for thousands of years. Commercial records were found in the ruins of Babylon; records of the Roman government dating back to 200 BC contain classifications of receipts and expenses into different categories (income and expense accounts).

During the Middle Ages developments in the accounting field took place mainly at the insistence of government and church officials. The first double-entry books known to exist date from 1340. These books reveal an excellent double-entry methodology, indicating that the system must have been in use for some considerable time.

In 1494 a Venetian monk, Luca Pacioli, explained the double-entry process in a book on mathematics. This publication, containing a comprehensive exposition of debit and credit principles and interaction, earned Pacioli the distinction of being the pioneer of double-entry bookkeeping.

After Pacioli's work, texts on the subject appeared in Germany, France and England. These early texts, however, only referred to buying and selling activities. The main objective of record-keeping was not for management purposes such as the comparison of costs and revenues, but the accountability of steward to master, the fixing of selling prices and the ascertaining of profit and loss.

Cost accounting

As with bookkeeping and accounting, the origin of cost accounting is unknown. With the growth in the 14th century of domestic industries — work done at home by artisans for capitalists — the need for some form of industrial accounting arose. Attempts to keep manufacturing accounts have been traced to this period. The capitalists needed to control the flow of materials to and from outside workers, to relate amounts paid to the workers to their individual productivity, and to check the profitability of different activities.

The rapid development of British industry due to the use of machines in the late 18th and early 19th century, known as the Industrial Revolution, replaced the domestic system with a factory system and resulted in phenomenal growth in production. The Industrial Revolution led to a vast improvement in accounting systems. A more intense and complex manufacturing and business environment demanded more accurate financial records, including new types of records and a serious need for cost accounting and budgetary control. Accountants had to respond to these demands.

Although manuals for double-entry bookkeeping were common before the 19th century, no proof of proper costing methods could be found until approximately 1830 in England when Charles Babbage presented a paper that stressed the need for serious cost accounting.

In the latter part of the 19th century and early 20th century developments in the cost accounting field were mainly attributable to engineers, who established concepts such as production centres, idle capacity charges, analysis of costs into fixed and variable components, setting and using of standards, and flexible budgets.

It is generally accepted that the present-day factory cost accounting structure was established before World War I. From the 1930s the magnitude of distribution costs compelled cost accountants to extend their production costing techniques to distribution activities. Costs were thus accumulated and allocated on bases such as tons warehoused, order size, method of delivery and specific related office activities.

As could be expected, cost control was relaxed during World War II. This arose from the well-known phenomenon that a war economy is not a controlled economy — emphasis is placed on production of all products that are deemed necessary, normally on excessive scales, and cost control is disregarded to a major extent. After the end of the war, however, increased competition necessitated proper cost control measures. This period also witnessed the development of expense-centre accounting by retailers and the creation of managerial accounting, focusing on corporate goals and performance measures.

World War II provided the stimulus for the development of operations research as well. This term was used by scientists in the USA and UK military who studied and disseminated military operations and logistics by applying mathematics. Operations research has since been designated to analyse complicated management problems. Applications which arose from operations research include inventory theory, queuing theory (waiting line), linear and non-linear programming, dynamic programming, modelling and probability theory.

Subsequently, uniform cost systems have generally been in use worldwide with regard to production and, to a lesser extent, distribution cost control and all related decision making. The main focus remained, however, on manufacturing cost. Conventional costing systems mainly focus on allocating cost of materials, labour and factory overheads to products, with no allocation for other overheads. Factory overheads are allocated to products according to a two-stage process on a labour or machine-hour basis (the plant-wide overhead allocation basis or so-called "peanut butter approach").

This approach worked well in its time as costs other than materials, factory labour and factory overheads were insignificant in relation to total organisational cost. This is portrayed by the following table of industrial income and concomitant expenditure (analysed into its major cost elements) in the USA from 1929 to 1940[1]:

TABLE 1.1: INCOME AND EXPENDITURE OF US INDUSTRIES 1929–1940

	$m	%
Total industrial income	625 971	100,0
Materials, fuel, supplies, etc	440 703	70,4
Salaries of employees	105 544	16,9
Replacement of plant	20 097	3,2
Interest and rent	9 401	1,5
Salaries of management	11 118	1,8
Taxes	17 603	2,8
Dividends to owners	21 505	3,4
	625 971	100,0

It is important to note from Table 1.1 that manufacturing-related costs (materials, salaries of employees and replacement of plant) constitute well over 90 % of total cost. A traditional cost system focusing on these main cost elements, using labour as a method of allocating overheads, could therefore calculate product costs fairly accurately .

Based on Table 1.1, a set of financial statements of a manufacturing concern could hypothetically be presented as in Table 1.2.

TABLE 1.2: ABRIDGED FINANCIAL STATEMENTS OF A MANUFACTURING CONCERN (CIRCA 1940)

Income statement	£	%	Comments
Sales	5 000 000	100,0	
Less: Manufacturing cost	4 435 000	88,7	1
Direct materials	3 250 000	65,0	2
Direct labour	750 000	15,0	3
Factory overheads	435 000	8,7	4
— Rent	25 000	0,5	
— Depreciation	160 000	3,2	5
— Other	250 000	5,0	
Gross profit	565 000	11,3	
Other expenses (selling, admin, etc)	205 000	4,1	6
Profit before interest and tax	360 000	7,2	
Interest	50 000	1,0	7
Profit before tax	310 000	6,2	
Taxes	140 000	2,8	
Distributable profit	170 000	3,4	8

Table 1.2 continued on next page

TABLE 1.2: Continued			
Balance sheet	**£**	**%**	**Comments**
Fixed assets	1 600 000	52	9
Current assets	1 500 000	48	
Raw materials and WIP	800 000	25	10
Finished goods	500 000	16	
Debtors	200 000	7	
Total assets	3 100 000	100	
Liabilities	1 100 000	35	11
Net assets	2 000 000	65	

Comments
1. Major proportion of total cost.
2. Substantial material cost.
3. Significant labour cost.
4. Approximately 10 % of manufacturing cost.
5. Low depreciation charge.
6. Almost insignificant non-manufacturing overheads.
7. Interest rate approximately 5 %.
8. Return on owners' funds approximately 8,5 % (satisfactory at the time).
9. Relatively low investment in mechanisation; mostly non-mechanised production processes.
10. Relatively high investment owing to high proportional material cost, low stock turnover and slow delivery systems.
11. Low gearing.

The position of cost accounting in this environment is thus under-standable. Conventional standard costing systems and conventional budgeting systems (also with a manufacturing cost focus) fulfilled a useful purpose. In general, cost accounting supported financial accounting — its primary objective was to supplement financial and taxation information, especially with regard to stock valuation and the short-term focus on financial period instead of the longer-term view of product life cycles.

The historical cost accounting systems can be regarded as appropriate for the era and the environment in which they were applied: proportionately high direct labour inputs; limited, simple product lines; low overheads; relatively expensive recording and processing of data.

CHANGES IN THE BUSINESS ENVIRONMENT SINCE 1940

The business environment changed dramatically after the 1940s. The world started rebuilding its infrastructures and production capacity after the devastating effects of World War II. Commodity prices started fluctuating considerably, especially as the gold standard (gold at \$32 an ounce) was no longer applicable. International trade in commodities flourished due to improved transportation. Fixed exchange rates between countries came under pressure and most countries adopted a floating exchange rate. This resulted in volatile and structural changes in prices of goods and services and a consequent striving by product developers to engineer material cost out of products. For example, the mass of motor vehicles, as of most other products, has been drastically reduced over the past few decades; alloys have been developed that cost up to one hundred times less than the traditional material used.[2] Smaller quantities of cheaper materials became the design criterion.

Improved communication and transportation systems brought about a much more competitive environment. Spending on marketing, communication and distribution costs soared. Companies became specialists in distribution (eg frozen products) and transportation of goods over long distances. Many "new" costs appeared such as market and other research, prototyping, training, etc. These costs may have existed earlier, but much more has been spent on these aspects in the last few decades.

The manufacturing environment was characterised by a move towards increased mechanisation and automation. People were replaced by machines and robots. Information technology was increasingly used in the production and development processes. Computer-aided design/computer-aided manufacturing systems (CAD/CAM), flexible manufacturing systems (FMS), numerically controlled machines (NCM), etc became commonplace in many manufacturing installations. More sophisticated manufacturing systems were introduced such as materials requirements planning (MRP I) and manufacturing resource planning systems (MRP II). This necessitated increased investment by organisations and consequently higher capital structures.

Information technology changed the way organisations conducted business. Large volumes of products, customers, etc required better planning systems for their movement and control. The increase in the complexity of organisational hierarchical structures required more controls and reporting between the levels of the organisation. This laid the foundation for a burgeoning bureaucracy in most organisations.

The above and other developments led to cost structures that differ considerably from the historical illustration quoted above. Considering the above developments, the financial statements of a modern organisation, striving to be a world-class company, can be hypothetically depicted as in Table 1.3.

TABLE 1.3: ABRIDGED FINANCIAL STATEMENTS OF A MANUFACTURING CONCERN (CIRCA 1990)			
Income statement	**£**	**%**	**Comments**
Sales	5 000 000	100,0	
Less : Manufacturing cost	2 750 000	55,0	1
Direct materials	1 500 000	30,0	2
Direct labour	350 000	7,0	3
Factory overheads	900 000	18,0	4
— Rent	75 000	1,5	
— Depreciation	560 000	11,2	5
— Other	265 000	5,3	
Gross profit	2 250 000	45,0	
Marketing, distribution and admin.	1 520 000	30,4	6
Profit before interest and tax	730 000	14,6	
Interest	400 000	8,0	7
Profit before tax	330 000	6,6	
Taxation	130 000	2,6	
Distributable profit	200 000	4,0	8
Balance sheet			
Fixed assets	2 800 000	68,3	9
Current assets	1 300 000	31,7	
Raw materials and WIP	250 000		10
Finished goods	550 000		11
Debtors	500 000		12
Total assets	4 100 000	100,0	
Liabilities	3 100 000	75,6	13
Interest-bearing debt	2 500 000		
Trade creditors	600 000		14
Net assets	1 000 000	24,4	15

Comments
1. Considerably reduced since 1940s.
2. Engineered down. Effect of quantity and price reduction.
3. Replaced by technology cost (depreciation and maintenance).
4. Increased, mainly due to increased mechanisation.
5. Technology costs higher; shorter economic and technological life spans of equipment.
6. Vast increases due to increased advertising, increased spending on information technology, distribution, customer services, etc.
7. Increased rates, increased investment requirements, higher gearing.

8.   Return on equity higher because of inflation, higher gearing and risk.
9.   Increased investment in technology and mechanisation.
10.   Considerably reduced because of lower consumption and better methodologies (just-in-time practices; material requirements planning).
11.   Increased investment due to increased variety, distribution and marketing channels.
12.   Increases due to competitive forces.
13.   Increases due to higher accepted gearing.
14.   Increases due to competitive forces.
15.   Lower equity due to market acceptability and higher fixed asset cover (by debt).

TRADITIONAL COST SYSTEMS IN THE MODERN ENVIRONMENT

Some very important conclusions can be drawn from the above in terms of the applicability of traditional cost accounting systems:

*   Product costing based on manufacturing costs alone today represents an unacceptably low proportion of total cost. Non-manufacturing product costs, such as product selling and product distribution expenses, are ignored for product costing purposes. This could lead to significant cross-subsidisation of costs as the consumption of the latter costs is not known. An ABC system addresses the treatment of all overhead-related costs. Material costs will still be treated as direct costs, except that **all** costs incurred in bringing the product to its current state and location will be included.
*   Labour, as a basis for assigning manufacturing overhead, is irrelevant as it is significantly less than overhead and many overheads do not bear any relationship to labour cost or labour hours. Using the labour base to assign overheads could thus severely distort product costs.
*   The cost of technology (improved, but complex production processes, eg robotics, computer-aided design, computer-assisted manufacturing and flexible manufacturing systems) is treated as a period cost and consequently expensed on a straight-line basis, irrespective of use. This cost is thus not assigned to products based on usage. Moreover, direct (labour) cost is replaced by an indirect (machine) cost.
*   Service-related costs have increased considerably in the last few decades. Professional services, banking services, insurance services and several internal services, such as personnel and accounting services, have expanded considerably in the past few decades. Costing for these services was non-existent. A much greater awareness exists among the providers of these services that their "products" also need to be costed to determine profitability. The only real difference between service and manufacturing businesses is that the product in a service business cannot be stored and inventory valuation is thus of no concern.

- Customer-related cost (finance, discounts, distribution, selling, after-sales service, etc) are not related to the product cost object. Customer profitability has become as crucial as product profitability.
- Direct labour is also replaced to some extent by information technology and systems. These costs are treated similarly to organisational over-heads and not related to products or other cost objects, such as customers.
- Costs affected or driven by time (interest and inflation) have increased significantly, yet time does not feature in traditional cost systems as a cost driver. Interest cost is treated as another period cost, whereas it may contribute significantly towards bringing the product (or customer) to its current status.
- The traditional short-term focus of the financial year (12 months) is still intact, yet most products and technologies have life cycles exceeding many accounting periods.
- Vastly increased competition world-wide, mainly brought about by increased productivity, economies of scale, better communication technology, improved transportation and marketing skills, have led to substantially increased marketing costs.
- Greater variety, diversity and complexity of products are not taken into consideration in traditional systems.
- A much more sophisticated market, which calls for the production of goods and rendering of services desired by the customer/client, and not those thought proper by the supplier, accentuates the lack of customer focus in traditional systems.

One of the more important paradigm shifts in cost accounting has been the utilisation of the factor which influences cost, namely the cost driver, to determine product costs and to serve as a mechanism for managing costs.

These and other issues have led to many commentators questioning the validity and applicability of traditional cost systems in the modern business environment. A lack of essential innovation in the field of cost and management accounting over the past 50 years has led to a situation where this supposed management tool fails to meet the inherent demands created by the changed environment.

RELEVANCE LOST

The undesirable state of affairs described above, evoked, *inter alia*, the following statements by Johnson and Kaplan in their book *Relevance lost: The rise and fall of management accounting*[3]:

- "Management accounting information is produced too late, too aggregated, and too distorted to be relevant for managers' planning and control decisions.

- Management accounting systems:
  - do not provide detailed information on process efficiencies,
  - focus too narrowly on inputs, such as direct labour, that are relatively insignificant in today's production environment, and
  - fail to provide accurate product costs."

Management accounting systems not only fail to provide timely, relevant information, but they also distract managers' attention from the key factors important for production efficiencies and distort the costs of individual products. The latter deficiency is caused by the simplistic measures which are applied when allocating costs to products — usually based on direct labour — which do not represent the demands made by each product on the enterprise's resources. This practice provides biased product cost information and brings about major cross-subsidisation of some products by others which, in turn, leads to misguided management decisions on aspects such as product pricing, product sourcing, product mix and responses to rival products. Furthermore, existing systems are regarded as restrictive by managers who want to streamline operations, boost productivity and implement advanced manufacturing techniques and modern information technology.

Johnson and Kaplan[3] also refer to another extremely important issue, namely that of contracting managers' horizons to the short-term cycle of the monthly income statement. Financial accounting systems treat many expenses as period costs even though such expenses will mainly benefit future periods, eg outlays for new products, improved processes, preventive maintenance, long-term marketing positioning, employee training and development of new systems. Pressure to meet short-term profit goals can then result in managers cutting back on these discretionary expenses which are, in fact, important investments to safeguard the future of the enterprise. Monthly management accounts compiled in accordance with practices employed for external reporting can thus produce increased profits while the long-term economic health of the enterprise has been compromised.

The concern about the ills of traditional cost accounting is appropriately summarised in the introduction to the book *The Goal: Excellence in Manufacturing*[4]:

> "Almost everyone who has worked in a plant is at least uneasy about the use of cost accounting efficiencies to control our actions. Yet few have challenged this sacred cow directly."

CONCLUSION

In summary, to be effective and appropriate, modern cost accounting systems and information should:

— resemble the physical business processes and not necessarily the functional proceedings;
— be detailed enough to ascertain reasonably true cost;
— provide information for life-cycle decision making;
— incorporate time as an important cost driver;
— provide a multi-dimensional focus on a multiplicity of cost objects such as customers, products, services, functions, processes and activities;
— incorporate physical measures such as quality, productivity and capacity, and follow the physical flow of the product or other cost object;
— have not only an input focus on cost but also an output focus (what has been achieved with those costs);
— measure wastage and induce the elimination of wastage;
— identify non-value-adding processes and expenditure;
— focus less on cost tracking and reporting and more on cost planning and control;
— entail value-added management accounting and focus on future value creation;
— use modern technology;
— reflect all special attributes attached to individual products; and
— support every key business decision, including sourcing, pricing, investment justification, efficiency and productivity measures, product elimination and new product introduction.

SOURCES CONSULTED

1. Kimball, DS & Kimball, DS. *Principles of Industrial Organization*, 6th edition. New York: McGraw-Hill, 1947.
2. News from the world of medicine: Dental breakthrough. *Readers Digest*, July 1993:11.
3. Johnson, HT & Kaplan, RS. *Relevance lost: The rise and fall of management accounting*. Boston, Mass: Harvard, 1987.
4. Goldratt, EM & Cox, J. *The Goal: Excellence in Manufacturing*. New York: North River Press, 1984.
5. *Encyclopaedia Britannica*. Chicago: William Benton, 1969.
6. Solomons, D. The historical development of costing, in *Studies in Cost Analysis*, 2nd edition. London: Sweet & Maxwell, 1968:3–49.
7. Emore, JR & Ness, JA. The slow pace of meaningful change in cost systems. *Journal of Cost Management*, Winter 1991:36–45.
8. Eiler, R, Goletz, W & Keegan, D. Is your cost accounting up to date? *Harvard Business Review*, Jul-Aug 1982:133–139.
9. Porter M. *Competitive Advantage*. New York: Free Press, 1985.
10. Johnson, HT. Activity-based management: Past, present and future. *Engineering Economist*, Spring 1991:219–238.

2

Conceptual framework of an activity-based costing and management system

INTRODUCTION

The objective of this chapter is to explain the important concepts underlying activity-based costing and management (ABC & M) and the structure or framework of the system. A proper understanding of these concepts is essential as it forms the basis of proficiency in ABC & M and of the practical implementation and operation of the system. Other relevant concepts will be explained in the context to which they apply.

The chapter also sets out the logic of the cost accounting process in the ABC & M system. The approach uses the activity which relates to processes or other constructs as a base of measurement. The objective is to determine the cost of a multiplicity of cost objects which are the domain of activity-based costing.

Due to the nature of the information used in the cost accounting process (financial and non-financial) and the fact that all facets of the business need to be (performance) evaluated and managed, several management concerns and systems can be integrated into the activity-based management system.

The approach which combines activity-based costing and activity-based management is thus referred to as Activity-Based Costing and Management (ABC & M) in this book.

VALUE CHAIN

An enterprise's activities convert inputs into outputs; value is added to inputs in order to convert them into outputs (products and/or services) which are purchased and used or consumed by customers. The chain of activities that is performed to add value to inputs in order to arrive at the final outputs, is referred to as the value chain. This concept was originally identified and defined by Porter[1].

If an enterprise wishes to enjoy a competitive advantage it must carry out its activities in a more cost-effective way than its competitors do. It is therefore clear that such an enterprise needs to have a value chain in which:

— there are a minimum number of activities;
— all activities are effective; and
— all activities are performed at a relatively low cost.

Porter classified the full value chain into nine interrelated primary and support activities. **Primary activities** can be related to actions which the organisation performs to satisfy external demands while **secondary activities** are performed to serve the needs of internal "customers".

Porter[1] depicts the value chain, comprising the above interrelated primary and secondary activities, as in Figure 2.1.

Figure 2.1: Porter's value chain

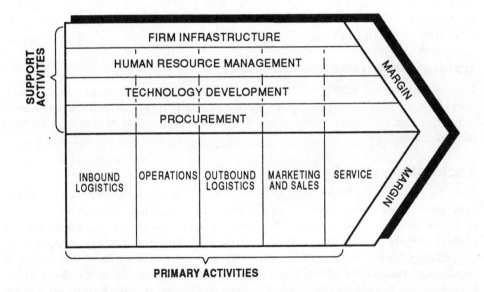

Primary activities are the fundamental activities performed by an organisation in order to be operative. They are:

— inbound logistics;
— operations;
— outbound logistics;
— marketing and sales;
— service.

Secondary activities are support activities, ie those activities required to ensure the efficient performance of the primary activities. Support activities are:

— infrastructure;
— human resources management;
— technology development;
— procurement.

The different value chain activities can be briefly described as follows:

Infrastructure

This consists of the the management structure which services the whole organisation as well as structures such as reception, general postal services, messengers, financial accounting and other general activities. An attempt to trace these costs to any specific cost object will result in an inordinate amount of work. The total amount of such cost should be relatively small in comparison with total cost and this cost is usually considered to be untraceable. The cost of the physical infrastructure (plant, equipment, etc) is considered part of the cost of activities where the infrastructure is used.

Human resources management

This is the basic activity of overseeing the acquisition, maintenance and severance of staff and principally services the primary activities. Personnel departments, in-house medical services and even sports clubs may be part of this major activity.

Technology development

The development of technology today may require large sums of money, take place over a lengthy period of time and ultimately benefit a multitude of users in the organisation. This cost must thus be seen as any capital project which cannot be charged to users before the project is operative. Technology development cost could thus be capitalised and expensed to users over the useful life of the project. Cost of operating technology must, however, be traced to users on a usage basis. An example may be a large computer project which may take several years to complete. Users will only benefit from the project once it is operative and there is no point in charging this cost before such time.

Procurement

The procurement activity services the organisation as a whole by acquiring all necessary goods and services which the organisation may require. If the activity is specifically related to the acquisition of, say, raw materials it could be seen as part of the inbound logistics process, ie a primary activity. If, however, the procurement activity cannot be linked to purchases for primary activities, it will be considered a secondary (support) activity.

Inbound logistics

Inbound logistics cover all the activities performed to have goods and services available for the operational processes as and when they will be required. This may include buying, transport, receiving, inspection, storage, etc.

Operations

These are the operations the organisation performs to convert its raw materials or products into a state for resale. In the case of a manufacturing concern these may be various production-related activities such as production control, machining, finishing, etc. For a retail business these may be the merchandising and display activities used to offer goods to customers for sale.

Outbound logistics

These are the activities performed to move merchandise between the seller and the purchaser. They may include selection, scheduling, transport, etc of deliveries. Some businesses such as cash-and-carry wholesalers may, for example, not have such activities as these tasks are performed by the customer.

Marketing

This includes all the activities performed to create a demand for the organisation's products and services and includes advertising, sales, market research, etc.

Service

Service pertains to the services rendered to the customer. These include financing services such as financing the outstanding balance, or after-sales service to products, or services to handle customer queries and complaints, etc.

The above value chain activities can, to a greater or lesser extent, be found in most businesses. The value chain serves as a useful mechanism to analyse an organisation in order to determine what activities it performs to convert inputs to outputs. It also helps to develop a good understanding of the primary and support activities.

In contrast, the customary functional divisions within businesses are principally :

— warehousing;
— production;

— marketing;
— distribution;
— administration.

This view is normally reflected in the hierarchical structures along which organisations are organised. It fails, however, to reflect the processes which the organisation executes to service its customers and represents a more vertical perspective of an organisation.

PROCESSES

Businesses are mostly organised and managed along the above-stated functional lines. However, the procurement, production and disposal of a product would normally require business processes across these functional lines. (An overall business therefore comprises a network of such business processes, which are performed to achieve its objective.) Consequently, if the cost system is designed and operated along functional lines, the real cost of individual business processes will be indeterminable. Also, it will be difficult to isolate ineffective, costly and/or unnecessary activities. This is sometimes referred to as the "silo" view of the business. Each functional executive primarily understands his own function (silo) and has little knowledge of what happens outside his function. The process view requires a thorough understanding of what happens throughout the process, irrespective of the function in which it takes place.

Figure 2.2 reflects a few processes and indicates where the activities relating to them are performed (e.g. procurement of raw materials could require that the following activities be carried out: requisitioning, ordering, inspection (of goods on receipt), issuing of goods received notes, conveying to stores, storing, checking of creditors' invoices, and settling creditors' accounts):

Figure 2.2: Process matrix

Process	Functions (in departments)				
	Warehousing	Production	Marketing	Distribution	Admin
Procurement	XXXXXX				XX
Manufacturing	XX	XXXXX			XXX
Storing	XX				X
Marketing			XXX		XX
Selling	X		XX		
Delivering	XXX		X	XX	X
Invoicing			X	X	XX
Debt collection			X		XXX

Figure 2.3: "Process" in a traditional functional organisation structure[2]

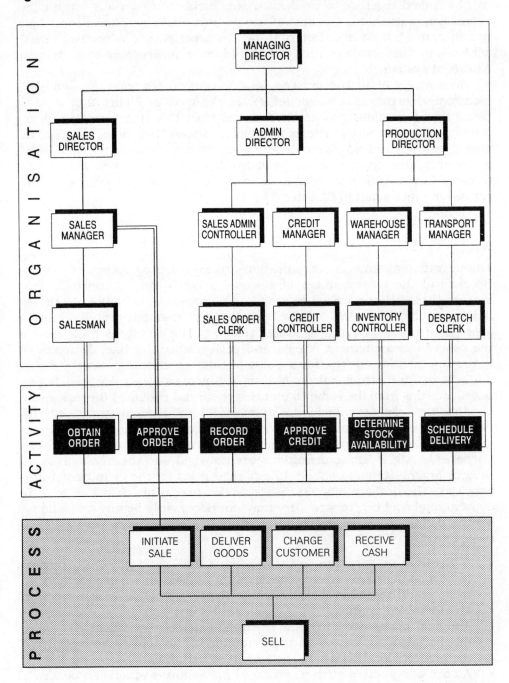

A **process** could therefore be described as a logical series of activities which can be linked together to produce a reasonably homogenous output (not necessarily a product). The cost of the process could be a basic cost objective in many businesses. Determining the process cost is normally easily achievable. This process analysis could be a forerunner to a detailed ABC & M system.

An example of such a process, as it is constructed from the functional hierarchical organisational structure, is depicted in Figure 2.3. It illustrates how the selling process is deduced from this structure by utilising the underlying activities. The exhibit clearly shows that the elements of the selling process, namely sales, ordering, credit approval, determining stock availability, delivery scheduling and invoicing are performed by different workers but are all part of the same selling process. Processes are described in more detail in Chapter 6.

ACTIVITIES

The operations within an organisation are executed by means of actions. Because of the great number of actions or tasks that are normally performed, these actions are aggregated into homogenous activities. All the actions required to pack finished goods, for example, could thus be aggregated to form an activity called packing. The activity is thus used as the basis of measurement of cost and performance. Michael Ostrenga referred to activities as "the focal point of total cost management".[3] Figure 2.4 sets out the structural analysis of a business enterprise that is proposed, starting from the value chain perspective and ending at the task level.

Activities are described by Computer Aided Manufacturing International (CAM-I) as work performed within an organisation and also as an aggregation of actions performed within an organisation which are useful for purposes of ABC.[4] These definitions are not rigid and the intention is not to force organisations to adhere to any rigid rules for the definition of their activities. The designer should rather be creative in his definition and the conventional cost centre structure may not necessarily be any indication of such a definition. Activities could possibly be defined from three perspectives, namely:

- A **physical perspective,** ie those actions that could physically be seen to be a homogenous group of tasks such as assembly. The assembly activity would resemble the physical assembly operation which produces an assembled product.
- A **logical perspective** such as the quality perspective where all quality-related tasks are viewed as the definition of the activity, irrespective of the physical location where the activity is performed.
- A **cost perspective** such as storage of inventories which can be viewed from the cost driver perspective. Storage costs can be affected by both

the place or time and value. Each of these views could thus be seen as separate activities.

Figure 2.4: Structural analysis of a business

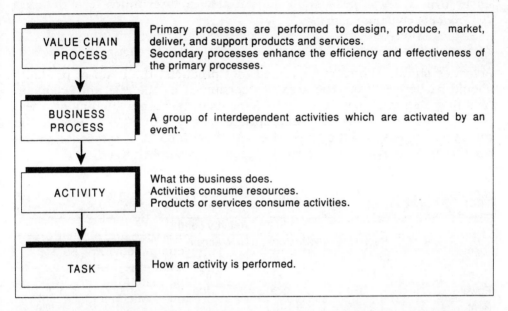

Robin Cooper[5] argued that conventional volume-based cost systems will distort product costs. Conventional systems generally use broadly defined cost centres and usually a plant-wide or uniform cost centre rate, to trace costs to products. He advocated instead that costs be traced first to the activity and second, utilising the specific cost driver of the activity to trace costs, to the product. In order to manage costs it is necessary to manage the activities. To understand the cost behaviour of activities it is necessary to understand the causes of cost, ie the cost drivers.

Examples of activities are :

— buying;
— receiving;
— storing;
— packing;
— selling;
— invoicing;
— distribution;
— debt collection;
— customer servicing.

These definitions will differ from business to business and will depend on the level of detail that is required of the ABC system. The term **activity** is pivotal to the concept of activity-based costing. An important point of departure is that :

> *Activities consume resources*; in other words, *activities cause costs.*
> In turn,
> *Products consume activities.*[6]

Activities should therefore be costed, not products; the costs of products should be derived from the activities consumed by the relevant products. As a first step to achieve this, cost elements or resources such as salaries, power, rent, etc are costed to appropriate activity centres to determine the full operating costs of the respective activities. Table 2.1 represents an extract from an activity cost matrix designed to accomplish that.

TABLE 2.1: Activity cost matrix

	Activity centre				
	Receiving	*Warehousing*	*Machine set-up*	*Inspection*	*Maintenance*
Salaries	6 530	18 600	9 350	11 720	14 270
Power	360	1 230	100	150	1 720
Rent	2 000	10 400	—	300	550
Insurance	300	7 970	50	—	180
Consumables	130	590	140	70	1 340
Depreciation	690	3 920	280	—	1 500
	10 010	42 710	9 920	12 240	19 560

After having identified the activities that incur costs and having assigned the costs to the relevant activities, the next step is to determine the justified bases on which the costs appropriated to the activity centres are to be traced to the organisation's products. Hence, in terms of activity-based costing, the cost of a product comprises the cost of the raw materials plus the cost of all the activities required to produce the product.

RESOURCES OR COST ELEMENTS

According to the CAM-I glossary of terms[4], **resources,** or cost elements, are economic elements directed towards the performance of activities. Resources are traced to activities utilising the resource cost driver. Examples of resources are labour, power and depreciation. The resource cost drivers could be time (for labour), kilowatts consumed (for power) and value of equipment employed (for depreciation).

PERFORMANCE MEASURES

Performance measurement is considered more useful than pure financial evaluation to evaluate overall organisational performance. The reasons for this statement will be explained fully in Chapter 10 on performance measurement. The principal reason for this is the fact that both financial and non-financial criteria, which must be met in order to service customers satisfactorily, are considered. The more important performance criteria which need to be measured are quality, time, cost and flexibility.

Quality management, productivity management systems and capacity management systems can thus be integral parts of an activity-based management system.

The measurement of these criteria indicates how well the organisation is meeting its customers' requirements. This measurement becomes very useful when comparisons with other organisations are made (if everything is measured at the same level, ie the activity level or the process level). Peter Turney describes this as a view that provides operational intelligence about the work going on in a company.[7]

COST DRIVERS

Traditional costing systems allocate overhead costs to products via a two-stage allocation process:

1. Assign overhead costs to cost centres (production divisions), based on appropriate measures (eg indirect salaries pro rata to number of employees in each cost centre, rent pro rata to floor space occupied and depreciation pro rata to value of machines and other equipment).

2. Allocate overhead costs from cost centres to the products. As a rule this allocation is based on labour hours or labour cost or, if the manufacturing process is fairly mechanised, machine hours.[8]

Although labour-related cost allocations might have been appropriate in the past when direct labour constituted a major part of the manufacturing cost of products, this premise is generally no longer applicable in present-day manufacturing operations. Currently direct labour cost represents a small fraction of corporate costs[9] — it very often does not exceed ten percent of the total cost of a product — whereas overhead costs generally account for approximately 40 percent of the cost of sales and are still increasing.[10] Because of an irrelevant cost relationship, cost allocations based on labour hours or labour cost can be totally unreasonable and result in product costs being incorrectly recorded. Consequently, substantial cross-subsidisation among the different products can take place.

The utilisation of machine hours as a basis of allocation can also be misleading. Machine hours do not necessarily bear a fair relationship to the total resources consumed by the respective products. Even the amortisation of machines can result in misleading cost figures if a time-based method is used. In this way cost is equated to time and amortisation (which increases overhead costs) continues even when little or no production takes place. By using a direct production-based amortisation method, such as units of production, costs are matched more accurately with products manufactured.

Moreover, when determining the number of units over which to amortise the relevant assets, only the planned production of the assets should be taken into account. Simply using the total lifetime capacity of an asset, if this does not correspond with the prospective total production, will clearly not lead to the correct cost allocation to the manufactured products. The total units on which the amortisation of an asset is based should therefore be limited by planned production, product demand and obsolescence of the asset's technology or the manufacturing process.[11]

Traditional costing systems are being criticised, *inter alia* because they merely allocate overhead costs on some arbitrary basis instead of focusing on the origination and causes of costs.

Activity-based costing comprises a different, more logical approach to determine product costs. It emphasises the need to obtain a better understanding of cost behaviour and thus ascertain what causes overhead costs, ie it relates overhead costs to the forces behind them. The forces behind overhead costs are described as **cost drivers**.

Cost drivers can be defined as those factors or transactions that are significant determinants of cost.[8] The following are examples of cost drivers:

- The number of purchase orders drives the costs of the purchasing department.
- The number of goods received notes drives the costs of the receiving department.
- The number of items in stock drives the costs of warehousing.
- The number of sales invoices drives the costs of the sales department, the dispatch department and the sales ledger department.

The above cost drivers may differ from business to business, depending on which causal factor is the most significant in each instance. For example, instead of the number of stock items, it may be more appropriate to use mass as the cost driver for warehousing costs, ie if the mass of stock handled and stored bears a better relationship to warehousing costs than the number of units does. Cost drivers are discussed in detail in Chapter 7.

Various types of cost drivers can be identified such as process cost drivers, activity cost drivers or resource drivers. Knowledge of the cost driver is useful for cost management purposes. This book makes a distinction between cost drivers and output measures. **Cost drivers** are the causal factors (such as a business policy) that cause costs of an activity to change. An **output measure** is simply the measurement of the output of an activity. Thus, where the cost driver is also the output of the activity, the cost driver and the output measure will be the same.

OUTPUT MEASURES

All activities and processes deliver outputs. If they do not, the continued existence or operation of the particular activity becomes questionable. Processes and activities should be designed to meet customer requirements (internal and external customers) at a cost which renders a satisfactory return to the shareholders.

Outputs from activities are measured as output measures. In many cases the output measure is the same as the cost driver, but it need not necessarily be so. The cost of the buying activity could be driven or determined by the purchasing policy of the company. The actual cost of the buying activity (within the constraints of the particular purchasing policy) will be influenced by the number of buying actions or tasks, which are most probably determined by the number of purchase orders. The output from the buying activity can thus be seen as the number of buying orders, which could then be used to trace the buying cost to the particular products which required the purchase orders. The cost of buying could then presumably be affected by influencing the number of purchase orders that are issued.

Activities should, in most cases, have a single output (measure); if not, the activity may need to be redefined. Output measures are thus principally used for cost measurement purposes.

COST OBJECTS

Although the most generic cost object is the physical product, various other cost objects may exist in an organisation for which separate cost accumulation (or cost measurement) needs to be done. The following cost objects, other than products, are typically found in businesses:

- **Services:** Many organisations do not sell a physical product but a service. This is nothing other than an invisible or intangible product. One main distinction is that this type of product is not held in stock.

- **Marketing channels:** An organisation may make use of different marketing channels such as a network of representatives and a set of wholesale outlets. It may therefore want to accumulate costs for this purpose in order to evaluate the alternatives.
- **Distribution channels:** The principles in this regard are very similar to marketing channels; products may, for example, be distributed by rail or by road and these costs may be evaluated.

- **Customers:** Many costs are customer-specific costs such as discounts, financing costs and commissions and it is thus relevant to determine relative customer profitability.

- **Processes:** Businesses typically consist of a series of processes which need to be evaluated and cost information may be required for this purpose.

- **Activities:** As activities are the focal point of an ABC & M system, the cost of the activity is normally very useful in analysing the business.

A number of other cost objects may be defined (eg projects, contracts or other work units). The multiplicity of objects or multidimensional views should be one of the main considerations in the design of a modern accounting system.

From the above discussion, the pictorial presentation of the basic structure of an activity-based costing system as depicted in Figure 2.5 should be followed. Resources are traced to activities which in turn are traced to cost objects. Processes, which can be viewed as consisting of a number of activities, are performed to ultimately satisfy customer requirements, as reflected in the performance measures.

Figure 2.5: Activity-based costing (CAM-I)

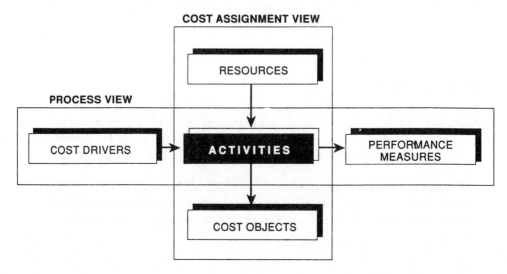

BILL OF ACTIVITIES

The bill of activities (BOA) is a description of the routing the product (or other cost object) takes through the activities in its path towards completion. This can be compared to the well-known concept of a bill of materials which contains the constituent parts, subassemblies, etc which are necessary to make a product. The BOA also itemises the number of units of the various activities that the cost object consumes in this process. A BOA therefore represents a list of all the activities and relative quantities required by a particular cost object.

Naturally the bill of activities will only include primary activities as secondary activities are not directly associated with the cost object. (Secondary activity costs are traced to primary activities.) Also useful in this regard is the sequence in which the activities are performed. This instrument helps to illuminate the cost structure of the cost object and enhances cost visibility compared to a traditional system. The explicit information on the activities, cost drivers, and quantities associated with particular cost objects thus facilitates better decision-making.

Example 2.1
The BOA of a subassembly may be as depicted in Table 2.2.

Sequence	Activity	Units consumed (of output measure)
1	Production planning	2
2	Buying	6
3	Receiving	12
4	Quality inspection – components	4
5	Assembling	8
6	Quality inspection – assembly	3
7	Storage	20

TABLE 2.2: The BOA of a subassembly

Table 2.2 illustrates that the cost of a subassembly will be determined by the above activities. The assembly typically consumes:

— two units of production planning;
— six units of buying (maybe the number of orders);
— twelve units of receiving (maybe the number of GRNs);
— four units of component inspection;
— eight units of assembling;
— three units of final quality inspection; and
— twenty units of storage (maybe square metres or days).

Units consumed will be the relevant measure of output for the particular activity.

ILLUSTRATIVE FRAMEWORK OF AN ACTIVITY-BASED COSTING AND MANAGEMENT SYSTEM

The elements and concepts of the ABC & M system can be depicted by the presentation set out in Figure 2.6. In this regard it is useful to note the difference between a simple activity-based costing system and a comprehensive activity-based management system. In Figure 2.6 the elements of the ABC system are indicated in black.

It is useful to note the descriptions provided by CAM-I[4] of the ABC and ABM concepts, which are:

- **Activity-based costing:** A methodology that measures the cost and performance of activities, resources and cost objects. Resources are assigned to activities, then activities are assigned to cost objects based on the use or consumption of the relevant activities. Activity-based costing recognises the causal relationships of cost drivers to activities.

- **Activity-based management:** A discipline that focuses on the management of activities as the route to improving the value received by the customer and the profit achieved by providing this value. This discipline includes cost driver analysis, activity analysis and performance measurement. Activity-based management draws on activity-based costing as its major source of information.

- **Activity-based cost system:** A system that maintains and processes financial and operating data on a firm's resources, activities, cost objects, cost drivers, and activity performance measures. It also assigns costs to activities and cost objects.

Cost elements or resources are traced to activities through the resource driver (discussed in Chapter 7). Direct costs such as material or packing material will be traced directly to the product. Some costs may remain untraceable, such as management cost or certain general infrastructure costs. As long as the untraceable portion remains small (5 – 10 %), relative accuracy will not be dramatically affected. For practical purposes a cost system that renders 90 % accuracy (ie 10 % is traced arbitrarily or remains untraced) will meet most demands.

Activity costs are then traced to cost objects utilising the output measure. This assumes that the cost object consumes the various outputs. For example, a product that requires far more inspection to ensure an appropriate degree of quality, should bear more inspection (activity) cost than a product that requires less inspection. The bill of activities indicates the quantity of outputs of each activity that the particular cost objects consume. It may indicate, for example, that one product requires 20 inspections and another only five. The BOA facilitates the calculation of the cost of the various cost objects such as customers, products, etc.

Figure 2.6: Conceptual framework of an activity-based management system

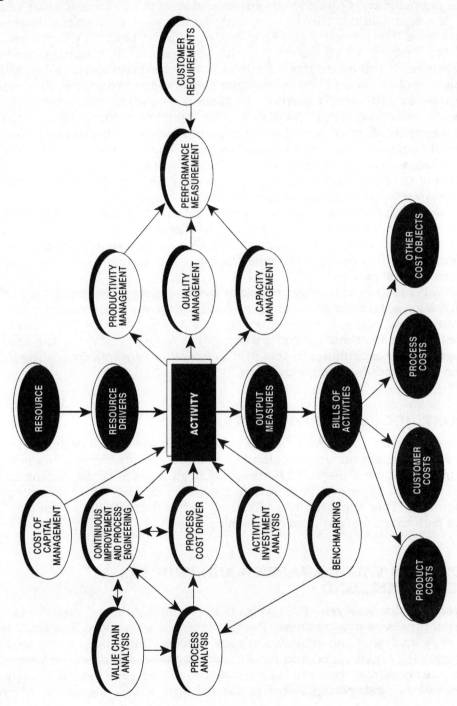

The horizontal perspective of the model indicates the process view of the organisation. Starting with an evaluation of the particular value chain of the organisation, this can typically be analysed into several business processes. The process focus in an organisation facilitates the improvement of the business by re-engineering the way business is conducted and by continuously improving the effectiveness of the organisation. The activities can almost be seen to be the building blocks of the process. Modern businesses are increasingly starting to focus on satisfying customer requirements effectively and profitably. The factors determining customer satisfaction will most probably never be precisely known but most studies reveal some common criteria such as price, quality and differentiation of the commodity, timely delivery, etc. These factors therefore form the nucleus of the performance management system and the ABM system should endeavour to measure and evaluate these elements.

Certain constraints may exist which limit the business' potential profit-earning capabilities. These factors may be shortage of funds or investment, capacity, etc. The ABM system should also endeavour to evaluate these constraints in order to overcome their limiting factors and to maximise shareholders' return.

This model is in no way perfect. In fact future research, practical implementation and experimentation may indicate many more useful ways to evaluate and manage an organisation. It is hoped that this book makes a contribution to stimulate and encourage the reader to advance the knowledge and the capabilities in this field. A few other concepts emanating from this model are also dealt with below.

CONTINUOUS IMPROVEMENT

Continuous improvement is aimed at upgrading the overall performance of the organisation in an evolutionary manner by improving efficiency in small, continuous steps. This means that all aspects of the organisation will continually be evaluated and improvement effected by a "salami slice" approach. This approach has ultimately led to dramatic improvements in the performance of Japanese companies.

PROCESS VALUE ANALYSIS AND PROCESS RE-ENGINEERING

Process value analysis (PVA) refers to the identification and analysis of the major processes of a business. The processes are subdivided into activities, and by analysing the activities in each process, the opportunities for improving the organisation and reducing cost become identifiable — *inter alia* by distinguishing between value-added and non-value-added activities. **Process re-engineering** refers to the redesign or reconfiguration of processes and/or the use of alternative processes. These aspects are dealt with more fully in Chapter 6.

Value-added vs Non-value-added activities

A value-added activity adds something that the customer wants to a product or service; a non-value-added activity adds cost and time to the product or service, but adds no value from the customer's point of view. The practical way to distinguish between value-added and non-value-added activities is therefore to approach them from the perspective of the customer (whether the customer is external or internal, such as another division of the business). If the customer is not willing to pay for the activity, then it does not add value.[12] Alternatively, ask yourself at each process step (activity) if eliminating it would detract in any way from the customer's satisfaction with the product. For example, a reduction in machine set-up time, the number of times materials are handled in the factory or the time the finished product is stored in the warehouse, would not upset customers; however, if the painting or the packaging step was eliminated, customers would quickly switch to another supplier.[13]

Apart from bringing about a better understanding of the business processes and related costs, PVA also focuses on meeting customer requirements, minimising cost and cycle time, and improving the quality of output.[3]

Process re-engineering aims to change (sometimes fundamentally) the structure of business processes to meet customer requirements. Business process re-engineering normally begins with an evaluation of the performance of the business processes in terms of meeting customer requirements such as timely delivery, quality of the product or service that it delivers, and the profit that can be made. Processes are then analysed to determine methods to meet requirements or to simplify them. Process re-engineering principles are discussed in Chapter 6.

ACTIVITY INVESTMENT ANALYSIS

In order to determine the cost of the use of assets (eg depreciation; wear and tear) or investments associated with activities, it is necessary to analyse assets according to the activity structure. Information about assets invested in each activity facilitates the evaluation of capital productivity and may eventually be useful in investment decision making. This almost has the effect of being able to see the balance sheet from an activity perspective, which also facilitates evaluation of the use of cost of capital.

COST OF CAPITAL MANAGEMENT

Cost of capital in many businesses represents one of the most significant cost elements. Because of the fact that a major part of cost of capital, namely return on shareholders' funds, does not necessarily represent a cash outflow, the cost of capital is seldom traced to cost objects. In Chapter 5 a model is proposed, using the residual income concept, to apply cost of capital to the costing system so that cost of capital is also reflected in the cost of cost objects.

LIFE-CYCLE ACCOUNTING

Life-cycle accounting refers to the logical concept whereby all costs relating to a product are charged to that product over its economic life cycle. This implies that the economic life cycle of the product needs to be predetermined, estimated or forecast in order to allocate certain costs to the product during such period, and not during the period in which the costs (eg research and development costs) were incurred.

Four steps are typical in the conventional life cycle of a product or service:[14]

1. Identification of an opportunity (by research or clear observation) .
2. Development, testing, promotion.
3. Introduction, growth, maturation, decline.
4. Withdrawal.

In general, overheads are relatively high in the early phases of product development, and then diminish over the life cycle of the product.[15] On the other hand, the main revenue stream is generated during phase 3 above. Consequently, by charging costs to the income statement as and when they are incurred, as is common in conventional accounting, serious mismatching with income is brought about.

CONCLUSION

This chapter sets out the more general concepts used in an ABC & M system. A basic understanding of the concepts and the structure of an ABC & M system is useful in following the activity accounting literature and the material contained in the ensuing chapters. Most of the concepts are discussed in more detail in later chapters of the book.

SOURCES CONSULTED

1. Porter, ME. *Competitive Advantage*. New York: Free Press, 1985.
2. Dilton-Hill, K & Glad, E. Business process management. *Accountancy SA*, Oct 1992: 317–321.
3. Ostrenga, MR. Activities: The focal point of total cost management. *Management Accounting* (US), Feb 1990: 42–49.
4. Raffish, N. & Turney, PBB. Glossary of activity-based management. *Journal of Cost Management*, Fall 1991: 53–63.
5. Cooper, R. The rise of activity-based costing – Part I: What is an activity-based cost system? *Journal of Cost Management*, Summer 1988: 45–54.
6. Jeans, M. & Morrow, M. The practicalities of using activity-based costing. *Management Accounting* (UK), Nov 1989: 42–44.
7. Turney, PBB. What an activity-based cost model looks like. *Journal of Cost Management*, Winter 1992: 54–60.
8. Drury, C. Activity-based costing. *Management Accounting* (UK), Sep 1989: 60–63; 66.
9. Cooper, R. & Kaplan, RS. Measure costs right: Make the right decisions. *Harvard Business Review*, Sep-Oct 1988: 96–103.
10. Bellis-Jones, R. & Hand, M. Seeking out the profit dissipators. *Management Accounting* (UK), Sep 1989: 48–50.
11. Peavey, DE. Battle at the GAAP? It's time for a change. *Management Accounting* (US), Feb 1990: 31–35.
12. Alexander, G, Gienger, G, Harwoord, M & Santori, P. The new revolution in cost management. *Financial Executive*, Nov/Dec 1991: 35–39.
13. Beischel, E. Improving production with process value analysis. *Journal of Accountancy*, Sep 1990: 53–57.
14. Atkinson, AA. Life-cycle costing. *CMA Magazine*, Jul/Aug 1990: 7.
15. Macintyre, DK. Marketing costs: A new look. *Management Accounting* (US), Mar 1983: 21–28.

3

Costing methodology for raw materials, products and services

INTRODUCTION

This chapter describes the cost accounting process applied in an ABC system. In order to follow the technique, it is essential to have a good understanding of the relevant concepts discussed and illustrated in the previous two chapters. Principally the same methodology can be applied to determine the cost of all cost objects.

METHODOLOGY

The basic steps applied in this methodology are:

1. Determine the nature of cost elements and analyse them between:
   — direct traceable costs;
   — activity-traceable costs;
   — non-traceable costs (or unallocated costs).
2. Account for all traceable costs per activity, distinguishing between primary and secondary activities. Consideration should be given to the treatment of non-traceable costs. These could either be traced to other activities on an arbitrary basis, or treated as part of the required profit margin.
3. Determine cost drivers for each activity and use output measures to calculate activity recovery rates. This must be done for primary as well as secondary activities.
4. Trace all secondary activity costs to primary activities so that the combined activity rates include all support costs. Secondary costs will be traced to primary activities utilising the secondary output measure.
5. Identify which cost objects are to be costed. Compile the bill of activities for each cost object.
6. Multiply the activity recovery rate by the quantity of output consumed as specified in the bill of activities. The sum of these calculated costs will give the activity-traced cost of the cost object.

7. Direct cost and non-traceable cost (where applicable) will be added to the cost calculated above to give the total cost of the cost object. Direct costs, such as material and packaging costs, can normally be associated with the cost object specifically. Non-traceable costs may be added on an arbitrary basis or provided for in the profit margin.

NATURE OF COSTS

For the purpose of developing a good costing system it is essential to understand the *raison d'être* of the cost element and its relationship to the cost object. Certain costs are traceable to the cost object directly — the occurrence of the cost is most probably the direct consequence of the manufacture of a product or the delivery of a service. These costs are typically raw material or other costs which have a direct relationship to the cost object and therefore the term **direct costs** is used. They can most probably be costed to the cost object mechanistically (such as in a bill of materials system) and do not normally pose a major problem from a cost system perspective.

Traceable and non-traceable costs are normally the major concern in the cost system because cost systems fail or succeed because of the way they treat these costs. In contrast with traditional cost systems, labour is normally not considered to be a direct cost of a cost object such as a product but rather as a cost associated with an activity. Because of the axiom "*activities consume resources and products consume activities*" the traceability of a cost element to an activity is the major concern of an ABC system.

Direct cost

Direct cost has traditionally been seen as direct materials and direct labour. These direct costs plus production overheads, incurred to bring the inventory to its current state and location, are used as the basis for valuing inventories (Statement of Standard Accounting Practice no. 9).

This view represents two important anomalies namely:

1. The actual cost of bringing a product to its current state and location may differ from the cost implied by SSAP9 (understood to be mainly manufacturing cost). The actual cost may logically include some administrative, finance and transport costs. This anomaly arose because of the assumption that the cost of creating the product has to correspond with the inventory valuation method. For this reason many costing systems serve no other purpose than to value inventories. Instead, the cost system should inform management of the cost incurred in bringing a product or service to its current state and location.

2. Material cost is seen as the so-called "landed cost". This is normally the cost of goods purchased, insurance and freight in. However, landed

cost does not, for instance, include the cost of activities associated with receiving, handling, storing or moving such items to make them available for production. Similarly the cost of all relevant activities incurred in the procurement process should also be included. The cost of direct inputs into production should logically include all costs incurred up to that point.

Cost to the point of input into production can be depicted as in Figure 3.1:

Figure 3.1: Cost of procurement process

MRP* activity	Buying activity	Receiving activity	Quality activity	Payment activity	Storage activity

(MRP= material requirements planning)

A summary of the cost of a particular product is illustrated in Example 3.1. To some extent this is comparable with the concept of landed cost as traditionally used in accounting, but there are also some important differences. Landed cost does not include any administrative activities such as production planning, receiving or the cost of storage (which includes finance charges). The ABC cost of the material placed in production can be reconciled to the generally accepted accounting practice (GAAP) inventory valuation by eliminating non-inventoriable activities (which could be indicated as such in the ABC system).

Example 3.1: ABC cost of material

	£
Purchase cost ex supplier	5 000
Material requirements planning	400
Buying activity	300
Receiving activity	480
Quality inspections	300
Payment activity	320
Storage activity	1 200
Cost of material (transferred)	8 000

Material costs are normally identifiable with the product and can be traced to the product utilising a bill of material which specifies the raw materials, components or subassemblies which are required to complete the product.

Labour costs can still be traced to products as direct costs. However, due to the relatively small percentage of total cost that it represents in most organisations, it may not be worthwhile to have a separate cost rate to cater specifically for this cost. A more obvious avenue could be to trace labour, like most other costs, to the activity concerned and then recover labour cost through the activity cost rate.

Traceable cost

Traceable costs are accounted for per activity. The link with the cost object is achieved via the related output measure which is utilised to trace these costs to the cost object. This relationship is useful as it can be validated scientifically and is normally well understood by people involved in operational activities. The resource driver is used to trace traceable cost to the activity.

Activities can be classified as primary or secondary activities. Costs traced to primary activities are used to calculate the primary rate, ie the rate which excludes secondary cost. The cost of primary activities can be related directly to the cost object — this normally being the product, service or customer. Secondary activities such as training or personnel services are performed to support primary activities and their cost should therefore be recovered from the primary activities that they serve. A rate called the combined rate will thus be calculated which includes the primary rate and will contain an element of secondary cost. This is explained more fully in the illustrated examples.

Non-traceable cost

Normally a small element of cost remains which is difficult to trace to any specific activity or cost object. An example of such a cost may be general management expenses or small sundry expenses such as postage which cannot be related to a particular activity with any accuracy. Such expenses are normally small in relation to total expenses (less than 5 % of total costs) and can be allocated to cost objects in proportion to other costs or may be covered by a small increase in the target margin.

The above issues are summarised in Figure 3.2:

Figure 3.2

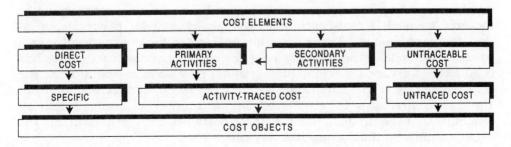

TWO-STAGE ALLOCATION PROCESS

The costing technique in an ABC system resembles that of a traditional costing system. Traditionally the costing technique is referred to as the two-stage cost accounting process. Each expense is classified into a cost element in a cost centre or cost department. This is referred to as the first stage in the cost allocation process.

The second stage in the allocation process recovers the costs which have been aggregated in the cost centre via the use of the recovery base. This can be illustrated as in Figure 3.3:

Figure 3.3

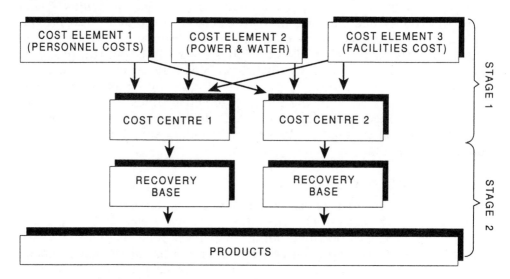

This framework has principally evolved within the responsibility structure of organisations. Cost centres or cost departments represent functional responsibilities, within which a number of tasks and actions are performed.

An example of such a cost centre in a manufacturing enterprise may be the machine shop. The machine shop may house several types of equipment such as lathes, drilling and milling machines. It may also be supervised by a manager and supervisors. Naturally, a variety of costs would be incurred for such a cost centre such as personnel costs, power, depreciation and consumables. These costs are aggregated for the cost centre as a whole. Traditionally the recovery base for costs from this cost centre has been either labour or machine hours, which may seem logical at first. The cost centre rate is therefore expressed as £ per labour or machine hour (for the cost centre as a whole). Based on the number of hours (labour or machine) that the product absorbs, these costs will then be allocated to the product, utilising the average recovery rate.

Due to the diversity of actions (or activities) and costs to be found in a cost centre, the cost centre rate used in a traditional cost system will relate to several types of output and the rate may thus not reflect the nature of the action it portrays.

Several arguments can be offered as to why this type of approach does not lead to accurate product costing. First, no homogeneity exists between the actions (activities) which are performed within the cost centre. In the above example, at the very least, the costs of turning (lathes), drilling and milling (the activities) and supervision need to be separated. Turning, milling and drilling are considered primary activites in this regard, ie directly related to the products or cost objects. The supervision activity serves the primary activities and its cost must be traced or recovered through the primary activities.

Second, the cost structures of the activities need to be analysed to determine the main cost components or elements and to obtain an understanding of the behaviour pattern of the cost of the activity. The determination of cost homogeneity is an important step in the proper analysis of cost. The behaviour pattern may give an indication of the factors which cause the costs of the activities to change, which may be an indication of what drives the cost up or down. Several factors may, at this stage, reveal reasons for cost variations such as set-up of machines, complexity of tasks as well as the volume of products that must be manufactured. Activity costs tend to be a homogenous collection of costs which result in a single output such as a set-up activity or a specific production activity.

A major consideration in the tracing of cost to the product is the use of the knowledge about the cost behaviour which is indicated by the output measure. It is logical that if a specific cause of cost exists, this causal factor be used to trace the cost of the activity to the product.

Activities do not necessarily fit into the responsibility structure. They quite often span functional boundaries. An example in this regard is quality control, which may take place throughout the organisation. Activities therefore do not equate to cost centres.

The axioms about ABC which can be deduced from the above reasoning are:

1. *Activities consume resources such as manpower, electricity, facility costs, etc.*

2. *Products consume activities such as turning or drilling.*

The above can be illustrated by Figure 3.4:

Figure 3.4

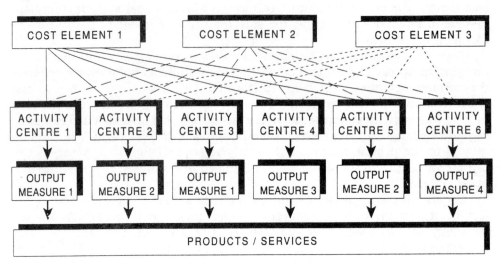

From Figure 3.4 it should be obvious that ABC requires a much more detailed analysis of the business than might have been performed traditionally. Also the underlying cause of the cost change is utilised to trace the cost to the product. (This is a very simplified view of an ABC system and assumes that all activities are primary activities.) In practice activities are often defined within the functional responsibility structures and another linking mechanism is used if activities span organisational boundaries. As businesses move more towards a process-orientated responsibility structure, the definition of activity structures may also develop different characteristics.

The two-stage allocation method as used in traditional costing is still used in ABC. In the first stage costs are traced to the activity and in the second stage they are traced through the output measure to the cost object.

WASTAGE

One of the main objectives of an ABM system is to help management determine the lowest possible cost at which a product or service can be rendered. This naturally implies that no wastage of any form is allowed to take place in the organisation. Wastage can be defined as anything over and above the minimum amount of resources and time absolutely essential to add value to the cost object (from the customer's perspective).

Wastage may be one of the most important cost factors in an organisation yet it fails to appear in most traditional accounting systems. An ABC & M system, however, should not only attempt to measure wastage but also to integrate this concept into the accounting system by treating it as a specific, manageable cost.

Identification and measurement of cost of wastage are particular problems in most businesses. Certain forms of wastage are obvious such as material or capacity waste. Others are less easy to detect such as time wastage or ineffective use of resources. Wastage could therefore be detected at various levels, ie the cost element level, activity level or facility level. This is a specific business problem and goes far beyond the mere accounting implications. The importance of wastage management obviously lies in the very direct effect that it can have on profitability.

DETERMINING THE COST OF RAW MATERIALS

Example 3.2 below describes the various steps followed in the ABC method. Starting with an extract from the general ledger of A Company, these costs are then traced through the various steps in the costing process to determine the cost of raw materials (the cost object in this case) as used in the manufacturing operations.

Example 3.2: Extract from general ledger of A Company:

Raw material purchases	£600 000
Salaries and wages	200 000
Power	50 000
Stationery	5 000
Rent	10 000
Depreciation	80 000

Step 1 — Analysis into activity centres

The first step in the costing process corresponds with the first stage in the two-stage process previously described. During this step costs must be traced to the respective activity cost pools. This will normally take place at the time of recording the basic transaction (as with cost centre accounting). The following information is extracted in respect of the above general ledger items:

Raw materials
Three raw materials are used in manufacturing process X, namely A, B and C. Respective purchases were:

A	£100 000
B	60 000
C	40 000

Salaries and wages

Most salary and wage systems have the facility to analyse and allocate these costs to the various cost pools and the following extract can typically be taken from this source:

MRP	£20 000 (2)
Buying	10 000 (1)
Receiving	6 000 (3)
Quality inspection	15 000 (3)
Stores	12 000 (4)
Personnel department	30 000 (3)
Accounting	25 000 (2)

The number of people employed in each activity appears in brackets.

Power

Wherever power represents a significant cost element it may be worthwhile for the company to invest in metering systems to measure power consumption in the more important activity centres. Alternatively, technical personnel can be asked to prepare a reasonable allocation of costs based on capacities of equipment installed, uptime of such equipment as well as work loads. The following allocation of power costs is assumed for this example:

MRP	£1 000
Buying	500
Receiving	3 000
Quality inspection	1 200
Storage	4 000
Personnel	800
Accounting	600

Stationery

This cost item most probably contains non-traceable items. In addition, the cost of tracing this cost to the various cost pools may well exceed the benefit. It can be provided for in each cost object using stationery as a small add-on percentage of cost or it could be covered by the product margin. However, if specific stationery costs, such as printing costs, can be traced to specific activities, this should be done. The cost of printing purchase orders or goods received notes (GRNs) can be traced directly to the appropriate activity such as buying or receiving.

Rent

Rent may be traced to the various activity centres in proportion to square metres occupied. The following is assumed as a reasonable split of rental cost:

MRP	£ 500
Buying	300
Receiving	600
Quality inspection	500
Stores	2 000
Personnel	800
Accounting	900

Depreciation

Depreciation will be traced on the basis of the investment in depreciable assets in each activity centre. This information is normally available from the fixed asset register. Assume the following costs:

MRP	£4 000
Buying	1 000
Receiving	6 000
Quality inspection	2 000
Storage	10 000
Personnel	500
Accounting	3 000

Activity cost matrix

From the above information the following activity cost matrix can be compiled:

Cost element	MRP	Buying	Receiving	Quality	Storage	Personnel	Accounting
Salaries	20 000	10 000	6 000	15 000	12 000	30 000	25 000
Power	1 000	500	3 000	1 200	4 000	800	600
Rent	500	300	600	500	2 000	800	900
Depr	4 000	1 000	6 000	2 000	10 000	500	3 000
Total	25 500	11 800	15 600	18 700	28 000	32 100	29 500

This matrix will, of course, be extended over the whole organisation and this is merely an extract of the activities which relate to the raw materials.

Step 2 — Determination of output measures

The next step in the costing process is to determine those factors which influence the behaviour of costs and the basis on which these may be traced – the output measure of the costs in the activity centres. A detailed discussion of output measures and cost driver analysis is given in Chapter 7.

For illustrative purposes it is assumed that the following output measures have been identified:

MRP	Number of material plans done
Buying	Number of purchase orders
Receiving	Number of goods received notes
Quality inspections	Number of quality inspections
Storage	Number of square metres of space
Personnel	Number of people employed

(No output measure could be identified for the accounting activity.)

The output measure is then used to determine the recovery rate of each cost pool. Two alternatives exist for this purpose:

Actual output
This method uses the actual output of the particular output measure during a particular period under consideration to determine output rates. This results in all costs being fully recovered by the cost object. With varying capacity utilisation rates from period to period this will result in recovery rates fluctuating (sometimes dramatically). This will also not highlight the cost of idle capacity which exists in the particular activity. The cost of the cost object may also fluctuate dramatically.

Capacity
Every activity has a certain capacity level and this could be used to determine the recovery rate. The effect of this will be that recovery rates will be reasonably consistent from period to period and the cost of the unused or idle capacity, which should be specifically reported, will be calculated. Idle capacity constitutes a form of wastage. The cost of the cost object will also not vary dramatically. This latter method is the preferred method and will be followed in this text.

In the above example the following capacities for the relevant activities are assumed:

MRP	50 plans (for 3 raw material items)
Buying	1 000 purchase orders
Receiving	2 000 GRNs
Quality inspection	1 500 inspections
Storage	1 000 square metres
Personnel	100 personnel members

Step 3 — Determination of activity rates

Activity rates can be determined utilising the above activity cost matrix and the output measure information. The rate is calculated as follows:

$$\text{Activity cost per unit} = \frac{\text{Activity cost}}{\text{Output measure capacity}}$$

Applied to the above example the activity rates are as follows:

MRP	= 25 500/50	= £510 per plan
MRP per material	= 510/3	= £170 per material
Buying	= 11 800/1 000	= £11,80 per purchase order
Receiving	= 15 600/2 000	= £7,80 per GRN
Quality inspection	= 18 700/1 500	= £12,47 per inspection
Storage	= 28 000/1 000	= £28 per square metre
Personnel	= 32 100/100	= £321 per personnel member

The above rates represent the primary rates of the various activities and do not provide for secondary costs. In the above example the following can be considered as primary and secondary activities relative to the raw material cost object:

Primary activities

> MRP
> Buying
> Receiving
> Quality inspection
> Storage

Secondary activities

> Personnel
> Accounting

Activity cost rates should provide for secondary activity costs as these (by definition) are performed to support primary activities. In this example therefore, personnel and accounting activity costs must be traced to the respective primary activities that they serve. Utilising the appropriate output measure of the personnel activity (number of personnel members) this cost can be traced to the appropriate primary activities based on the number of personnel members employed in each activity (as was indicated in the extract from the salary and wage system). The cost of the accounting activity is considered to be an untraceable cost and will therefore be estimated on an arbitrary basis.

Personnel activity costs can be traced to the primary activities as follows:

MRP	2 × £321	= £642
Buying	1 × £321	= £321
Receiving	3 × £321	= £963
Quality inspection	3 × £321	= £963
Storage	4 × £321	= £1 284

Primary activity rates will therefore have to be recalculated to recover these costs. This can be done taking the cost structure from the activity matrix above:

Activity	Primary cost	Secondary cost	Total cost	Output measure units	Combined rate
MRP	25 500	642	26 142	50	£522,84
Buying	11 800	321	12 121	1 000	£12,12
Receiving	15 600	963	16 563	2 000	£8,28
Quality	18 700	963	19 663	1 500	£13,11
Storage	28 000	1 284	29 284	1 000	£29,28

Note that, for example, the cost of a material requirements plan is now £522,84 as opposed to the £510 primary rate.

Step 4 — Compilation of the bill of activities

Once the activity rates have been established these rates can be used to calculate the cost of the particular cost object. However, the consumption of the activities by the various cost objects needs to be known. This consumption pattern is described in the bill of activities.

For example, the bill of activities of the three raw materials under consideration may be as follows:

Activity	A	B	C
Material requirements planning	2	2	2
Buying	24	16	60
Receiving	80	60	240
Quality inspection	80	24	40
Storage	50	150	500

This structure indicates, for example, (material A) that 2 production plans are required per period, 24 purchase orders may be necessary, 80 GRNs will be issued, 80 quality inspections will be performed and 50 square metres of storage will be required for this stock.

Step 5 — Calculation of cost of object

The cost of the three raw materials will therefore be calculated as follows:

Activity		A	B	C
MRP	(2 × £522,84/3)	348,56	348,56	348,56
Buying	(24 × £12,12)	290,88	193,92	727,20
Receiving	(80 × £8,28)	662,40	496,80	1 987,20
Quality	(80 × £13,11)	1 048,80	314,64	524,40
Storage	(50 × £29,28)	1 464,00	4 392,00	14 640,00
Total "add-on" cost		3 814,64	5 745,92	18 227,36
Direct material cost		100 000,00	60 000,00	40 000,00
Raw material cost		103 814,64	65 745,92	58 227,36
Units purchased		20 000	30 000	40 000
Cost per unit		£5,19	£2,19	£1,46

SUMMARY

The above steps can be summarised in the following schedule:

			PRIMARY			SECONDARY
Cost element	MRP	Buying	Receiving	Quality	Storage	Personnel
Salaries	20 000	10 000	6 000	15 000	12 000	30 000
Power	1 000	500	3 000	1 200	4 000	800
Rent	500	300	600	500	2 000	800
Depreciation	4 000	1 000	6 000	2 000	10 000	500
Total	25 500	11 800	15 600	18 700	28 000	32 500
Secondary cost reallocation	642	321	963	963	1 284	−32 100
Total cost	26 142	12 121	16 563	19 663	29 284	
Output measure	50 x 3	1 000	2 000	1 500	1 000	
Recovery rate	174,28	12,12	8,28	13,11	29,28	
BOA - Mat A	2	24	80	80	50	
Add-on cost	£348,56	£290,88	£662,40	£1 048,80	£1 464,00	

This is comparable with the calculations set out in the above steps for material A. A similar process can be followed for other cost objectives such as products, processes, marketing or distribution channels, customers, etc.

DETERMINING THE COST OF MANUFACTURED PRODUCTS

The principles of ABC can be further demonstrated by the calculation of the cost of a manufactured product X. Continuing the example, product X contains raw material A (2 units). The product is manufactured in a machine shop in three stages starting with cutting on a bandsaw, then turning on the lathes and lastly, the drilling of holes. Both the bandsaws and the lathes need some set-up of the machines. Products are cut in batches of 50 on the bandsaws and each batch takes 0,5 hours to produce. The bandsaws are set up by robots and set-up time is negligible (as is the case with the drilling machines). Set-up time on lathes normally amounts to 0,2 hours per set-up and 10 % of total operating hours. Product X takes 2 minutes to turn on a lathe and machine set-up is checked after every 1 000 products. Each product requires 3 holes to be drilled and drill capacity is 60 holes per hour. Practical machine capacity amounts to 160 hours per period per machine (all machines). Assume product X is the only product manufactured in the machine shop.

The following costs are incurred in the machine shop:

Salaries and wages	£50 100
Power	9 000
Depreciation	14 000
Machine tools	17 000
Cleaning material	3 400
Rent	5 400
Maintenance	25 000
	123 900

The following additional information is supplied:

Salaries and wages
One supervisor, earning £5 100 per month, is employed to oversee the whole department. The staff complement and the respective average salary per operator are as follows:

Bandsaws	(3)	2 000
Lathes	(6)	3 000
Drilling machines	(8)	2 625

Each operator occupies one machine. Secondary personnel-related costs remain the same as in Example 3.1 (ie £321 per person).

Power
Power costs consist of electricity capacity costs (kilovolt-hours) of £6 000 and consumption costs (kilowatt-hours) of £3 000. Bandsaws have a maximum capacity of 3 000 Kvh, lathes a capacity of 6 000 Kvh and drilling machines 1 000 Kvh. This is considered a fair basis for tracing Kvh cost to machines. Consumption based on operating hours is estimated as follows:

Bandsaws (820 batches)	400 hours	(7,5 Kw/hr)
Lathes	900 hours	(10 Kw/hr)
Drilling machines	1 200 hours	(15 Kw/hr)

Depreciation
According to the fixed asset register this is as follows:

Bandsaws	4 000
Lathes	8 000
Drilling machines	2 000

Machine tools expensed
The following issues of machine tools were made during the month:

Bandsaws	3 500
Lathes	8 500
Drilling machines	5 000

Cleaning material and rent
According to the supervisor of the machine shop, the space occupied by the various machines is approximately the same and the amount spent on cleaning material per machine is also very similar.

Maintenance
A planned maintenance system is in operation and maintenance costs are charged to the machine shop based on operating hours (see electricity).

The objectives of the ABC system are to:

1. Determine the cost of a product manufactured in this department. (25 000 products were actually manufactured.)
2. Calculate all forms of wastage which may be occurring.

The procedures to achieve these objectives are:

1. CALCULATION OF PRODUCT COST

Step 1 — Determination of activity cost matrix (ACM)

Before an ACM can be constructed the relevant activities need to be defined. In the above example it can be reasoned that the following activities must be defined:

Primary activities
*   Cutting
*   Turning
    — set-up (10 %)
    — operating (90 %)
*   Drilling

Secondary activities
*   Supervision
*   Personnel

Cost element	Cutting	Turning Set-up 10%	Turning Op. hrs 90%	Drilling
ACTIVITY COST MATRIX (Primary activities only)				
Salaries	6 000	1 800	16 200	21 000
Power				
— Kvh	1 800	360	3 240	600
— Kwh	300	90	810	1 800
Depreciation	4 000	800	7 200	2 000
Machine tools	3 500	–	8 500	5 000
Cleaning material	600	–	1 200	1 600
Rent	900	180	1 620	2 700
Maintenance	4 000	–	9 000	12 000
Primary cost	21 100	3 230	47 770	46 700

Note: It is argued that machine tools and cleaning materials will only be required when the machines are operated and not necessarily during set-ups.

Step 2 — Determination of output measures

Cutting
It can be argued that the number of batches may be the output measure. Should fairly large batches of equal quantities be manufactured, the number of batches may correlate with machine hours. Batches which are not fully utilised would constitute wastage and should be measured separately, if this occurs frequently. Batching planned for a month would be:
3 machines x 160 x 2 (batches per hour) = 960 batches.

Turning set-up
The output measure in this case is most probably the number of set-ups. Set-ups amount to 10 % of 6 x 160 hours = 96 hours or 480 set-ups.

Turning operating hours
The output measure is probably the number of machine hours, which amounts to 90 % of 960 hours or 864 operating hours.

Drilling
The output measure is probably the number of holes drilled. Drilling capacity amounts to 8 machines x 160 hours x 60 holes = 76 800 holes. This could probably also be expressed in terms of machine hours.

Personnel cost
As in the previous example this can be taken as the number of people employed in each activity.

Supervisory cost
This can most probably also be related to the number of people supervised (or sometimes the complexity of tasks performed).

Step 3 — Calculation of activity rates

Primary cost rates
As in the previous example the activity rates can be determined as follows:

Cutting	21 100/960	= £21,98	per batch
Turning set-up	3 230/480	= £ 6,73	per set-up
Turning operating hours	47 770/864	= £55,29	per hour
Drilling	46 700/76 800	= £ 0,608	per hole

Combined cost rates

Activity	Primary cost	Personnel cost	Supervision cost	Total cost	Output measure	Combined rate
Cutting	£21 100	£963	£900	£22 963	960	£23,92
Turning s/u	3 230	193	180	3 603	480	7,51
Turning op	47 770	1 733	1 620	51 123	864	59,17
Drilling	46 700	2 568	2 400	51 668	76 800	0,67
	£118 800	£5 457	£5 100	£129 357		

Step 4 — Compilation of bill of activities

The bill of activities for a product will be determined by observing the consumption of the activities by the product. This could be as follows:

	Per batch (50)	25 000 units
Cutting	1 batch	500 batches
Turning set-up	1 set-up	500 set-ups
Turning operating	1,67 hours (50 x 2/60)	833 hours (25 000 x 2/60)
Drilling	3 holes x 50	75 000 holes (25 000 x 3 holes)

Step 5 — Calculation of product cost

Cost of product X:

	Per batch (50)			**25 000 units**
Material cost	519,00		25 000 × 2 units @ £5,19	259 500
Cutting	23,92		500 batches @ £23,92	11 960
Turning set-up	7,51		500 × £7,51	3 755
Turning operating hours	98,62	(1,67 × £59,17)	833 × £59,17	49 289
Drilling	100,50	(50 × 3 × 67p)	75 000 × 67p	50 250
Cost of 25 000 units	749,55			374 754
Units	50			25 000
Cost per unit £	14,99			14,99

2. CALCULATION OF WASTAGE

Calculation of wastage is a very important element in an ABC & M system. Wastage includes all forms of wastage such as material, manpower, capacity or any other. In this case wastage is measured simplistically in terms of capacity. Costs are calculated below:

Capacity wastage:

Bandsaws	$(960-50) \times £23,92$	11 003
Lathes		
— set-up	$(480-500) \times £7,51$	(150)
— operating	$(864-833) \times £59,17$	1 834
Drilling machines	$(76\ 800 - 75\ 000) \times 67p$	1 206
Total capacity wastage		13 893
Per unit	$(\div 25\ 000)$	0.56p

This implies that 56p per product was lost due to the wasted capacity. Products thus actually cost £14,99+56p = £15,55.

It is recommended that a cost system calculate product cost with and without wastage. This draws management's attention to the cost savings that could be accomplished if wastage was eliminated.

Reconciliation:

Material cost	£129 500
Total cost (per example)	123 900
Personnel cost (17 x R321)	5 457
Cost for 25 000 units	388 857
Cost per unit	£ 15,55

CONCLUSION

This chapter sets out the calculation of the costs of two important cost objects, *viz* raw materials and manufactured products. It describes the nature of costs (direct, traceable and non-traceable) and illustrates how the different types of costs should be treated in an ABC system. It defines the fundamental principle of ABC, namely that **activities consume resources** and that **products consume activities**. This principle is then used in clearly set-out steps to perform a cost calculation for the two cost objects. The ABC system also demonstrates that costs, which in a traditional costing system would be considered as general overheads, can in fact be traced to cost objects such as materials and products. Other cost objects such as customers and marketing or distribution channels are discussed in later chapters.

4

Customer and market profitability

STRATEGY SHIFTS

Companies throughout the world have fundamentally changed strategies in the last few decades. Company profits up to World War II were predominantly inhibited by limited production capacities and it was therefore logical that most organisational strategies were focused on the elimination of production constraints. Increased competition and lower population and economic growth rates have increasingly forced companies to shift from these internally focused strategies to externally focused strategies which have as their focal point the meeting of customer requirements (at a profit).

Western companies facing intense competition from the East, have learned at great cost (loss of market shares, etc) that customers *must* be the prime focus of all strategies. This is particularly evident in the so-called "push" vs "pull" inventory strategies. "Push" strategies endeavour to move merchandise to customers by creating a demand for products which the company may have available for resale. The "pull" strategies, however, interpret customer requirements and let those requirements "pull" merchandise through the business to the customer.

This shift in strategy requires a new look at the mechanisms of servicing customers such as different marketing and distribution channels, after-sales service methods and market segmentation. Most of the costs associated with servicing the customer have previously been included in overheads (sales and general expenses) which were not taken into consideration in evaluating the effectiveness of customer-focused strategies. In many organisations a major proportion of total cost is spent beyond the factory and any cost system focusing predominantly on manufacturing cost will lead to inaccurate results.

Activity-based costing and management (ABC & M) systems can play a particularly useful role in measuring and evaluating the effectiveness of the expenses incurred in meeting customer requirements. This is done by the specific identification of customers, marketing channels, marketing segments, distribution channels, etc as cost objects. These cost objects are then used to evaluate the contribution of the marketing mechanisms towards overall organisational profitability. Cost accounting is thus extended as close to the customer as is practically possible.

CUSTOMER SATISFACTION

No enterprise can survive without sufficient customers and the adage that customers are the most valuable asset of a business is a widely known truism. Profits are generated from customers and products are merely means of converting customer requirements into profits. A cost system that focuses solely on product profitability thus ignores the important customer dimension. Internationally, a shift from product-focused to customer- and market-focused organisations, ie understanding what customers want and how to satisfy them, is evident.[1] Companies are generally "getting closer" to their customers. Good customer service can make the difference between success and failure.

To improve overall performance, management needs valid information. As regards customer satisfaction (ie fulfilling *all* customer requirements as perfectly as possible) ABC & M methodologies can, *inter alia*, make an enormous contribution towards measuring the following important customer-related issues:

— superior quality;
— products conforming to customer requirements and specifications;
— availability;
— reliable, timeous delivery;
— after-sales service;
— warranties;
— continuous performance measurement;
— continuous improvement (overall);
— effective systems (eg customer communication channels, responses to customers' needs, and immediate handling of problems, should any arise).

The wellspring of an organisation's strength lies in its superior ability to contribute value to customers.[2] The above attributes and factors are clearly paramount in ensuring customer satisfaction which will, *inter alia*, lead to stronger customer loyalty. The latter can, in turn, give rise to additional beneficial spin-offs, eg lower marketing costs and relatively higher selling prices, without losing customers to competitors.

Attempting to satisfy all customer demands without regard for the financial implications can, however, have disastrous consequences for an organisation. Management has to be able to determine what the impact on profitability will be if *all* customer demands are met, what the ideal (most profitable) situation will be for the organisation, and then strike the right balance.

A customer-based ABC model can be an exceptional tool in deciding when a customer's needs should not be satisfied, at least at the current price.[1] Although a key strategic objective of an organisation should be to find ways of enhancing customer satisfaction, management also needs to know how well customers satisfy the organisation, ie how profitable the customer is for the organisation.[3] *Customer profitability* refers to the profitability of an organisation's customers for the organisation (and not the profitability of the customers *per se*). In other words, an organisation's profits are derived from its customers and its ultimate profitability will depend on how profitable its customers are for the organisation. Often a large proportion of an enterprise's profit is derived from relatively few customers.[4]

CUSTOMER AND MARKET FOCUS

A multitude of cost objects can be identified in most organisations such as:

— market campaigns or projects;
— branches, regions, countries and other geographical classifications;
— marketing channels or methods;
— distribution channels;
— customers or segmented groups.

These mechanisms are sometimes presented as an hierarchical marketing framework, but it is probably more relevant to be able to present these in various dimensions, combinations and structures. In order to evaluate organisational profitability it may be necessary to determine the relative contribution of any of these mechanisms towards serving and meeting customer requirements. The most important of these is most probably the customer as cost object.

CUSTOMER AS COST OBJECT

A very important principle is that the customer is the ultimate profit object. An organisation's profit is generated by its *customers*, and not by its products; the products are only the means by which the organisation reaches its customers. No profit is made until the product is finally sold and delivered to the customer.

Historically, cost control systems tended to focus on manufacturing and product costs. Although the control of these costs is indeed crucial for an enterprise to be competitive, a significant portion of the total cost is incurred beyond manufacturing, before a profit is finally made. This is often overlooked when attributing costs to cost objects or in exercising control over costs. Direct and indirect marketing, selling, distribution, administration and financing expenses often constitute 50–60 % of the total cost of products. Consequently, the non-manufacturing cost factor plays a major role in the overall competitiveness and financial viability of products and customers, and also justifies proper analysis, planning, measurement and control.

For various reasons, profitability per customer can vary to a high degree; in fact, while some customers may be most profitable to an organisation, others may be served at a loss. By aggregating income and expense items and reporting along functional lines, conventional accounting is not equipped to disclose the aforesaid profit variation from customer to customer. Nor is it sufficient to measure individual customer profitability by gross profit less trade discount. *All* traceable costs relating to the business relationship with a customer need to be taken into account in order to determine the actual profit or loss produced by the particular customer. Therefore, to obtain a more meaningful understanding of costs and profitability at customer level, customers should also be treated as cost objects.[5]

MICRO-COST STRUCTURE

An organisation's resources are consumed in different ways and to varying degrees by different customers. Examples of organisational resources at the disposal of customers are the following:

— information services;
— promotional and selling activities;
— order-taking and execution;
— volume discounts;
— trade discounts;
— delivery;
— merchandising;
— stockholding;
— financing;
— account administration (including credit control);
— settlement discounts;
— warranties.

Some of the above resources consumed by customers in general cannot be traced to individual customers on a justifiable basis and no attempt should be made to do so if a cost allocation cannot be properly substantiated. A discretionary cost allocation may distort the true profit situation in respect of particular customers and cause management to arrive at unfounded conclusions and make the wrong strategic decisions about those customers. (Some costs may be more applicable to some of the other marketing cost objects such as marketing and distribution channels.) Therefore, *all* costs that can be *directly* related to a particular customer and that can be apportioned to the customer on a *sound basis* should be traced to the customer. An example of a customer profit statement is shown in Table 4.1.

Table 4.1: Customer profit statement

	£	%
Sales to customer	50 000	100,0
Less: Cost of sales*	35 000	70,0
Gross margin	15 000	30,0
Less: Discounts	5 000	10,0
Trade	3 000	6,0
Volume	2 000	4,0
Adjusted margin	10 000	20,0
Less: Activities consumed	6 000	12,0
Directly traceable:		
Selling (commission)	1 000	2,0
Delivery	400	0,8
Financing	1 600	3,2
Insurance	50	0,1
Settlement discount	750	1,5
Activity-traced:		
Administration	450	0,9
Collection	200	0,4
Credit control	50	0,1
Merchandising	700	1,4
Warranty	800	1,6
Net margin	4 000	8,0

* *Cost of products as determined by ABC system*

As a further refinement customer profitability analysis could also incorporate a product or product group analysis as demonstrated in Table 4.2.

CUSTOMER AND PRODUCT ANALYSIS

One of the most valuable reports that can be produced in a customer-
focused organisation is the combined customer and product profitability
report. This report features the trading position with a particular customer,
taking into account the specific products which have been sold to the customer and the customer micro-cost structure. Products or customers with
relatively high marketing costs are thus easily identifiable.

Table 4.2: Product or product group analysis – Customer X										
Product/ Product group	Sales	COS	Gross Margin	Discount		Adj Margin	Directly traceable	ABC- traced	Total con- sumed	Net margin
				Trade	Vol					
A										
B										
C										
D										

TRACING OF COSTS TO CUSTOMERS

Direct costing

A number of cost factors are easily identifiable with specific customers and are directly traceable to the respective customers. These costs can therefore be accurately traced to the customers who absorb them. Examples are:

— volume discounts;
— trade discounts;
— delivery costs;
— commissions;
— financing costs;
— settlement discounts.

Application of ABC techniques

The most rational system of tracing customer support costs to customers is likely to be based on ABC principles. Not only will this system bring forth new cost information, but it also produces very different results from systems based on generally accepted accounting principles.[6] The fundamental ABC procedure as set out in Chapter 3 is also applicable in this instance[7]:

1. Establish the activities performed, eg:

— advertising;
— selling;
— order-taking;
— packing;
— shipping;
— warehousing.

2. Accumulate the specific activity costs for each activity.

3. Determine the cost driver and output measure for each activity, eg :

— for *advertising*, the cost driver could be the advertising policy and the output measure the quantity of units sold or the specific products promoted;

— for *selling*, the cost driver could be the number of customers targeted and the output measure the orders received, or number of sales calls (whichever has the main causal effect on cost variability);

— for the activities *order taking, packing, shipping* and *warehousing*, the cost driver and output measure could be number, weight, volume or size of units;

— for the activity *account administration* the cost driver could be the credit policy and the output measure the number of customer orders.

4. Determine the unit cost of each activity by dividing the total activity cost by the output measure selected. For example:

Activity:	Packing
Output measure:	Quantity (No of units shipped)
Total quantity:	20 000
Total cost:	£24 000
Unit rate:	£1,20

5. Trace the other costs to the individual customers on the basis of activities consumed by the respective customers.

PROFIT CONTRIBUTION BY CUSTOMER

By allocating both primary and secondary costs to customers, the total cost responsibility of each customer is determined. When this amount is offset against the gross income (sales less cost of sales) generated by doing business with the customer, the customer's profit contribution will be produced.

Example 4.1

Transactions during the first quarter of 19.1: X Ltd and three of its customers, K, L and M:

Table 4.3: Details of transactions

Customers:	K	L	M
Sales £	120 000	150 000	90 000
Number of orders	13	66	39
Number of units	300	500	450
Volume of goods (m³)	30	40	25
Number of deliveries	13	27	40
Distance per delivery (kms)	10	22	17
Average amount outstanding on account £	55 000	120 000	20 000

Additional information:

X Ltd's gross profit percentage on sales: 30 %.
Trade discount: 7 %.
Volume discount: 3 % if purchases exceed £40 000 per month.
(Only L qualified for this discount.)
Settlement discount policy: 5 % for payment within 7 days and 2½ % for payment within 30 days from date of statement. During the first quarter of 19.1 K, L and M were credited with discounts of £2 650, £1 100 and £4 500 respectively.
Commission payable to representatives: 6 % on sales.
Delivery costs are £4 per kilometre.
The company's opportunity cost of capital is 20 % per annum (pre-tax).

Relevant details in respect of activity-traceable costs:

Table 4.4: Activity-traceable costs

Activity	Output measure	Unit rate £
Order-taking	Quantity of orders	13,00
Packing	Quantity of units	4,20
Dispatch	Quantity of units	3,45
Warehousing	Volume (m^3)	10,60
Account administration	Quantity of orders	19,00

Customer profit statements

Table 4.5: Customer profit statements

	K		L		M	
	£	%	£	%	£	%
Sales	120 000	100, 0	150 000	100,0	90 000	100,0
Less: Cost of sales	84 000	70,0	105 000	70,0	63 000	70,0
Gross margin	36 000	30,0	45 000	30,0	27 000	30,0
Less: Trade discount	8 400	7,0	10 500	7,0	6 300	7,0
Volume discount	—	—	4 500	3,0	—	—
Adjusted margin	27 600	23,0	30 000	20,0	20 700	23,0

(Table 4.5 continued on next page)

Table 4.5: Continued	K		L		M	
	£	%	£	%	£	%
Less: Traced cost						
Directly traceable:						
Selling	7 200	6,0	9 000	6,0	5 400	6,0
Delivery	520	0,4	2 376	1,6	2 720	3,0
Financing cost	2 750	2,3	6 000	4,0	1 000	1,1
Settlement discount	2 650	2,2	1 100	0,7	4 500	5,0
Activity-traced:						
Order-taking	169	0,1	858	0,6	507	0,6
Packing	1 260	1,1	2 100	1,4	1 890	2,1
Dispatch	1 035	0,9	1 725	1,2	1 553	1,7
Warehousing	318	0,3	424	0,3	265	0,3
Account admin	247	0,2	1 254	0,8	741	0,8
	16 149	13,5	24 837	16,6	18 576	20,6
Net margin	11 451	9,5	5 163	3,4	2 124	2,4

Comprehensive analysis

To ensure accurate customer profitability evaluation and efficient improvement strategies, appropriate data such as portrayed in Table 4.5 should be generated in respect of *all* customers. This end could be achieved with relative ease by utilising present-day computer systems. Most organisations adapt their sales and debtors systems to accommodate an appropriate customer profitability structure. Alternatively, a separate ("stand alone") customer profitability system could be set up without much effort after the required variables and factors have been established.

The final product could be in the format reflected in Table 4.5, ie:

Income/expense items   **Customers 1 ... n**

   1
   .
   .
   .
   n

or in a converse format, ie:

Customers   **Income/expenses 1 ... n**

   1
   .
   .
   .
   n

The latter style will most probably facilitate ranking (eg in order of sales volume, adjusted margin, resources consumed (expenses) or net margin) and interpretation of the data.

Profit erosion

Ranking of customers from the most profitable to the least profitable (and commonly loss-producing) will typically depict the following:

Figure 4.1: Profit erosion graph

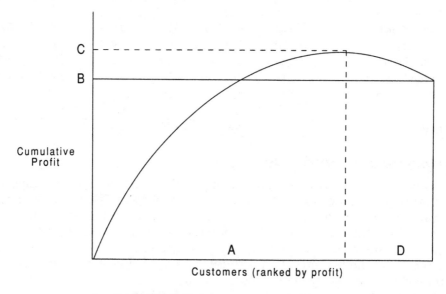

A = Profitable Customers
B = Current Profit
C = Invisible Maximum Profit
D = Unprofitable Customers

Figure 4.1 clearly illustrates how customer profitability analyses frequently identify examples of profit erosion to the extent of 10–20 % of profits which have already been generated.[8]

Customer profiles

A primary business objective, especially in a competitive environment, must be the effective management of resources. As a general rule, a sensible course will mean investing in customers that generate high profits and eliminating customers that do not generate sufficient revenues to justify the expenses required to support them.[3]

In order to perform *customer engineering* (as discussed in the following section) and to be able to make the required decisions with regard to customers, management must understand each customer's resource consumption and profitability. A general misconception exists that an enterprise's highest sales volume customers are its most profitable. Experience and analyses indicate, however, that the most profitable customers are more often those just below the top tier, who have relatively high sales volumes but do not require significant levels of support,[3] as is also demonstrated by the above example.

Apart from various rankings and other data reproductions with regard to customer attributes, an analytical matrix can also be extremely useful in the overall portrayal of an organisation's customer profiles and the ensuing customer engineering. An appropriate matrix may be as shown in Table 4.6.

Table 4.6: Analytical matrix of customer profiles

Margin	Sales volume					
	>£50 000		£10 000–£50 000		<£10 000	
>20 %	A	4(1,2%) 21,3 % £12 968	B	38(11,8 %) 21,0 % £6 277	C	33(10,2 %) 22,3 % £1 528
10 %–20 %	D	17(5,3 %) 14,4 % £9 251	E	80(24,8 %) 14,5 % £4 282	F	51(15,8 %) 15,1 % £1 073
<10 %	G	31(9,6%) 7,2 % £4 640	H	15(4,6 %) 7,8 % £2 315	I	54(16,7%) 4,6 % £251

In Table 4.6 the data provided in blocks A to I are, from top to bottom:

— number and percentage of customers;
— average net margin percentage per customer;
— average net margin per customer.

For example, block E: In the sales range £10 000 to £50 000, eighty customers, constituting 24,8 % of the total customer base of 323, yielded net margins of between 10 % and 20 % of sales (an average of 14,5%), ie an average net margin of £4 282 per customer.

Customer engineering

The improved quality of customer information will enable management to plan and act positively in order to enhance total profitability.

With reference to Table 4.6, the general objective would be to move customers up and to the left. To accomplish this, micro strategies in respect of each customer will have to be effected and activities and traceable costs relating to customers will have to be managed properly in order to increase profitability.

The initial procedure on the micro level will entail a close examination of all disproportionate items in each customer's profit statement. For example, in Table 4.5, the expenses relating to customer M's delivery, order-taking, packing, dispatch and account administration are all out of line if compared with those of customer K, who appears to be an ideal customer. Likewise, customer L's delivery, order-taking, account administration and, to a lesser extent, packing and dispatch are also out of line. (A comprehensive printout of customers' profit statements will, of course, facilitate the quantification of acceptable norms.) Furthermore, X Ltd's policy regarding quantity discounts most probably also warrants some re-thinking. A policy whereby almost 50 % of the net profit (before quantity discount) yielded by a customer (L in the example) is sacrificed, does not appear to be a sound one.

Transformation of an item in a customer's profit statement to an acceptable norm will usually be accomplished by:

— an analysis and proper understanding of the particular item, including the cause thereof (cost driver in the event of an expense item);
— improved productivity and cost efficiency;
— due consideration of possible alternatives; and
— most important, persuasive negotiations with, and co-operation of the customer, including trade-offs, if necessary.

For example, the following cost-efficiencies may be effected:

Deliveries

Determine the reason for the relatively large number of deliveries to the customer. This would automatically also involve the number of *orders* placed by the customer. The underlying causes may vary, eg:

— sheer habit/routine;
— a practice initiated and encouraged by the selling organisation's own staff;
— a lack of storage space;
— a lack of working capital;
— security problems.

In the first two instances the point at issue should be easily solved by agreement with the customer; the other "problems" will have to be addressed and resolved in the most feasible and, sometimes, ingenious ways.

This would include, at times, making sacrifices on the one hand in order to gain on the other hand, eg an additional 1 % trade discount may be granted to a customer on condition that he places his orders and takes deliveries only twice per month instead of twice per week. Apart from the favourable impact on the order-taking and delivery expenses relating to the particular customer, this will also have a positive effect on account administration, resulting in total cost savings of, say, 2,7 % of the customer's turnover, and therefore a net 1,7 % increase in profitability. Furthermore, the higher trade discount may also stimulate sales to the particular customer.

Unconventional solutions may have to be found for some of the obstacles, eg a customer's lack of security: Assist the customer (including financial assistance) to rectify the problem if a feasibility study indicates positive results arising from increased sales, less orders, less deliveries and decreased account administration. Similarly, a customer may be assisted to overcome his storage space problems if the net result would be positive.

Packing

A proper understanding of this cost and its driver should facilitate appropriate engineering. Depending on the product and individual customers' requirements, a satisfactory compromise might be reached whereby meaningful efficiencies could be achieved. For example, some customers in the retail trade may be satisfied:

— with less costly packing material for particular products; and/or
— that certain products may be packed and freighted in bulk.

In the first instance material costs would be reduced and in the second both material and labour costs with regard to the expense item *packing* would be reduced. Substantial changes to the packing process may eventually also alter the cost driver (eg from number of units to mass handled).

MARKET PROFITABILITY

The principles reflected above can be employed most profitably in other areas as well, eg:

1. Profit statement by market segment (eg territory)

Table 4.7: Territories

	North	South	East	West	Total
Sales					
Less: Cost of sales					
Gross margin					
Discounts:					
Trade					
Volume					
Adjusted margin					
Less: Resources consumed:					
Directly traceable:					
....					
....					
Activity-traced:					
....					
....					
Net margin					

2. Profit statement by market channel

Table 4.8: Market channels

	Wholesale	Retail	Agents	Mail-order	Total
Sales					
Cost of sales					
etc					
...					
...					
Net margin					

3. Profit statement by product line

Table 4.9: Product lines

	A	B	C	D	Total
Sales					
Cost of sales					
etc					
...					
...					
Net margin					

CONCLUSION

A primary business objective, especially in a competitive environment, must be the effective management of all resources and the activities that consume those resources. One of the tools at management's disposal is customer profitability analysis. In order to perform customer engineering and be able to make the required decisions with regard to customers, management has to understand each customer's resource consumption and profitability.[9]

The ABC model can be utilised most effectively to conduct customer and other market-related profitability analyses, and to highlight areas that may require managerial attention. However, before taking action on any re-engineering course, it is essential that management be satisfied that the information generated is sufficiently accurate. Only thereafter can the required courses of action for improvement be proceeded with and implemented.

Getting rid of a customer or portion of a market should be the *last resort* and should only be taken if a customer or market segment remains unprofitable after every effort has been made to reverse the situation. It may be sensible to retain unprofitable customers or markets for various reasons, eg the potential future growth of business or the strategic importance of an involvement with the relevant customer or market. On the other hand, marketing and sales efforts may be better directed towards prospecting for new customers/markets rather than attempting to satisfy unprofitable customers/markets. Marketing and selling personnel should be fully involved in decision making about customers and markets.

SOURCES CONSULTED

1. Kaplan, RS. In defense of activity-based cost management. *Management Accounting* (US), Nov 1992: 58–63.
2. Reeve, JM. The impact of continuous improvement on the design of activity-based cost systems. *Journal of Cost Management*, Summer 1990: 43–50.
3. Howell, RA & Stephen, RS. Customer profitability as critical as product profitability. *Management Accounting* (US), Oct 1990: 43–47.
4. Booth, R. Activity analysis and cost leadership. *Management Accounting* (UK), Jun 1992: 30–31.
5. Morrow, M. & Hazell, M. Activity mapping for business process redesign. *Management Accounting* (UK), Feb 1992: 36–38.
6. Sharman, PA. Activity-based management: A growing practice. *CMA Magazine*, Mar 1993: 17–22.
7. Lewis, RJ. Activity-based costing for marketing. *Management Accounting* (UK), Nov 1991: 33–38.
8. Bellis-Jones, R. Customer profitability analysis. *Management Accounting* (UK), Feb 1989: 26–28.
9. Becker, H. Understanding customer profitability. *Accountancy SA*, Oct 1993: 15–19.

5

Income measurement

INTRODUCTION

This chapter sets out a methodology for determining income in terms of activity-based costing (ABC) for management reporting purposes. Residual income theory principles are applied to the model as well as various other management methodologies such as total quality management, productivity management and capacity management. For this purpose the important differences between ABC and traditional accounting will be noted.

The chapter comprises three parts, namely:

1. The value chain approach.
2. Features of an activity-based management system.
3. ABC & M methodology using the residual income approach.

PART 1: THE VALUE CHAIN APPROACH

Traditional accounting systems present summarised accounting information in the form of manufacturing and trading accounts with other expenses summarised as general, selling and administrative expenses. This is a functional perspective of the business (manufacturing, marketing, finance, administration) and does not necessarily focus on the flow of business. The flow of the business is very well depicted by Porter's value chain as shown in Figure 5.1 (next page).

A brief reiteration of the elements of the value chain is warranted.

Primary activities
Porter's value chain sets out the logical flow of a business as consisting of the following major activities:

Inbound logistics
This entails all procurement activities which the firm may engage in to secure raw materials or products for manufacture or resale.

Operations
This includes manufacturing or merchandising, or similar activities, which are performed to prepare products for sale to the customer.

Figure 5.1: Porter's value chain

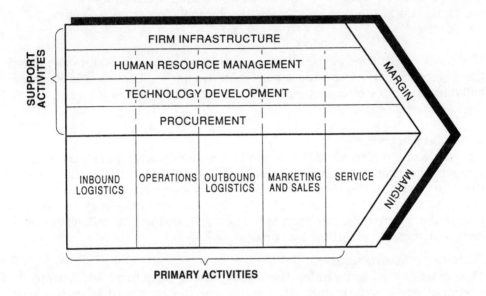

(Porter, ME. *Competitive Advantage*, New York Free Press, 1985.)

Outbound logistics
These are distribution-related activities which serve to convey goods from the business to the customer.

Marketing
These are the activities related to creating and fulfilling customer demands.

Service
This includes all customer service-related activities and may entail customer after-sales service, carrying of customer accounts, customer administration, etc.

It is important to realise that all the above activities have an external focus such as the market, the customer, the distribution channel or the product which is delivered to the customer. From a costing perspective it is relatively easy to identify the cost of a particular activity with a cost object. The relationship between the supplier of the service and the consumer is fairly direct and should not be problematic. For the above activities the following cost objects could be identified:

— Inbound logistics   Raw materials/products
— Operations   Products/services
— Outbound logistics   Distribution channels/customers
— Marketing   Marketing channels/products/ services
— Service   Customers

The relative sequence of the above activities is not considered important for the determination of cost in a particular business. The specific sequence will depend on the circumstances of the particular business.

Secondary activities

The value chain also identifies secondary activities which are performed to support the primary activities. It should be noted that the relationship of these activities to the cost objects mentioned above (products, raw materials, customers, etc) is fairly weak. The relationship between the secondary and primary activities, however, is particularly strong. The following secondary activities are identified by Porter:

Business infrastructure
This most probably includes the management structure, accounting department, switchboard and other structures necessary to keep the business going. The relationship between these activities and their "customers" is particularly weak.

Human resource management
This is the support structure which organises and manages all personnel-related matters. The customers in this case are most probably the various activities in which the personnel are employed.

Technology development
This could include operational and information technology development which service the primary activities of the firm.

Procurement
Procurement is very closely linked to the inbound logistical activity and in some cases could be directly related to this process.

Because of the strong relationship between the secondary and the primary activities, it appears more logical, from a costing perspective, to trace the costs of the secondary activities to the primary activities. These costs will ultimately be recovered in the cost object via the cost of the primary activities. Endeavours to trace secondary costs directly to cost objects such as products, customers or raw materials could be fairly arbitrary and misleading. The philosophy of tracing support costs through the primary activities is accepted throughout this text.

PHASES IN THE ACCOUNTING CYCLE

The value chain structure is very much in evidence in most organisations and is considered more representative of the flow of the business than the conventional functional view of marketing, manufacturing, finance and administration.

Traditionally two phases were distinguished in the accounting cycle, namely production and non-production (which included all other). This led to the main classification of costs as either product or period costs. In an ABC & M system the various primary activities defined by Porter in his concept of the value chain, can be used as an indication of the distinct phases which can be identified in an ABC & M accounting cycle. The primary activities can be related to the following phases in an accounting process:

PORTER'S PRIMARY ACTIVITY	PHASES IN ACCOUNTING PROCESS
Inbound logistics	Procurement and goods receiving
Operations	Manufacturing/operations
Outbound logistics	Distribution
Marketing	Marketing
Service	Customer support

As indicated above, various cost objects can be identified such as raw materials, products, distribution channels, marketing channels or customers. In order to determine the ultimate profit of the company it will be essential to determine transfer prices between phases. This can best be illustrated in the **integrated performance measurement model** which is used, *inter alia*, to determine profitability (see **Figure 5.2** which is an insert at the back of the text).

In Figure 5.2 a number of well-known management techniques are put together in a single model. An ABC model is taken and deployed on a value chain basis to give a particular strategic perspective of the organisation. The process view of the organisation features prominently in this design and productivity management and quality management systems are integrated into the measurement system to form a comprehensive performance measurement system. Life-cycle accounting and the residual income theory are applied to facilitate specific views on the management process. The objective is to get as much synergy as possible, but above all to achieve a comprehensive approach to managerial issues. This approach will be reconciled with the conventional income measurement philosophy.

Relating the new model to traditional reporting, the following analogy could be drawn in the case of a manufacturing company:

VALUE CHAIN APPROACH	**TRADITIONAL APPROACH**
Inbound logistics	
plus	Manufacturing account
Operations	
Marketing	Trading account
Service	
Outbound logistics	Profit and loss account
Support services	

This relationship is not absolutely precise but gives an indication of the resemblance between the two methodologies. The more important differences between the traditional approach and the application of ABC in the above model are:

- ABC focuses on the value chain concept in its determination of the phases in the accounting process.
- ABC ignores the constraints placed by GAAP (generally accepted accounting practice) on its determination of inventory valuation and in its recording of a transaction.
- Life-cycle accounting could specifically be incorporated in the ABC income determination process.
- The element of time may feature specifically in the ABC process but is largely ignored in traditional accounting.

EXPLANATION OF THE MODEL

The model is divided into five distinct accounting phases as indicated by the dotted lines. (This is described in more detail below.) These phases are found in most businesses and accounting systems for them will help a business focus on its area of competitive advantage. The first two columns in the model indicate the primary and secondary activities. Cost of secondary activities which can be traced to a primary activity, are traced to the cost object via the rate of the primary activity. This is a rate which combines the relevant primary and secondary cost. Management cost, which may not be traceable cost, is taken "down" the model and deducted from customer profits in the determination of residual income (see Table 5.11).

The characteristics of the various phases are as follows:

Phase 1: Procurement phase

The principal cost object during this phase is the raw materials or products procured. The purpose of this phase is to collect costs via the activity structure associated with the procurement and inbound logistical processes. The activities chosen for this example are buying, receiving, storage and payment. Many other activities are equally relevant but these are considered adequate for the purpose of this exercise.

Costs are conveyed via the output measure to the cost object. Buying cost is calculated per purchase order. The buying cost per raw material will be based on the number of purchase orders that were required for the particular raw material. Storage cost will be determined by two cost drivers, namely space and time. Space cost will be traced to the raw material based on the square metres of storage space occupied by each material. The proposed system takes account of time by charging the raw materials for the "time" costs (cost of capital for the time period) associated with the raw material. Raw material A may have been in stock for three months while raw material B has been in stock for only two weeks. A proportionate amount of time costs will be traced to the two raw materials on a "real-time" basis. This implies that time costs, such as interest or cost of capital, may be charged to the raw materials on a day-to-day or real-time basis. (See Time-based Accounting and Residual Income Theory later in this chapter.)

The result of this phase is to provide the *procurement and holding costs* of the various raw materials. To this is added the direct cost of the raw materials and this becomes the *transfer price* at which the raw materials are transferred to the operations phase. Holding and procurement costs are thus calculated per specific raw material. Holding costs are therefore not hidden away in general overhead costs, which often happens in traditional systems. If the raw material, procurement and holding costs are deducted from sales, a *procurement margin* is calculated which is not dissimilar to the value-added margin which is often calculated in the traditional approach. The **procurement margin** is defined as:

Sales less the purchase price, procurement cost and holding cost of raw materials.

This indicates how much is available to be spent in other phases of the business *and* to provide for the desired profit.

Phase 2: Operational phase

The principal cost object becomes the product or service which is sold. As input it may receive the transfer costs of various raw materials as calculated in the previous phase. It adds costs via the operational activities of engineering and development, various production activities, quality control, operations administration and storage (of the final product). Cost of time absorbed by this phase of the model is charged to the various products based on the applicable cost of capital rate and the time each product spends in this phase. (See example in section on Time-Based Accounting.) The intention with this calculation is to identify those products which ultimately do not *break even* or recover all costs. Interest cost is not charged to this model as it is implicit in the cost of capital calculation. (See reconciliation of two methods at end of chapter.)

As in the above phase costs are conveyed to the cost objects (products) via the output measures of the various activities. The rates of the various activities once again include a proportionate share of secondary activity costs. Certain costs (for example storage activity) will also be traced to the products on a "real-time" basis. (Time costs, such as interest or cost of capital, are thus traced to products on a day-to-day or real-time basis.) This model could therefore also be referred to a real-time cost model. Products that take longer to produce or are kept in stock for a longer period will be charged proportionately more time costs. This is very important in determining which products are disproportionate consumers of time-based cost (cost of capital).

The result of this phase is to produce the *operational and holding cost* of the finished product. This can be deducted from the *procurement margin*, calculated in phase one, to determine product profitability (or a type of operational margin) before other organisational expenses are calculated. The **operational margin** can thus be defined as:

> *The procurement margin, less operational and holding costs of the finished product.*

This can be compared (to some extent) with the gross margin as was traditionally calculated.

Phase 3: Marketing phase

The principal cost object could be the marketing channels or the product, depending on circumstances. Cost of marketing activities could thus be traced to marketing channels (or products or even customers). Products or customers, in turn, consume the activities of the marketing channels. In certain cases the customer could also become a cost object as marketing channels could be dedicated to specific customers.

This phase receives as input the cost of the finished product/service produced in the operational phase. The result of this phase is to produce the marketing cost per channel/per product. Product profitability can thus be taken a stage further than in phase two. The **marketing margin** can be defined as:

> *The operational margin less the cost of marketing activities.*

The marketing margin indicates the amount available for spending on distribution of the product, serving the customer, and profit.

Phase 4: Distribution phase

The principal cost object could be the distribution channel or the customer, depending on the organisational structure. Distribution costs are sometimes customer-specific. Input into this phase is the transfer cost of the product as it has moved through the first three phases. The distribution channels or customers will consume costs via the distribution activities.

The result of this phase is the cost of distributing products through various distribution channels or to different customers (or products, depending on circumstances). Product profitability can thus be calculated before customer-specific costs and other non-traceable costs are calculated. Distribution channel profitability can thus be determined.

The **distribution margin** can be defined as:

The marketing margin, less cost of distribution activities.

This indicates the margin that remains after distribution activity cost, but before the cost of serving the customer is taken into account.

Phase 5: Customer phase

The principal cost object in this phase is the customer. It receives as input the product with the cost it collected in the previous four phases. It consumes cost from a variety of customer-related activities (of which only two are indicated in the integrated performance measurement model). One of the important time-related costs it consumes is the cost of financing the customer's account.

The result of this phase is the determination of *customer profitability* or the customer margin. At this point the business' income before non-traceable and "waste"-related costs can be determined. The **customer margin** can be defined as:

The distribution margin, less customer-related cost.

This margin indicates the amount of profit that is left before wastage and untraceable cost are accounted for.

Phase 6: Determination of residual income

Residual income is determined by deducting from an organisation's revenue not only its operational costs but also the cost of funding the organisation.

Funding cost consists of cost of borrowed funds as well as cost of equity (owners' expected return). These funds are invested in various assets in the firm, the main classifications of which are:

— fixed assets (buildings, plant, vehicles, etc);
— current assets (debtors and inventory).

Cost of capital is affected by the amount of capital involved and the time it is utilised. This principle is applied to the conceptual model by charging the appropriate amount of cost of capital to all activities utilising the capital. Manufacturing activities utilising plant would thus be charged cost of capital on the investment in such plant. Inventory or products in process in a particular phase will accordingly be charged cost of capital for the time spent in the phase. In this manner the total amount of cost of capital that the firm must produce is recovered in the cost objects (raw materials, products, customers). The business that thus produces a positive residual income (ie after providing for cost of capital) will be able to satisfy all its fund providers. It is often said that such a business then adds value to the owners by providing a return higher than that expected by the owners (and if not, it destroys value).

Residual income is determined by taking the *customer margin* (from phase 5) and *deducting* from this the *non-traceable cost* (management cost and other) as well as all *wastage* which has been calculated in the activities. Wastage is not absorbed into the cost of a cost object.

The sequence of the various phases is not necessarily important and each business may choose its own relative sequence.

PART 2: FEATURES OF AN ACTIVITY-BASED MANAGEMENT SYSTEM

The focus in an activity-based management system is not only to calculate cost, but also to facilitate management of the organisation via an understanding of the activities and processes of which they form a part. Cost can, to a certain extent, be managed by managing the causes of cost or the activity levels.

STRATEGIC SUPPORT

The design of the system starts with an evaluation of organisational strategies. Fundamentally the accounting system should support the implementation and evaluation of strategies. This has been a pertinent shortcoming of traditional systems, because of the incomplete information produced by such systems.

Organisations usually strive to achieve a number of strategies. Generically these may be classified as internally- or externally-focused strategies. Examples of internal strategies are improvement of quality, productivity, and lead times, and management of finance or other costs. The accounting system should incorporate measures to evaluate the progress of such strategies. External strategies may aim to increase market share or to improve the organisation's image. This chapter does not focus on external strategies.

The ABC & M system thus finds the link between strategic planning and operational reporting, normally through feedback on the critical success factors.

TIME-BASED ACCOUNTING

Traditional accounting fundamentally ignores the time value of money in its cost measurement process, except in so far as the transaction date may relate to an accounting period. Costs incurred six months ago are measured and compared with current costs. It is, however, common knowledge that these costs are not comparable because of the time value of money. This situation is aggravated in a highly inflationary environment. The deficiencies in the accounting process which uses historical costs originate from this weakness.

The foregoing gives rise to the underlying flaw in traditional accounting which remains input-focused, ie focused on the date when resources were put into the system. An advertising campaign may start on 20 December of a financial year which ends on 31 December. The full cost of the campaign (if invoiced before 31 December) will be charged to the income statement of that year. The outcome or the output produced by this campaign is of no relevance to conventional accounting.

Many ABC & M systems lend themselves excellently to the introduction of time-related costs. Time in itself must be considered to be an important cost driver. If this notion is accepted then a methodology must be found to change the monetary result of a transaction over time.

Two products (of the same cost) may be purchased for resale at different times during the financial year and be held in inventory for different periods.

Table 5.1: Illustration of effect of cost of capital		
	Product A	**Product B**
Period in inventory	3 months	6 months
Cost price £	1 000	1 000
Carrying cost @ 20 % pa	50	100
Cost at date of use £	1 050	1 100

In the traditional model the so-called "cost" of both products will be £1 000. The integrated performance measurement model uses the principle of time-differentiated costs, ie Product A will be charged to cost of sales at £1 050 and Product B at £1 100.

In the integrated performance measurement model all activities that "consume" time-related costs, such as cost of capital, will be charged with such costs. It can be argued that basically three types of assets exist in the normal business which consume such costs, namely fixed assets, inventories and debtors. Fixed assets mainly provide the infrastructure to perform activities. The cost associated with these assets will thus be charged to the appropriate activities where the assets are employed. Inventory costs can be differentiated between raw materials, work-in-progress and finished goods. As these items move through the various accounting cycles they will attract costs on a real-time basis. Costs will virtually be incurred or charged on a daily basis. This will, of course, necessitate fairly sophisticated computer systems but provide a particular dynamism to the costing process.

Similarly, customers will attract cost of capital for each day their accounts remain outstanding. This will be taken care of in the customer profitability module of the ABC & M system. The issue can be illustrated by the following example: If the profitability of a customer must be determined, time-related costs must be taken into consideration. Two customers, A and B may have bought similar goods from the company at a price of £10 000. If the cost of these goods were £8 000 in both cases, the ostensible "profit" is £2 000. However, if customer A pays cash but customer B takes three months to pay his account, the profits on the two customers' purchases are obviously not the same. The profit generated by customer B should be reduced by the time "loss" on the goods that were carried for three months. If a notional interest rate of 15 % is accepted this amounts to £300 (15 % × £8 000 × 3/12). The cost driver is therefore the time (three months) that the costs were financed by the company. (An opportunity cost approach can also be applied in this case, ie that the company has actually lost the opportunity income on the sales of £10 000.)

This method is called the real-time accounting approach, which is an integral part of the proposed integrated performance model, and can be successfully applied to adjust all time-affected costs and assets or liabilities. Assets such as inventories, debtors and fixed assets will, for instance, be charged this notional cost. If this notional cost is then recovered through the product cost a more "real" profit will be determined. Such notional charges will naturally be reversed at year-end to determine conventional accounting profits. The specific cost of capital of the organisation may be applied to the situation resulting in a residual income or loss.

RESIDUAL INCOME

The *integrated performance measurement* (IPM) model lends itself perfectly to the application of the residual income theory in a very practical way. If the cost charged to the assets is indeed cost of capital and not merely external finance, the income remaining after this all-inclusive cost has been deducted from sales, is the residual income. The reasoning is that positive residual income adds value to the business and negative residual income destroys value. This model therefore facilitates the identification of products, customers, etc which do not add value to the business.

Residual income is determined by taking into consideration as an expense the cost of the various sources of capital the business may employ. Cost of capital is determined by calculating not only the cost of external sources of funds (borrowed funds) but also the cost of internal sources (mainly equity and retained income). These sources of funds are employed in two main categories of assets, namely fixed assets and current assets, the latter consisting of debtors and inventories.

The principle that is applied in this model is that the relevant activities which consume the capital will be charged the cost of capital rate applied to the capital employed in the respective assets. Fixed assets may, for example, be employed mainly in the production activities, which will bear this cost. Inventories may partially be employed in the procurement phase (raw materials) as described above or in the operations phase (finished goods). Debtors will be employed in the customer phase. Products or customers will consume cost of capital on a time basis as they pass through the various activities.

The intention with residual income theory is for the organisation to break even on this basis, which implies that the demands by all the providers of capital for an appropriate return can be met. All products or customers will therefore include an appropriate share of the cost of capital. It should be evident which products/services/customers do not provide this required return. Time-based accounting is, however, a prerequisite for the application of residual income theory.

PROCESSES

The value chain phases can normally be analysed or broken down into their constituent processes. Operations may, for instance, consist of several manufacturing processes or the customer phase may consist of a credit management process, a debt collection process and an account administration process. It is also imperative, from a strategic perspective, to understand the business processes (the way the business is conducted) as alternative or better processes may be more profitable to perform.

Although the various business processes are not indicated on the above model, these form the heart of the activity structure. Processes stem from the basic desire to satisfy customer requirements. Process structures are normally achieved by a linking mechanism in the ABC & M system. A process is usually a chain of activities performed in order to achieve a specific business purpose. An example of such a business process may be the sales process with activities as indicated in Figure 5.3.

The process definition and process costs are considered necessary in order to evaluate the optimal performance of the business. Processes are usually put in motion by a trigger external to the process, which may not necessarily be one of the activity cost drivers. The sales process trigger may be the result of a management decision to start selling in a new market segment. The cost driver of this process will be the number of customers who will be targeted in this market segment. The costs of virtually all the activities in the selling process would therefore be affected by this decision, for example, the cost of activities such as customer calling, order processing, order make-up and credit checking will all increase. A comprehension of this perception is essential from a cost management perspective. Total cost of the process as well as the cost per common denominator (such as the cost per sales invoice) may be important.

Figure 5.3: Sales process

Process matrices may be drawn of the business which will indicate all process links, as in Figure 5.4.

The number indicated in the blocks in Figure 5.4 merely indicates the sequence of activities that are performed for a particular process. Although not common in practice, it may be possible for various processes to have common activities.

Figure 5.4: Process matrix

PROCESS	ACT 1	ACT 2	ACT 3	ACT 4	ACT 5	ACT 6	ACT 7
A	1		2	3		4	5
B		1		2	4	3	
C			1	4	3		2

The value chain of any business can be broken down into a number of business processes. These processes should theoretically consist only of processes which are conducted to contribute to customer satisfaction.

LIFE-CYCLE COSTING

The life-cycle approach should also be applied to certain costs such as research and development (R & D). The cost of R & D may be related to several accounting periods or several activities or products and a particular approach should be developed to trace such costs to cost objects over the different accounting periods (during their life span).

COST DRIVERS AND OUTPUT MEASURES

One of the important features of an ABC system which distinguishes it from a traditional costing system is the fact that it uses the specific relationship which exists between the activity and the cost object, also to trace cost to the cost object. As is explained in Chapter 7, the cost driver may be excellent for cost management purposes but less useful as a "conveyor" of cost. Cost drivers are useful indicators of what determines the cost structure of an activity, but may be difficult to measure in some instances. It may therefore be more practical to use a different mechanism called the **output measure** to trace costs to the cost object. Output measures reflect the executional capability of an activity *within* the structural constraints set by the cost driver. This may relate to the relevant range concept in cost-volume-profit relationships. If the cost object is, for example, the customer order, then the cost driver for ordering costs may be the number of order lines. However, the profitability of the customer may be expressed per order and it may therefore be more appropriate to use customer orders as the mechanism to convey costs.

The concepts of cost driver and output measure could also be related to the credit management process for credit cards. The management decision relating to the threshold of transactions which require specific credit approval (say all transactions above £300) may determine the whole cost structure of the credit management process. Based on this limit a certain number of transactions will have to be approved and if the level is reduced to say £200, many more transactions will have to be approved. The cost driver is thus the credit policy. The output delivered by the process is the actual number of transactions approved and this can thus be used as the output measure to convey cost to the product.

Cost drivers and output measures could also be explained in the context of a purchasing activity. The cost driver of the purchasing activity could be the management policy to replenish stocks, say at weekly intervals. If this policy is changed to replenishment at monthly intervals, it can be expected that a different cost (infrastructure) will result. However, the output measure may be defined as the number of purchase orders, which may be an acceptable mechanism to convey costs to the cost objects/items purchased which "consume" purchase orders. Within a reasonably relevant range, ie subject to the underlying cost structure not being affected, this may be a fair basis for linking cost to the cost objects.

WASTAGE AND QUALITY MANAGEMENT

One of the important reasons for developing an ABC & M system may be to measure and report on wastage that has occurred in the organisation. Most forms of wastage are measurable, whether they be material waste, manpower or machine waste, time waste, process waste or product waste. Management of wastage is a prime concern in most organisations and it is therefore imperative that details on wastage should feature prominently in the financial system.

One of the objectives with this model is to measure wastage wherever it may occur in the organisation. Wastage does not normally feature in a conventional accounting system and vanishes amongst other expenses. Most quality management systems measure wastage and other non-quality factors but in a physical manner (number of defects). The ABC & M system should help to quantify this price of non-conformance (PONC) into financial terms for integration into the costing system. Also the measurement of quality activities (quality assurance) can be done fairly easily by identifying these as separate activities.

PRODUCTIVITY MANAGEMENT

Productivity of manpower, materials and capital is of major concern to most organisations. ABM should facilitate measurement and reporting of productivity criteria through its activity structures. All the relevant elements of productivity measurement such as time criteria, capital turnover, etc are normally measured in an ABC & M system. In some cases it may be necessary to drop down one more level of detail (to the task level) in order to facilitate productivity management.

CAPACITY MANAGEMENT

As is the case with productivity management, most of the information required for a capacity management system is also in evidence in an ABC & M system. A capacity management system, with measurement of capacity at activity level, is normally quite feasible.

MULTIPLE COST FOCUS

The conventional focus on costs is on cost elements (salaries, power, stationery, etc) within the responsibility framework of the organisation. A properly designed ABC & M system will provide a number of views of costs such as the normal cost element and cost centre focus, and also various others such as process and activity focuses and whether these add value to the organisation, etc. The different points of view are only limited by the imagination of the designer of the ABC & M system.

PART 3: PROPOSED METHODOLOGY

The application of the methodology can best be illustrated by an example which also illustrates the difference between the conventional approach and the ABC & M approach.

Example 5.1: Manufacturing company

The accountant has just finalised the accounting entries of the company and provides the following information relating to income and expenses:

Table 5.2: Extract from company records		
Materials purchased:	A (4 000 units)	£410 000
	B (7 000 units)	230 000
	C (5 000 units)	678 000
Production cost:	Personnel cost	450 000
	Facility cost	188 000
	Energy cost	350 000
	Consumables	179 000
	Repairs & maintenance	272 000
Non-production cost:	Personnel cost	590 000
	Facility cost	354 000
	Energy cost	207 000
	Consumables	135 000
	Repairs & maintenance	122 000
	Interest	130 000
	Transport	116 000
	Computer services	70 000
	Consulting fees	136 000
	Audit fees	30 000
	Petty cash expenses	20 000
	Bad debts	12 000
Revenue:		3 965 000
Additional information:		
Closing stocks:	Material A	300 units
	Material C	800 units
Manufactured units:	Product 1	60 000 units
	Product 2	115 000 units
Closing stock:	Product 1	3 000 units
	Product 2	15 000 units

Production costs can be split 40 % for product 1 and 60 % for product 2. Product 1 uses 0,06 units of raw material A and 0,03 units of C whilst product 2 uses 0,06 units of B and 0,02 units of C. Opening stocks may be ignored. Because of quality defects, 1 000 units of product 2 had to be scrapped. The normal selling price of product 1 is £30 and that of product 2 £25.

The company markets its products to agents and wholesalers and uses both rail and road transport to deliver its products.

TRADITIONAL INCOME DETERMINATION
This is fairly straightforward and will be as follows:

Table 5.3: Traditional income determination model		£	£
Revenue			3 965 000
Materials consumed			1 178 770
Purchases	(410 + 230 + 678)		1 318 000
Less: Closing stock			139 230
	A (410 000/4000 x 300)	30 750	
	C (678 000/5000 x 800)	108 480	
Value-add margin			2 786 230
Production cost of sales			1 197 020
Conversion cost [1]	(450+188+350+179+272)		1 439 000
Less: Closing stock	(see [2])		241 980
	Product 1	59 130	
	Product 2	182 850	
Gross margin			1 589 210
Non-production cost	(590+354+207+135+122+1		1 922 000
	30+116+70+136+30+		
	20+12)		
Loss			(332 790)
1. Conversion cost:	Product 1	Product 2	Total
Percentage allocation	40 %	60 %	
Cost £	575 600	863 400	1 439 000
Units produced	60 000	115 000	
2. Total cost per unit			
Conversion cost per unit £	9,59	7,51	
Raw material cost			
Material A	6,15*		
Material B		1,97	
Material C	4,07	2,71	
Total cost per unit	19,71	12,19	
Finished goods inventory	3 000	15 000	
Value £	59 130	182 850	241 980

*Raw material A 410 000/4 000 × 0,06 = £6,15; other materials calculated in the same manner.

It must be noted that a certain amount of raw material waste occurs in this example. This can be calculated as follows:

Table 5.4: Raw material inventory reconciliation

	Purchases	Consumption	Stock	Wastage	Value of wastage
A	4 000	3 600	300	100	10 250
B	7 000	6 900	—	100	3 286
C	5 000	4 100	800	100	13 560
Total raw material waste £					27 096

The cost of wastage in the traditional system is included in the cost of materials consumed as calculated in Table 5.3. Table 5.4 presents the calculation of wastage of raw materials, valued at purchase cost only. The amount arrived at above (£27 096) will differ from the value of wastage determined under an ABC & M model because the latter includes activity-traced costs and not only direct costs. (Refer to the appendix to this chapter — raw material waste calculation under (A).)

Income measurement under the ABC & M system could possibly be determined as follows (utilising the integrated performance measurement model). This model is referred to as the IPM model. The accounting treatment of cost or determination of income is seen as a subset of the IPM model and will be referred to as the ABM model. The IPM model can also be applied to the broader concept of performance measurement, but this is not dealt with in this chapter.

ACTIVITY-BASED MANAGEMENT APPROACH

Step 1— Tracing of resources to activities

The same costs as above could be divided into the relevant activities: See Step 1 in **Table 5.5** which is an insert at the back of the book.

It is assumed that costs can be divided between the activities that are defined for the various phases in the ABM model. In practice this process will involve setting up the necessary activity structures in the general ledger or analysing existing cost centres into activities. Costs must preferably be traced from source (wages system, creditors' invoices, cheque payments, etc). A notable difference at this stage concerns the treatment of interest. Interest being a cash or accrued expense will be treated as a period cost in conventional accounting. In the residual income model this is replaced by the cost of capital of the organisation, which obviously includes the remuneration for owners' funds. Cost of capital being a notional cost will have to be substituted by interest cost in the eventual report to external stakeholders. This will specifically be shown in the reconciliation between conventional and ABM profits. (Cost of capital is assumed to be £329 000 in this example.)

Step 2— Identification of wastage (other than capacity waste)

Various forms of wastage may occur in an organisation such as waste of manpower, time, energy or capacity. Many different wastage identification systems may be applied and definitions of what constitutes wastage will be dependent on the organisation. For the purpose of the example it is assumed that wastage has already been defined by the organisation (see step 2 in Table 5.5). Wastage in each activity can be deducted from other activity costs to determine normative costs, or costs that are chargeable to products. Product costs should therefore exclude all forms of wastage.

Capacity waste is calculated in step 5 once the combined activity rates have been calculated. Capacity waste, like material waste, or other forms of process waste, should also not be included in product cost.

Step 3— Trace secondary cost to primary activities

In accordance with the procedures previously described, the costs of secondary activities need to be traced to primary activities. Four secondary activities are shown in the model (Table 5.5), namely management, information services, personnel management, and research and development. (These may consist of several individual activities, but have been confined to the stated few activities for this example.)

Management activity is considered to be untraceable for this example and will be shown in the income statement as such. It is therefore not traced to primary activities. Most organisations have developed specific costing systems for tracing information technology (IT) costs to the users and this system (a type of technology accounting system) will be used for tracing this cost to user activities. Personnel-related activities such as payroll preparation, security, canteen, etc may be grouped together and traced to activities on a per head basis. Research and development costs usually benefit several years and such costs may probably be traced to products in several accounting periods. A life-cycle accounting system may be developed for this purpose. In order not to complicate this example too much, R & D costs are assumed to be applicable to a single accounting period in the example and are also considered to be untraceable. Consequently only personnel and IT costs will be traced to primary activities.

In this example personnel activity costs amount to £210 per head and are traced to the activities where people are employed (see Step 3 in model). IT services are charged to "user" activities at 64p per transaction.

Step 4— Calculation of combined rate

Primary and secondary traced costs are added together to calculate the combined rate for primary activities as set out in the attached table. This rate can then be used to calculate the costs of the various cost objects. The rate facilitates visibility of the various cost components which have been traced to it. For example, the combined rate of the buying activity of £17,73 consists of its prime rate of £14,00 and £3,73 for secondary activities. The £3,73 can once again be analysed into its components of personnel and IT (£0,53 for personnel and £3,20 for IT cost). This provides some "visibility" of the support cost structure.

Steps 5 and 6— Calculation of capacity and total wastage

Capacity waste poses a slightly different problem in that the organisation has to decide on practical capacity levels. Some organisations may prefer to recover costs on actual capacities. This implies, however, that if capacity utilisation is relatively low, unit costs may be extremely high. To overcome this problem it is recommended that costs be recovered on a realistic capacity and that unutilised capacity be treated as wastage.

In the example, capacity waste is specifically calculated and an assumption is made about other forms of wastage in order to illustrate the relevance of reporting wastage. (All costs are assumed to be affected by capacity utilisation.) Note the specific reporting of wastage in the ABM income statement.

Once again, in order to simplify the example, no capacity waste is calculated for marketing, distribution or customer activities. However, the same principles of calculating capacity waste would apply.

Step 7— Calculation of cost per cost object

The detailed calculations of the various cost objects are set out in the appendix to this chapter. A summary of these costs is as follows:

Cost of raw materials — (A in appendix)

Material A	434 611	108,65 per unit
Material B	312 108	44,59 per unit
Material C	762 414	152,48 per unit
	1 509 133	

Cost of manufactured products (production and holding cost) — (B in appendix)

Product 1	731 581	£12,19 Unit conversion cost
Product 2	791 338	£ 6,88 Unit conversion cost

Cost of marketing channels — (C in appendix)

Agents	201 260
Wholesalers	118 090
	319 350

Cost of distribution channels — (D in appendix)

Road	188 000
Rail	216 370
	404 370

Cost per customer — (E in appendix)

Customer P	101 700
Customer Q	48 150
Customer R	16 500
	166 350

Henceforth the profit figures determined using the traditional approach (Table 5.3) and the ABM model (Table 5.5) are reconciled.

Table 5.6: Income statement – ABM model	£	£
Sales		3 965 000
Less: Cost of procuring and holding raw material		1 323 982
Direct material cost	1 318 000	
Buying	33 687	
Receiving	19 440	
Storage	79 320	
Payment	58 686	
	1 509 133	
Raw material inventory	(154 579)	
Raw material waste	(30 572)	
Procurement margin £ c/f		2641 018

Table 5.6: Continued			
Procurement margin	b/f		2 641 018
			1 251 289
Engineering		76 458	
Production activity 1		545 948	
Production activity 2		244 870	
Production activity 3		398 151	
Quality control		22 768	
Operational admin		36 120	
Storage		198 604	
		1 522 919	
Finished goods inventory		(259 020)	
Quality defects		(12 610)	
Operational margin (product profitability)			1 389 729
Marketing channel cost			319 350
Market research		46 260	
Advertising		35 050	
Sales		157 930	
Sales administration		80 110	
Marketing margin (marketing segment profitability)			1 070 379
Distribution cost			404 370
Delivery		350 530	
Distribution administration		53 840	
Distribution margin (distribution channel profitability)			666 009
Customer costs			166 350
Customer administration		125 500	
Customer collections		40 850	
Customer margin (customer profitability)			499 659
Untraceable cost			474 000
Research & development		74 000	
General management		300 000	
Other untraceables		100 000	
Profit before wastage			25 659
Wastage			525 060
Raw materials		30 572	
Quality defects		12 610	
Capacity (rounding – £61)		100 878	
Manpower		143 000	
Energy		77 000	
Time		56 000	
Other resources		105 000	
Residual income			(499 401)

Table 5.7: Reconciliation of traditional and ABM profits	£
Conventional income	(332 790)
Cost of capital less interest (329 000 – 130 000)	(199 000)
Raw material inventory difference (154 579 – 139 230)	15 349
Finished goods inventory difference (259 020 – 241 980)	17 040
Residual income/(loss)	(499 401)

CONCLUSION

This chapter sets out the methodology of measuring income using the activity-based management model. It utilises the residual income theory, ie
charging cost of capital to the income statement instead of interest. Costing
for various cost objects such as raw materials, products, marketing channels, distribution channels and customers is explained. Lastly a reconciliation is done between the conventional profit calculation and that of the
ABM approach, proving that the two methods could lead to vastly different
financial results. The difference is mainly attributable to:

— taking account of cost of capital instead of only interest;
— tracing of certain activity costs to inventories which traditionally are
   not included in inventory valuations;
— the identification and treatment of wastage which is traditionally in-
   advertently absorbed in inventory valuations.

No attempt has been made to interpret the above information as this is
covered in Chapter 8 on Cost Management.

Appendix

Calculation of cost of cost objects

All calculations refer to Example 5.1 described in Chapter 5. Activity costs and other relevant figures are derived from Table 5.5 which is an insert at the back of the book.

(A) Cost of raw materials

The cost of raw materials can be calculated by referring to the bill of activities (BOA) of raw materials. This is as follows:

Table A5.1: Bill of activities (BOA) — raw materials				
Raw material	**Buying**	**Receiving**	**Storage**	**Payment**
A	300	450	400	400
B	700	1 650	1 400	1 480
C	900	900	2 200	900
	1 900	3 000	4 000	2 780

The BOA merely represents the "consumption" of the outputs of the activities by the various raw materials. Raw material A has, for example, consumed 300 output units from buying activities, 450 output units from receiving activities, 400 output units from storage activities and 400 output units from payment activities. The cost of the various activities as calculated above could be used to determine the cost of all procurement activities that should be added to the direct material cost. (Example: Buying activity material A: 300 × £17,73 = £5 319.) This can be set out as in Table A5.2.

It is also interesting to note the treatment of capacity cost, or waste in this example. The buyer or buying activity, for example, has a capacity to execute 2 000 orders (see step 5, Table 5.5, which is inserted at the back of the book). However, from the bill of activities above, it is evident that only 1 900 orders were executed, or that a capacity loss of 100 orders occurred. This capacity waste is then valued at the full output measure rate of £17,73 per order, resulting in a capacity waste of £1 773 for this activity. Similar calculations are done for other activities.

Table A5.2: Calculation of cost of procured raw material				
Activities	**Material A**	**Material B**	**Material C**	**Total***
Buying (£17,73)	5 319	12 411	15 957	33 687
Receiving (£6,48)	2 916	10 692	5 832	19 440
Storage (£19,83)	7 932	27 762	43 626	79 320
Payment (£21,11)	8 444	31 243	18 999	58 686
Procurement cost	24 611	82 108	84 414	191 133
Raw material cost	410 000	230 000	678 000	1 318 000
Total cost	434 611	312 108	762 414	1 509 133
Units	4 000	7 000	5 000	
Per unit	108,65	44,59	152,48	
Raw material inventory:				
Units	300	—	800	1 100
ABC value	32 595		121 984	154 579
Conventional value	30 750		108 480	139 230
Difference	1 845		13 504	15 349

* Please note that capacity waste is not traced to cost objects. For example, in the case of the buying activity £33 687 is traced to cost objects which represents the total cost of the activity (£35 450) less capacity waste. (£1 773 – rounding difference £10.)

The ABC valuation is not a valuation for external reporting purposes but merely of the costs incurred to bring inventories to their current status. By indicating in the cost system which activity costs are not "inventoriable" for external reporting purposes, an easy reconciliation with conventional valuations can be made.

Raw material waste

Raw material waste which occurred in the manufacturing process should also be valued at the above rate.

Table A5.3: Raw material waste			
Material	**Wastage**	**Cost/unit**	**Value of wastage £**
A	100	108,65	10 865
B	100	44,59	4 459
C	100	152,48	15 248
Total raw material waste			30 572

Wastage normally results from resource waste (manpower, energy, time, etc — see step 2, Table 5.5 inserted at the back of the book) or process waste (such as raw material or capacity waste in process) or product waste (products become redundant, obsolete or are simply lost).

(B) Cost of products

The following bill of activities applies to products 1 and 2:

Table A5.4: Bill of activities – manufactured products

Activity	Product 1 Quantity	Product 1 Cost	Product 2 Quantity	Product 2 Cost	Total Quantity	Total Cost
Engineering	200	43 690	150	32 768	350	76 458
Production act. 1	35 000	181 983	70 000	363 965	105 000	545 948
Production act. 2	34 000	177 140	13 000	67 730	47 000	244 870
Production act. 3	75 000	170 636	100 000	227 515	175 000	398 151
Quality control	400	4 554	1 600	18 214	2 000	22 768
Operational admin	100	12 900	180	23 220	280	36 120
Storage	340 000	140 678	140 000	57 926	480 000	198 604
Conversion cost		73 158		791 338		1 522 919
Units		60 000		115 000		
Conversion cost per product £		12,19		6,88		

To this cost should be added the appropriate amount of raw material cost which was consumed in production. The material cost is as follows:

Table A5.5: Bill of materials

Raw material	Product 1 Per unit	Product 1 Units	Product 1 Cost	Product 2 Per unit	Product 2 Units	Product 2 Cost
A (£108,65)	0,06	3 600	391 148			
B (£ 44,59)				0,06	6 900	307 644
C (£152,48)	0,03	1 800	274 464	0,02	2 300	350 710
			665 612			658 354

The cost of the manufactured product and inventory is thus as follows:

Table A5.6

	Product 1	Product 2	Total
Raw material cost	665 612	658 354	1 323 966
Conversion cost	731 581	791 338	1 522 919
Total product cost	1 397 193	1 449 692	2 846 885
Units produced	60 000	115 000	
Cost per unit	23,29	12,61	
Inventory	3 000	15 000	
Inventory value	69 870	189 150	259 020

Quality

Quality defects can be measured in a similar way. Quality management systems primarily evaluate quality from a physical perspective (number of defects). An ABC & M system can play a significant role in the measurement of quality activities and the evaluation of the price of non-conformance (PONC). Assume the quality defect (1 000 units of product 2) is valued at full cost, the quality deviation is thus $1\,000 \times £12{,}61 = £12\,610$.

(C) Cost of marketing channels/marketing cost per product

Calculating the cost of a marketing channel may be a specific objective in order to evaluate the most effective way of marketing a company's products. This can be done by analysing the relevant activities to determine to what extent the activity costs have been consumed by the relevant channels. (A marketing channel bill of activities may be established for this purpose.) Based on the above example the marketing activity costs may be assumed to be as follows (assuming the wholesalers are owned by the company):

Table A5.7: Marketing activity costs

	Agents	Wholesalers	Total
Market research	15 260	31 000	46 260
Advertising	—	35 050	35 050
Sales	133 000	24 930	157 930
Sales administration	53 000	27 110	80 110
Total marketing cost	201 260	118 090	319 350

The extent to which this cost is then "consumed" by products has to be ascertained. Assume this is as follows:

Table A5.8: Cost consumption by product

	Product 1		Product 2		
	Agents	Wholesalers	Agents	Wholesalers	Total
Market research	5 000	—	10 260	31 000	46 260
Advertising	—	14 500	—	20 550	35 050
Sales	60 000	12 000	73 000	12 930	157 930
Sales admin	13 000	17 000	40 000	10 110	80 110
Total	78 000	43 500	123 260	74 590	319 350
Products sold	15 000	42 000	34 000	65 000	
Cost per product £	5,20	1,04	3,62	1,15	

Assume customer and distribution information is as follows:

The company has three customers P, Q and R and the following sales were made to these customers:

Table A5.9: Sales per customer by product					
Customer	Product 1		Product 2		Total
	Units	£	Units	£	£
P	30 000	850 000	35 000	795 000	1 645 000
Q	20 000	580 000	50 000	1 200 000	1 780 000
R	7 000	210 000	14 000	330 000	540 000
Sales	57 000	1 640 000	99 000	1 830 000	3 965 000

Customer P buys all his requirements through wholesalers while customer Q buys 40 % of his requirements through agents and the balance through wholesalers. Customer R only buys through agents.

Distribution of products to customer P is by rail whilst 50 % of products to customer Q is by road. All products distributed to customer R are by road. This information is used in section E to determine profits derived from each customer, also referred to as customer profitability.

(D) Cost of distribution channels/distribution cost per product

Assume distribution activities can be traced to distribution channels as follows (a distribution channel bill of activities may be used for this purpose):

Table A5.10: Distribution cost					
	Road		Rail		Total
	Product 1	Product 2	Product 1	Product 2	
Delivery activity	110 000	50 000	26 000	164 530	350 530
Delivery administration	16 000	12 000	6 000	19 840	53 840
	126 000	62 000	32 000	184 370	404 370
Products distributed	17 000	39 000	40 000	60 000	
Cost per product £	7,41	1,59	0,80	3,07	

The above information could also be seen as a decision tree containing the following information to determine ultimate profitability:

Table A5.11: Product costing decision tree

	Product 1				Product 2			
Production cost	23,29				12,61			
Marketing cost	5,20 (Agents)		1,04 (Wholesale)		3,62 (Agents)		1,15 (Wholesale)	
	28,49		24,33		16,23		13,76	
Distribution cost	7,41 (Road)	0,80 (Rail)	7,41 (Road)	0,80 (Rail)	1,59 (Road)	3,07 (Rail)	1,59 (Road)	3,67 (Rail)
Cost	35,90	29,29	31,74	25,13	17,82	19,30	15,35	17,43
Selling price	30,00	30,00	30,00	30,00	25,00	25,00	25,00	25,00
Profit / (loss)	(5,90)	0,71	(1,74)	4,87	7,18	5,70	9,65	7,57

This decision tree presents a clear picture of which product distribution route will be more or less profitable. Distribution activity costs may also be seen to be customer-related activities especially where customers are widely dispersed in many different geographical locations. These geographical areas may also become cost objects if they are important from the organisation's perspective.

(E) Cost per customer

Assume that customer-related activities can be traced to the customers as follows (a bill of activity may be defined for each customer):

Table A5.12: Customer activity costs per customer

Customer	Customer admin	Customer collections
P	80 700	21 000
Q	37 300	10 850
R	7 500	9 000
	125 500	40 850

A summary of all product-related costs is as follows:

Table A5.13: Determination of total product-related cost

	Product 1		Product 2	
	Agents	Wholesale	Agents	Wholesale
Production cost	23,29	23,29	12,61	12,61
Marketing channel	5,20	1,04	3,62	1,15
Total	28,49	24,33	16,23	13,76

Similarly a summary of customer-related costs and the calculation of customer profitability is as follows:

Customer profitability

Customer P

Calculation of the profitability of customer P is relatively easy as:

— this customer bought all stocks through the wholesaler; and
— all deliveries are made by rail;

Table A5.14: Customer P					
	Product 1		**Product 2**		**Total**
Units	30 000		35 000		65 000
	Per unit	*Total*	*Per unit*	*Total*	
Sales – gross	30,00	900 000	25,00	875 000	1 775 000
Cost ex wholesale	24,33	729 900	13,76	481 600	1 211 500
Marketing margin	5,67	170 100	11,24	393 400	563 500
Discount	1,67	50 000	2,29	80 000	130 000
	4,00	120 100	8,95	313 400	433 500
Distribution cost					
Rail	0,80	24 000	3,07	107 450	131 450
Distribution margin	3,20	96 100	5,88	205 950	302 050
Customer costs					
Admin					80 700
Collections					21 000
Profit on customer P					200 350

Customer Q

The calculation of the profitability of this customer is slightly more complex as:

— this customer buys through wholesalers and agents; and
— deliveries are made by rail and by road.

Table A5.15: Customer Q — Product 1

| | Product 1 | | | | |
	Agents		Wholesale		Total
Units	8 000		12 000		20 000
	Units	Total	Units	Total	
Gross sales	30,00	240 000	30,00	360 000	600 000
Cost of sales	28,49	227 920	24,33	291 960	519 880
Marketing margin	1,51	12 080	5,67	68 040	80 120
Discount					20 000
Distribution cost	—Road 10 000 × £7,41				74 100
	—Rail 10 000 × £0,80				8 000
Distribution margin	Product 1				(21 980)

Table A5.16: Customer Q — Product 2

| | Product 2 | | | | |
	Agents		Wholesale		Total
Units	20 000		30 000		50 000
	Units	Total	Units	Total	
Gross sales	25,00	500 000	25,00	750 000	1 250 000
Cost of sales	16,23	324 600	13,76	412 800	737 400
Marketing margin	8,77	175 400	11,24	337 200	512 600
Discount					50 000
Distribution cost	—Road 25 000 × £1,59				39 750
	—Rail 25 000 × £3,07				76 750
Distribution margin Product 2					346 100

Table A5.17: Summary — Customer Q

Distribution margin — Product 1		(21 980)
— Product 2		346 100
		324 120
Less: Customer costs		48 150
Customer admin	37 300	
Customer collections	10 850	
Profit on Customer Q		275 970

Customer R

Calculation of the profitability of customer R is similar to customer P, except that this customer buys solely through agents instead of wholesalers.

Table A5.18: Customer R

	Product 1		Product 2		Total
Units	7 000		14 000		21 000
	Per unit	Total	Per unit	Total	
Gross sales	30,00	210 000	25,00	350 000	560 000
Cost ex agents	28,49	199 430	16,23	227 220	426 650
Marketing margin	1,51	10 570	8,77	122 780	133 350
Discount			1,43	20 000	20 000
			7,34	102 780	113 350
Distribution cost					
Road	7,41	51 870	1,59	22 260	74 130
Distribution margin	(5,90)	(41 300)	5,75	80 520	39 220
Customer costs					
Customer admin					7 500
Customer collections					9 000
Profit on customer R					22 720

Table A5.19: Total customer profits

Customer: P	200 350
Q	275 970
R	22 720
Total ABM profit	499 040
Profit per ABM model	499 675
Difference	635
Difference is due to rounding of unit cost in terms of:	
Product costs	665
Marketing cost	160
Distribution cost	(190)
	635

6

Process and activity analysis

VALUE OF PROCESS AND ACTIVITY ANALYSIS

Process and activity analysis (PAA) is at the heart of activity-based management (ABM). It facilitates a comprehension of an organisation's processes and activities which affords management the opportunity to understand and manage the business of the organisation in order to achieve the overall business objectives. Properly documented, PAA portrays an intelligible frame of reference of an organisation's processes, activities, cycle times, wastage, resources consumed and all costs related to these elements.

An overriding objective in successful organisations is to meet customer requirements. Effective business, therefore, is about the combination of processes and activities that are harnessed to meet those customer requirements at minimum cost. To optimise these requisites the processes and activities that govern the organisation's performance have to be most effective, which can only be engineered once proper PAA has been conducted. (Although a comprehensive discussion of process re-engineering falls outside the scope of this text, sufficient reference is made to its core elements to convey an appreciation of the discipline, its attributes and its fields of application.)

Apart from the above-stated valuable benefits, the process and activity analysis and related documentation also serve as an ideal basis for the design and implementation of an activity-based costing and management system.

IDENTIFYING PROCESSES AND ACTIVITIES

The processes that an organisation consists of can be identified in various ways such as observation, interviews, questionnaires, existing organisation charts, flow charts, operation schedules and route sheets. A combination of these options will normally be utilised to assist in identifying and defining the processes and their underlying activities. However, irrespective of the *modus operandi*, the following salient points should be adhered to in order to ensure a sound and reliable portrayal of an organisation's processes and activities:

- *Practical observation* of the processes and activities should always be part of the identifying and defining procedure, whether it be the initial step, the main tool, or the final checking mechanism to ensure that all relevant information has been accounted for and is correctly documented.
- The *actual situation* at the time of conducting the analysis must be documented, not scenarios of what should or could be.
- Finally, cross-checks and verifications should be done to ensure that the final product contains all the required factors and data and that this information is reliable. Procedures with regard to this aspect are discussed in point 10 of this chapter.

PAA METHODOLOGY

Process and activity analysis comprises the following methodology:

1. Value chain analysis and process definition

The logical starting point for PAA is to ascertain and define the processes of the particular organisation to be analysed. Properly documenting all processes and their flows will provide the building blocks for the gathering and attachment of the remainder of the information.

A *process is a series of activities that can be linked and that add value to an input in order to produce an output to an internal or (in the final instance) external customer* (see Figure 6.1).

Figure 6.1: A process

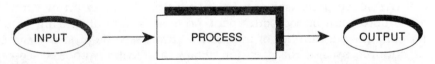

Whereas enterprises are traditionally organised along functional (vertical) lines, processes have no organisational boundaries and flow horizontally, ie across the functional lines (see Chapter 2). It can be depicted as in Figure 6.2.

Examples of key *primary* processes are the following:

- procurement;
- operations;
- marketing;
- distribution;
- customer service.

Figure 6.2: Process flows

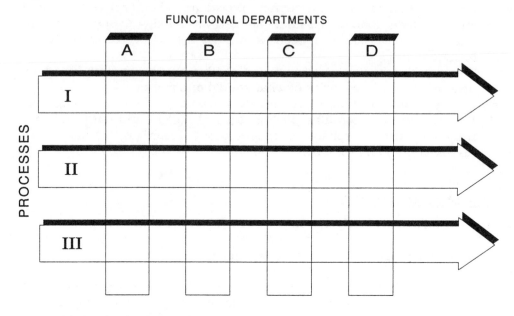

In addition to its primary processes, an organisation also has *secondary* processes, ie processes *supporting* the primary courses of action, for example:

— management, planning and co-ordination;
— technology support;
— human resources management.

Some of the above processes can be in multiple form, eg an organisation can have more than one procurement process; a manufacturing concern will normally have a number of operational processes (ie process segments and/or subprocesses). Processes (or, where applicable, process segments or subprocesses) consist of activities which, in turn, comprise tasks. The fundamental structure can be depicted as in Figure 6.3.

In practice all processes (ie primary processes, supporting processes, subprocesses and process segments) are commonly referred to simply as "processes".

Example 6.1

In order to clearly illustrate the concepts and principles of PAA a basic example (Example 6.1) is used and referred to in this chapter, namely that of a simplified opencast gold and silver mining operation.

The following is an elementary outline of the mine's primary processes:

OPERATIONAL
I   Blasting
II   Ore accumulation
III   Crushing and stamping
IV   Extraction
            — Gold
            — Silver
            — By-products
V   Refining
            — Gold
            — Silver
VI   Waste disposal
VII   Environmental rehabilitation

MARKETING
VIII   Selling

DISTRIBUTION
IX   Delivery

Figure 6.3: Structure of a process

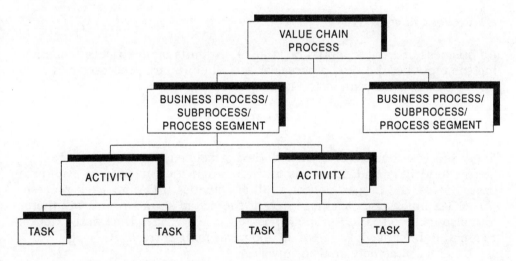

2. Process output definition

The next step is to draw up an exact exposition of what is "produced" by each and every process (ie the outputs of the respective processes), for example in the above-stated mining operation the ore crushing and stamping process produces:

> 100 metric tons
> of ore particles
> 0,17 mm and finer
> per nine hour shift.

3. Process input requirements

Outputs from one process form the inputs of another. Although the outputs supplied by one process are normally deemed to correspond with the inputs demanded by a subsequent process (or processes), this is not always precisely the situation.

The purpose of this step is to determine the inputs that a process *really requires* from the preceding process(es) and the support processes (not the inputs actually produced and tendered by them). For example one of the inputs required by the extraction and refining processes is certain manpower, including particular scientists. (This will be one of the outputs of a support process, *viz* human resources management.)

4. Process flow chart

All business processes should be linked — outputs of one process comprising the inputs of the next process(es), etc. The primary processes can thus be depicted in a diagram as in Figure 6.4.

5. Activity analysis

Every process consists of activities. Having defined the processes the next step is to identify and define the individual activities involved in each process, that is, the preparation of a bill of activities (BOA) for each process. The BOAs must, once again, represent the *actual* situation and will therefore also include the "noise" activities, ie those activities that would not be required if the process were set up and performing correctly.[1]

Essentially, activity analysis involves:

— the decomposition of processes into their constituent elements, ie activities;
— ascertaining and costing the resources consumed by each activity; and
— preparing an appropriate diagram in respect of each process, depicting the relevant activity details and the linkages between the activities, ie the chain of activities that forms the process.

Figure 6.4: Process flow chart

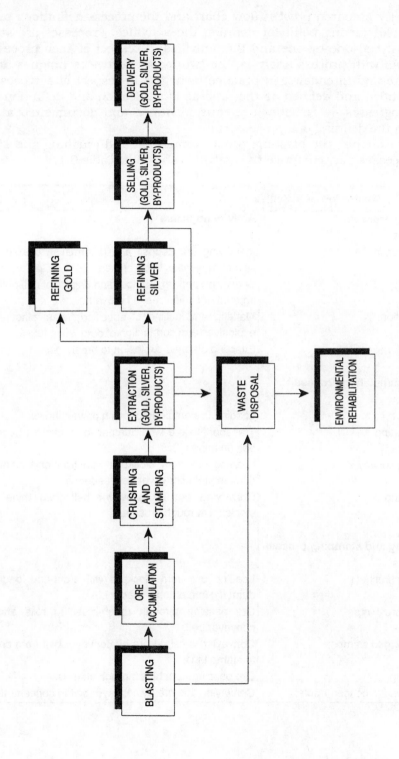

A properly prepared process flow chart and the process definitions provide a suitable starting point for defining the activities. Processes are studied and analysed one by one and the activities in respect of each process are listed. As with process analysis, the two most effective techniques are observation and interviews. In practice, activities in respect of a process can be identified and defined as the process identification and definition function progresses — activities are thus identified and documented at each stage in the defining of a process.

For example, the blasting, ore accumulation and crushing and stamping processes may comprise the activities shown in Table 6.1.

Table 6.1: Illustration of activities	
Blasting process	**Activity objective**
Activities	
Rock examination:	Identifying ore deposit and determining character and size of rock mass to be broken.
Planning :	Specifying pattern, number and depths of drill holes and amount of explosives to be used.
Preparation:	Marking and drilling of specified holes; placement of explosives and connection of detonating fuses.
Detonation:	Effecting planned explosion to break rock.
Ore accumulation process	
Activities	
Loading :	Loading ore onto dumper with power shovel.
Transporting:	Transporting ore with dumper to stockpile at conveyor belt (in mine pit).
Feeding conveyor:	Loading ore from stockpile with front-end loader and dumping into conveyor belt feeder bin.
Conveying:	Conveying ore by conveyor belt from mine pit to stockpile at rough crushers.
Crushing and stamping process	
Activities	
Feeding crushers:	Loading ore from stockpile with front-end loader and dumping into crusher feeder bin.
Rough-crushing:	Ore passing through rough-crushing rolls and onto conveyor belt.
Conveying to stamps:	Conveying crushed ore by conveyor belt from crushers to stamp bins.
Stamping:	Ore passing from bins through stamps.
Conveying to concentrators:	Conveying fine ore by conveyor belt to concentrators.

6. Activity diagrams

After having identified and defined the activities of each process, the next step would technically be to detail the resources consumed by each activity and attach costs thereto, whereafter diagrams would finally be prepared of the activities that make up the respective processes. However, from a practical point of view, it may be more feasible to prepare the diagrams first and then add all relevant information. This procedure should bring about a better perspective and make the activities and related information more "visible".

The respective chains of activities of the ore accumulation and the crushing and stamping processes can be depicted as in Figure 6.5.

7. Resource consumption

The fundamental approach in determining resource consumption and related costs is to regard the respective activities as cost objects. Resources and their cost elements are thus traced to the relative activity centres.

In order to facilitate and enhance decision-making it is most important that a clear and reliable picture is portrayed in this regard. A practical approach is to arrange and elucidate the key information on the activity diagrams in an orderly way. Such disclosure will also simplify the verification of data (see point 10).

Resources refer to all economic and human elements that are applied and used in the performance of activities. They thus include the use of capital assets, the consumption of other assets (ie expenses) and the utilisation of manpower. For example, the resources and cost elements in respect of the activity *feeding conveyor* in the ore accumulation process are the following:

Resource	*Cost element*
Front-end loader	Depreciation
	Wear and tear
	Maintenance
	Fuel
Driver	Salary
	Fringe benefits

In addition to the above cost elements an amount will also be traced to this activity centre from the supporting processes. Furthermore, it will be burdened with the cost of capital relative to the capital tied up in the activity centre.

Note that conventional "depreciation" is split into two elements: depreciation, representing the devaluation of the asset brought about by obsolescence and the passage of time, whether it is utilised or not; and wear and

Figure 6.5: Chains of activities

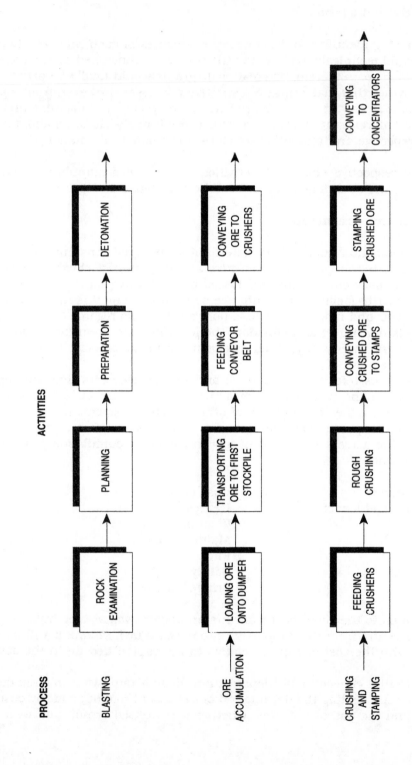

tear, representing the decrease in value sustained because of the actual use of the asset (based on work performed, eg number of hours operated or production mass). Moreover, in addition to providing for depreciation and wear and tear, provision should also be made for the replacement of the asset. This provision will be equal to the increase in price during the period of a new, similar (in respect of production performance) piece of equipment. Such provision is required to maintain the organisation's capital, ie to ensure that it can, in due course, replace assets to maintain its activities at the existing levels.

8. Cycle times and unutilised capacities

Further factors to be determined (primarily by observation) and documented are the cycle time of each activity and the maximum capacity available. From this the unutilised capacity (or capacity waste) can also be determined. For example, with regard to the activity *feeding conveyor:*

— the front-end loader takes 45 seconds to load 1,2 cubic metres of ore from the stockpile and dump it into the conveyor belt feeder bin;
— because of the capacity of the feeder bin and the regulated flowing speed of ore onto the conveyor belt, the loading activity ceases for approximately 10 minutes after every 15 loads.

From the above the following can be concluded:

Continual running time	11,25 minutes
Waiting period between continual runs	10 minutes
Operating time per 9 hour working day	4,76 hours
Cycle efficiency	53 %
Total capacity per day	864 cubic metres
Actual capacity per day	457 cubic metres
Capacity waste	407 cubic metres (or 47 %)

(The actual capacity per day (457 cubic metres) will also serve as a cross-check when the actual capacity of the next activity of the ore accumulation process, *conveying*, is determined.)

The above situation will deteriorate (from a wastage point of view) if the loading is further delayed from time to time because of insufficient quantities of ore on the stockpile. Depending on the magnitude of such shortages of ore, the cycle efficiency may be severely influenced. The activity's time consumption may then resemble the pattern shown in Figure 6.6.

Figure 6.6 reflects:

— the activity's productive time consumption;
— the normal capacity waste; and
— the abnormal wastage.

Figure 6.6: Time consumption of activity

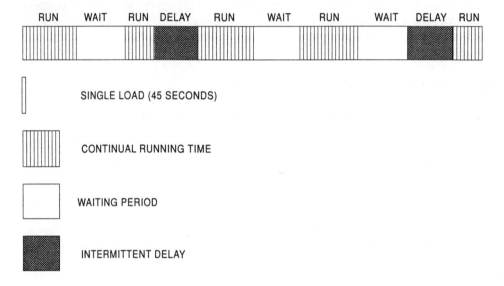

Whereas the cost and effect of normal capacity waste are restricted to the particular activity, the abnormal interruptions will not only affect the activity, but will also have far-reaching consequences down the line, ie for the remaining activities in the process, and for the subsequent processes.

Furthermore, the operating (running) times as such may also be ineffective. If so, normal, effective times are also to be established in order to give a true reflection of the real pattern of time consumption.

To document and portray cycle efficiencies a summary of all process and activity times is made. An example of this, pertaining to the time taken to execute a customer's order, is reflected in Table 6.2.

Table 6.2: Process: Execution of a customer's order			
Activity	**Processing time (hrs)**	**Effective time (hrs)**	**Cycle time (hrs)**
1	0,2	0,2	1,5
2	4,3	3,8	24,0
3	0,3	0,2	28,0
4	1,1	0,9	17,0
5	0,8	0,8	6,0
	6,7	5,9	76,5

Although the customer only received the goods 76,5 hours after having placed the order, the actual time spent on receiving and processing the order and delivering the goods amounted to only 6,7 hours, and even this can be improved upon.

9. Activity classification

An important function to perform in the final stage of PAA is that of classifying activities into value-adding (VA) and non-value-adding (NVA). Since an overall objective must be to satisfy customer requirements in the most effective and efficient way, the fundamental approach should be to rate activities from a customer's perspective. A *value-added activity* would therefore be one which *contributes to the customer's perceived value of the product or service*; a *non-value-added activity* would be one which, if eliminated, *would not detract from the customer's perceived value of the product or service*.[2] (In this regard it is to be noted that there are two types of customers: internal, eg another division, process or activity centre, and external.)

Classifying activities can be more problematic than may appear on the surface. Technically some activities may not add physical value, but the customer may nevertheless be prepared to pay for the activity. For example, although transporting a product does not add to its physical value, the customer is prepared to pay for the transportation as such activity makes the product attainable. Activities that customers are prepared to pay for can thus be referred to as *customer value-added* activities. However, an organisation will normally also have to perform activities which do not add value from a customer's perspective, but are essential for the effective running of the business, eg credit authorisation. These activities can be referred to as *business value-added* activities. *Non-value-adding* activities are worthless for both the customer and the business; they therefore represent the futile consumption of resources — activities destroying value.

10. Detailed diagrams

After having:

- — completed the necessary investigations,
- — gathered the relevant information,
- — prepared diagrams in respect of all processes, and
- — annotated certain particulars on the aforesaid diagrams,

the said diagrams can be finalised to portray a meaningful delineation of the organisation's business processes. To illustrate this, Figure 6.7 finally depicts the *crushing and stamping* process.

Figure 6.7: Detailed diagram: Crushing and stamping process

Value-adding / Non-value-adding
(B = Business)
(C = Customer)

Capacity utilization ■
Capacity waste □

	(B)VA Feeding crushers	(C)VA Rough crushing	(B)VA Conveying crushed ore to stamps	(C)VA Stamping crushed ore	(B)VA Conveying to concentrators
Equipment	Front-end loader	2 Crushers	Conveyor belt	2 Stamps	Conveyor belts
Cycle efficiency	34 %	46 %	67 %	80 %	66 %
Manpower	Driver Charge-hand	Charge-hand Assistant	Overseer	Charge-hand Assistant	Overseer
	£	£	£	£	£
Cost elements and costs:					
Depreciation					
Wear and tear					
Prov. for replacement					
Maintenance					
Fuel					
Electricity					
Salaries					
Fringe benefits					
....					
Traced cost of supporting activities					
Cost of capital					

Process delineations in this format provide a suitable basis for and greatly facilitate the next logical measure, *viz* process re-engineering. In addition, however, it also integrates the conventional accounting system and provides cross-checks and verifications. All assets, human resources and expenses are analysed and traced to their relative activities, for example:

— equipment is allocated to the respective activities performed by each;
— manpower is assigned to its relative activities (based on full-time equivalents (FTEs) to accommodate the situation where employees are involved in different activities);
— expenses are traced to the different activities by virtue of the equipment, employees and other resources consumed by the relevant activities.

The cross-checks and verifications are occasioned by the fact that all assets and expenses are to be allocated; for instance, the equipment and employees assigned to the activities should tally with the organisation's asset register and total number of employees respectively; the depreciation and wear and tear of equipment traced to the activities should correspond with the depreciation of equipment recorded in the accounting records; likewise, salaries traced to activities should tally with the total salary account, etc.

PROCESS RE-ENGINEERING

Process and activity analysis can be used to support many areas of decision making and management action programmes. It is eminently suited to aid business process redesign, leading to process improvement and greater cost effectiveness. Long-term cost effectiveness emanates from optimising the way a business operates rather than just pressing harder on traditional, financially orientated cost controls.[3] The overall objectives should therefore be to make the business processes:

— *effective*, ie to produce the desired results;
— *efficient*, ie to minimise the resources used;
— *adaptable*, ie to change and conform to changed business and customer needs.

Processes should be analysed to identify any of the following symptoms in order to isolate processes which should be considered for re-engineering:

— excessive cost (via benchmarking; value-added analysis);
— quality problems (via a quality and wastage management system);
— time problems (via delivery and cycle time analyses);
— bottlenecks (capacity and logistical issues);
— customer satisfaction.

Directional focus

Before embarking on a process redesigning course it is imperative to ensure that any actions taken in this regard will remain within the organisational philosophies. Whatever re-engineering is done should therefore
ultimately be in line with the organisation's:

- — mission;
- — goals;
- — strategies;
- — values;
- — management philosophy.

An individual aspect of importance that needs to be focused on throughout
is customer satisfaction.

Process improvement strategies

The essential means of redesigning business processes are:

- Streamlining the business processes;
- Simplifying the business processes;
- Reducing frequencies;
- Eliminating non-value-adding activities;
- Reducing cycle times;
- Eliminating wastage;
- Eliminating constraints;
- Evaluating alternatives;
- Reducing cost.

Streamlining

In its wider sense it incorporates the majority of the above actions; in its
narrow sense it refers to the smooth running of the processes by the elimination of duplications and start/stop/start practices.

Reducing frequencies

Reducing the frequency of activities may result in less consumption of resources by products. For example, set-up activity frequency can be reduced
by better production planning, and the frequency of ordering can be reduced by changing the purchasing policy.

Simplifying

This refers to making activities and processes easier to understand and
perform, for example by replacing an activity with a less complicated one.

Eliminating non-value-adding activities

This is obviously an extremely important and beneficial method of effectively and efficiently improving processes. Apart from eliminating unnecessary resource consumption it is also conducive to streamlining and simplifying the processes.

The relevant principles can be illustrated on the basis of H Thomas Johnson's value creating exhibits.[4]

The VA/NVA activities of a process may be portrayed as in Figure 6.8.

Figure 6.8: The VA/NVA activities of a process

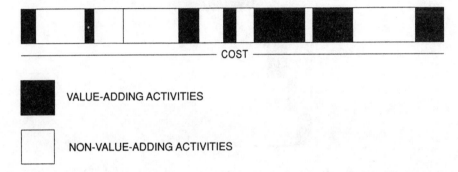

The above can be depicted on a VA graph as in Figure 6.9.

Figure 6.9: VA graph of activities

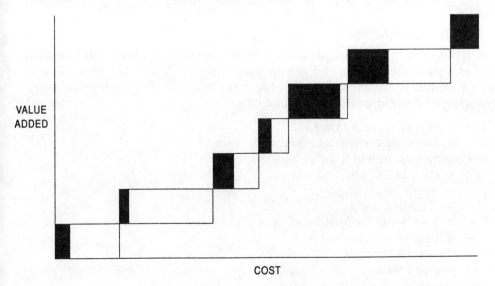

The ideal would be to eliminate all NVA activities, which would result in a phenomenal contraction of the cost line:

Figure 6.10: NVA activities eliminated

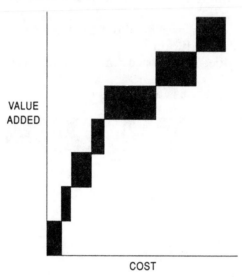

This ideal situation will hardly ever be practically achievable. However, the objective should always be to:

— eliminate non-value-added activities;
— minimise business value-added activities;
— optimise real (customer) value-added activities.

Reducing cycle times

This represents another major avenue for process improvement. It can also be the most underrated. The axiom that time is money is fully effective when it comes to business processes and profitability. Reduced cycle times throughout an organisation will, *inter alia*:

— reduce processing times;
— enhance customer satisfaction;
— reduce all inventories
  — raw materials
  — work in progress
  — finished goods;
— ensure better utilisation of infra-structure;
— disengage surplus capacities;
— eliminate wastage;
— reduce costs;
— reduce capital requirements.

To be most time-efficient the goal must be to have materials, components, products, etc move from value-adding station to value-adding station without interruption, ie from the input of raw materials to the delivery of the finished product to the customer. All activities that cause interruptions/delays must be eliminated[5] or accelerated.

Eliminating wastage

This is a self-evident course of action to be taken in the re-engineering process. Wastage of resources can be encountered in different forms, *viz:*

— wastage owing to ineffectiveness;
— defects and reworking;
— non-compliance with specifications;
— non-compliance with customer requirements;
— obsolescence;
— pilfering;
— misuse;
— misapplication;
— unproductive manpower;
— unproductive capacity;
— unproductive capital;
— administrative red tape.

Each of the above wastage possibilities must be addressed and, where applicable, suitable measures put in place in order to eliminate them as far as practicable. Examples of such measures are:

— market research to determine customer requirements;
— exact and lucid product specifications and job descriptions;
— proper training and apposite empowerment of employees, which should have various positive results, *inter alia*:
    — more effective use of all resources;
    — improved quality;
    — less defects;
    — better productivity;
    — decreased red tape;
    — less supervision and inspection;
    — a committed workforce with job satisfaction.

(This development will represent a major step towards the Japanese *Kaizen* philosophy — to do something right the first time and better every time thereafter);

— redesigning of processes, including consideration of alternatives and outsourcing, to eliminate wastage as well as capacity waste (eg

using a smaller electricity-driven machine instead of a bigger fuel-driven machine with excessive capacity);
— redesigning organisational systems to eliminate red tape.

Eliminating constraints

This means the removal of any limitations on the free flow of activities and on capacities required to produce the desired outputs. Capacity constraints can be illustrated as in Figure 6.11.

Figure 6.11: Capacity constraints

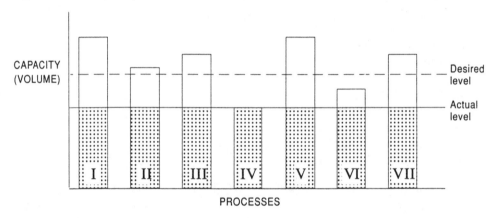

Figure 6.11 clearly shows the so-called bottleneck in the process chain. The current ultimate output is limited to whatever process IV can produce. Although process VI can cope with the current volume, its capacity will have to be increased together with that of process IV to reach the desired level.

When analysing individual processes a similar graphic presentation can be prepared in respect of each process — depicting the capacities of the *activities* of the relevant process. Such a portrayal will expose the constraining activities that will have to be attended to in order to increase the operating capacity of the process as a whole.

Evaluating alternatives

This should be an entrenched procedure in re-engineering of any kind. In addition to all other measures, alternatives should be considered when, for instance, streamlining, simplifying and improving processes and activities. Outsourcing and the use of subcontractors are two important alternatives to consider. Moreover, replacing an existing process with a new one could be a feasible solution in some instances.

Reducing cost

By their very nature the above measures will impact favourably on costs. An additional technique is to examine and evaluate the cost items and amounts relative to each and every activity. In essence it is tantamount to focusing on and reducing input costs of activity centres, resulting in lower output costs. This approach must, in consequence, also extend beyond the normal boundaries of the operation, ie to suppliers on the one end and customers on the other end — the so-called supplier and customer linkages — whereby the co-operation and participation of these parties (where feasible) are obtained. (For example, acquiring components from suppliers in an unpainted state at a lower cost as the final product is re-painted anyhow, and delivering goods in cheap containers and without labels to some customers who remove the manufacturers' expensive labels and replace them with their own.)

CONCLUSION

ABC & M's process and activity analysis is one of the most powerful tools at the disposal of management. It facilitates proper "visibility" of an organisation's processes and activities, leading to a better understanding of the business. Accordingly, PAA facilitates the effective streamlining of business processes by means of process re-engineering to improve overall efficiency and competitiveness. Finally, PAA provides the logical starting point for designing and implementing an ABC & M system.

SOURCES CONSULTED

1. Dale, D. Activity-based cost management. *Australian Accountant*, Mar 1991: 64–69.
2. Convey, S. Eliminating unproductive activities and processes. *CMA Magazine*, Nov 1991: 20–24.
3. Morrow, M & Hazell, M. Activity mapping for business process redesign. *Management Accounting* (UK), Feb 1992: 36–38.
4. Johnson, HT. Activity management: Reviewing the past and future of cost management. *Journal of Cost Management*, Winter 1990: 4–7.
5. Northey, P. Cut total costs with cycle time reduction. *CMA Magazine*, Feb 1991: 19–22.
6. Beaujon, GJ & Singhal, VR. Understanding the activity costs in an activity-based cost system. *Journal of Cost Management*, Spring 1990: 51–72.
7. Beischel, ME. Improving production with process value analysis. *Journal of Accountancy*, Sep 1990: 53–57.
8. Booth, R. Activity analysis and cost leadership. *Management Accounting* (UK), Jun 1992: 30–31.
9. Cyr, J. Building success through process improvement. *CMA Magazine*, Mar 1992: 24–29.
10. Dale, D. ABCM: Challenging tradition. *Australian Accountant*, Apr 1991: 25–34.

11. Greenwood, TG & Reeve, JM. Activity-based cost management for continuous improvement: A process design framework. *Journal of Cost Management*, Winter 1992: 22–40.
12. MacErlean, N. A new dawn for western management? *Accountancy*, Jun 1993: 40–41.
13. Maira, A. Rebuilding US manufacturing industries for sustainable performance acceleration. *Journal of Cost Management*, Spring 1993: 68–72.
14. Ostrenga, MR. Activities: The focal point of total cost management. *Management Accounting* (US), Feb 1990: 42–49.
15. Ostrenga, MR & Probst, FR. Process value analysis: The missing link in cost management. *Journal of Cost Management*, Fall 1992: 4–13.
16. Raffish, N & Turney, PBB. Glossary of activity-based management. *Journal of Cost Management*, Fall 1991: 53–63.
17. Sharman, PA. Activity-based management: A growing practice. *CMA Magazine*, Mar 1993: 17–22.
18. Turney, PBB & Reeve, JM. The impact of continuous improvement on the design of activity based cost systems. *Journal of Cost Management*, Summer 1990: 43–50.

7

Cost driver and output measure analysis

INTRODUCTION

A cost driver is an aspect of the business that, if changed, will result in a change in the cost of a process or activity. A cost driver must be distinguished from an output measure. An output measure is used to trace costs to cost objects. The **cost driver** is concerned with cause and effect. The **output measure** is devised to influence the behaviour of the users of the activity's output. Activity-based costing is specifically concerned with cost drivers and output measures to the extent that it affects the cost of individual processes, activities or products.

Various viewpoints exist as to what the concept of a cost driver actually means. John K Shank[1] distinguishes between structural and executional cost drivers. *Structural cost drivers* resemble the strategic issues which drive a firm's competitive capability such as economies of scale, levels of integration, relative experience and technological advances. These factors may have explicit effects on the cost structures of products. The management of a telephone information system may decide to provide services for any number of hours during a day, up to 24 hours. Depending on the number of hours they decide upon (the structural cost driver) they may determine whether personnel will be employed for one, two or three shifts per day. The cost of the service (per hour) could be very cost-effective on a single shift (prime time), but less cost-effective on a three-shift basis.

Executional cost drivers relate to the organisation's capabilities in executing its affairs efficiently and effectively. Examples are quality management programmes, effective utilisation of capacity, effectiveness of design and work force participation. An understanding of these organisational cost drivers is useful in evaluating the competitive advantage or disadvantage of the firm.

Ostrenga and Probst[2] describe a cost driver as the root cause of an activity. They argue that this could be the fact, event, circumstance, or condition prevalent in the process that causes the activity. It can be operational, policy-related, or environmental; it need not be a quantifiable basis of cost assignment. Although it is necessary to determine and understand the effect of the cost driver on the cost structure, it is not always possible to measure the resultant outcome in terms of the cost driver. The inventory replenishment policy of a company may be the real cost driver for the purchasing process. For example, a policy to review stock levels weekly, as opposed to monthly, may result in different numbers of purchase orders executed. It is thus difficult to trace cost to the cost object using the cost driver. Instead, the output measure is used for this purpose. In this case it may be the number of purchase orders required by each product. In some cases, the cost driver may be the same as the output measure. Cost driver is used as the broader concept in this text.

Although cost measurement is done at resource or activity level, this merely serves as a collection base to evaluate various cost impact decisions. Costs accumulated in an activity may be linked to various other activities. Various combinations of activities may provide a variety of insights into organisational issues. Examples of these may be the impact of cost in design activities on ultimate manufacturing cost, the cost of certain activities in a process on other activities in the same process or the impact of the cost of distribution activities on customer satisfaction.

This chapter focuses on cost behaviour patterns and how they are affected by activity levels. The various types of cost drivers and their uses are explained. The methods for identifying and validating the drivers are described and an indication is given of the number of drivers to be chosen. The output-based focus and the relevance of output measures are also explained.

COST BEHAVIOUR

Cost behaviour in traditional accounting is usually seen as the distinction between fixed and variable costs. A certain grey area always existed which was typically classified as an incremental cost or semi-variable cost. The semi-variable cost was seen as a bulk increase in capacity ie an additional resource with a capacity to produce many units of output. Variable cost was seen to change in direct proportion to production volumes or output. This led to the establishment of break-even analysis or cost–volume–profit relationships as depicted in Figure 7.1.

Many businesses have come to realise that the fixed/variable classification of cost in relation to the volume of output is simplistic and misleading. Volume of output is normally determined by many different products which all have different impacts on fixed and variable cost. Costs do not behave in such a smooth and homogenous manner as is depicted by Figure 7.1. The fact that a multitude of factors (cost drivers) affect costs and cause change in cost is fundamental to the ABC philosophy. Furthermore, the time horizon could also have an effect on the behaviour of cost as most costs are changeable over the longer term. The preferred term for fixed cost in the activity-based costing and management (ABC & M) terminology is long-term variable cost as opposed to short-term variable cost.[3]

Figure 7.1: Cost–volume–profit relationships

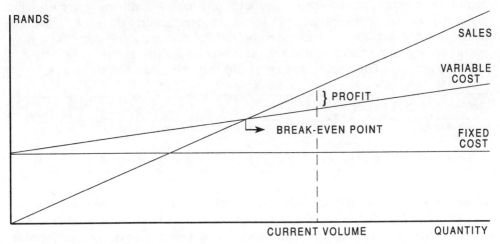

Factors that could affect cost behaviour include mass, quantities, decisions, policies, movement and volume. Cost accounting for decision making should consider the implications of these factors on cost structures. These factors could be grouped into the following levels of variability[3]:

- **Unit level:** Costs vary in proportion to changes in units produced. The cost driver will be a volume indicator such as kilograms or units.
- **Batch level:** Costs vary in proportion to the number of times preparation for any process will be required. The cost driver could be the set-up time on machines or the number of batches. Batch level variability also includes actions on groups of items, for example, orders and invoices often consist of more than one line item.
- **Product level:** Costs will vary when a change is effected in the product or model. The cost driver could constitute changes to products or designs.
- **Process level:** Costs will vary when process changes take place, such as maintenance to the process or re-engineering of the process. The cost driver would be the number of such changes.
- **Plant level:** Costs are incurred to sustain the facilities and premises such as security, insurances and rental. Cost drivers could include time, decisions, space, etc.

While the above variability levels pertain to product costs, similar views could be given for customer costs by classifying such costs between order level cost, marketing channel cost, distribution channel cost and customer cost.

The design and classification of the activities will determine to what extent the above type of costs could be present in a single activity. Ideally an activity should only contain a single level of variability. Within a process, all the batch-variable activities could be identified as one activity or all the plant-related expenses could be classified as another activity. However, this is not always the most logical approach and one activity may account for costs pertaining to several activity levels. Understanding the cost behaviour of the activity implies an understanding of the cost variability levels. It may be necessary to perform cost driver analysis on all the elements of a multi-variable activity. The cost structure could thus be viewed in two ways:

Table 7.1: Activities categorised by variability level				
Unit level	**Batch level**	**Product level**	**Process level**	**Plant level**
Activities	Activities	Activities	Activities	Activities
M1-M2-M8	M3-M4-M6	M5-M7-M9	M10-M14-M15	M11-M12-M13

M denotes various machine and cost centres. Unit level costs are, for instance, found in machine centres 1,2 and 8. The unit-related costs could be classified as one activity. This view is, however, not always determinable in practice.

Another view could be obtained by classifying cost at resources level as each resource is entered into the activity. See Table 7.2.

Table 7.2: Activities analysed by resource category			
	Activity 1	**Activity 2**	**Activity n**
Unit level costs			
Material			
Electricity			
Packaging			
Labour			
Batch level costs			
Labour			
Tools			
Electricity			
Product level costs			
Design cost			
Special packaging			
Special dies			
Process level cost			
Process design cost			
Supervision			
Plant level			
Maintenance			
Insurance			
Rental			
Total cost			

Both the views illustrated in Table 7.1 and Table 7.2 facilitate good decision making as the cost impact of different decisions can be easily evaluated. Unit level variable cost resembles variable cost as defined in traditional accounting, while plant level variable costs to some extent resemble fixed cost. Batch, process and product level variable costs represent the so-called grey area of cost which was previously difficult to define. Further research into cost behaviour patterns may well indicate many more meaningful levels of variability.

Cost–volume calculations

Cost-volume relationships are not as easy to define as was assumed in the traditional approach. Costs could be affected for a given volume by altering the batch sizes, or costs could be affected by volume as well as process level and plant level changes. To find the appropriate cost for a given set of circumstances it is necessary to understand the levels of variability of relationships and apply this knowledge to the situation. Thus, in order to manufacture a product, it will be necessary to determine the units to be manufactured (for unit variable cost), the number of batches, which products, and what process or facility changes will be necessary in order to predict cost. Alternatively a cost simulation model may be built which incorporates these relationships.

Cost modelling and target costing

Many of the variability factors could have a direct influence on determining the lowest possible cost at which a product can be produced. Companies whose objective is reaching a target cost may find cost modelling a feasible aid contributing to this goal.

Methods to identify the cost relationships are discussed later in this chapter.

TWO-STAGE COST DRIVERS

Two stages of cost drivers are identifiable, one at resource level and one at activity level. This can be explained as follows:

Resource driver/stage one cost driver

Most accounting systems are set up with a multiplicity of accounts to classify information for various reasons. A good example is the different types of payroll accounts which may be held in an accounting system. Payroll costs could be classified under the following account headings:

Normal salaries
Overtime salaries
Sick/holiday pay
Bonuses
Employer contributions: Pension
                         Medical
                         Car allowance

This categorisation is necessary for control purposes, but normally only at organisational level and not at activity level. From a costing perspective it is not necessary to distinguish between all the above cost elements as they are all payroll-related costs. These costs could be summarised (aggregated) or included in a cost pool before being traced to the primary activities. The stage one cost driver is used for this purpose. Diagrammatically this can be presented as in Figure 7.2.

Figure 7.2: Stage one cost drivers

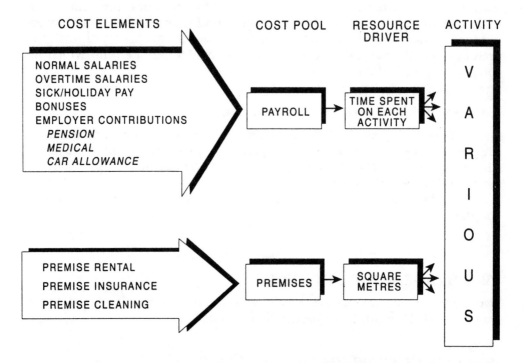

The resource driver therefore describes the relationship between the cost element and the activity, or how the activity "consumes" the cost element. ABC & M systems require a much more detailed analysis of costs into activities versus departments or cost centres. If the same level of detail as is required for control purposes is built into the costing system, a tremendous "explosion" of ledger accounts will occur. Use of the cost pool concept alleviates this problem as more than 10 cost pools will seldom be required per activity.

Activity driver/stage two cost driver

Products consume activities and the stage two cost driver describes this relationship. The relationship is important for cost management purposes as the understanding and management of the cost driver should help to manage activity costs down. An activity may be to carry the finished product in stock. The cost driver of this activity will predominantly be the time the product is held in inventory. Therefore, if the time the product is held in stock is managed down, product costs ought to come down as well. This relationship is normally defined with the output measure (see section on output measures).

Referring to Example 5.1 in Chapter 5 (procurement of raw material) with the activities buying, receiving, storage and payment, the following cost drivers could be relevant:

Buying

It could be argued that the cost of buying is largely influenced by management policies such as buying once a week or buying only when inventories reach a certain level. The number of purchase orders and other outputs by the buying activity would thus be directly influenced by these policies. The buying policy is therefore considered to be the cost driver. (The output measure to trace cost may be the purchase order.)

Receiving

The number of receipts is most probably a consequence of the buying policy, but it could also be the subject of an independent management policy such as a just-in-time delivery schedule. This schedule will, in this case, be considered to be the cost driver. (The output measure to trace cost may be the receipt of goods.)

Storage

Storage costs are mainly affected by the period that inventory items are held in stock (the stock turnover) and this may be the result of delivery lead times of suppliers or safety stocks. Any of these arguments could be considered to be cost drivers. (The output measure to trace cost may be the average time in inventory.)

Payment

Payment could be effected per invoice or per statement, once or twice a month. The payment policy will be the cost driver. (The output measure to trace cost may be the number of payments.)

From the above discussion it should be apparent why an understanding of the cost driver is necessary to appreciate a particular cost structure and why this understanding is useful in managing costs.

PROCESS DRIVERS

A series of activities that can logically be linked together to produce a significant and complete output is called a **process**. The collective cost of this group of activities may be influenced by one important factor such as a policy decision or management action. It is equally important for cost management purposes to understand this influence as all the costs in this chain (or process) may be affected.

The reason why the process is put in motion is referred to as a process trigger. A *process trigger* is often also a cost driver for the process as a whole. If the total cost of the process changes as the cost driver changes, this cost driver is a valid process cost driver. Managing the process cost driver ought to affect the cost of the process in total.

The term "cost driver" is preferred as the factor influencing a whole process and "output measure" as this relates to cost changes in a single activity. In the above example, the cost structure of all the activities in the buying process may be influenced by the process cost driver (buying policy) but individual activity costs will be influenced by their specific output measures.

OUTPUT MEASURES

The output measure is a term used in conjunction with the cost driver and in many cases is the culmination, or end result, of a particular cost driver. The output measure is thus simply the medium to convey cost from the activity to the cost objects. Using the above example again, the following output measures could be identified:

*   **Buying:** Although the buying policy is the main factor affecting costs, the cost has to be expressed as a unit of output which, in this case, could be argued to be the number of orders placed by the buying activity. Cost of buying is therefore expressed as an amount per purchase order. This cost is then conveyed or traced to the product based on the number of purchase orders it required (or consumed).

- **Receiving:** The unit of output for the receiving activity could be the number of items received, the physical volume or even the number of goods received notes handled. Whatever is decided, this mechanism will also be used to trace the receiving costs to the product or cost object.
- **Storage:** Storage activity costs are normally broken down into physical storage costs (premises, etc) and monetary storage costs (holding costs). The latter are mostly affected by the amount of inventory held and the time period for which it is held. The output of this activity could thus be expressed as the cost-per-£ value of inventory held per day/week/ month. Physical storage cost could possibly be expressed as the cost per square or cubic metre of space.
- **Payment:** Depending on the payment policy followed (statement/invoice) the output of this activity could be expressed as the payment cost-per-statement/invoice. Cost will thus be traced to the product or cost object based on the number of invoices/statements it required.

Output measures should be understood by users so that they can select the level of use. A decrease in the use of an output measure should in the long run result in a decrease in total activity costs and in the unit variable costs. Capacity and the relevant range concept must be considered in the determination of all other costs. If predetermined activity rates are used to convey costs to cost objects, it is necessary to consider the impact of cost recovery if full capacity is not achieved. For example, in the case of a specific activity only unit variable and facility level (plant level) costs exist — these are similar to fixed and variable costs. If these costs are recovered through the output measure at practical capacity, the situation illustrated in Figure 7.3 can result.

Figure 7.3

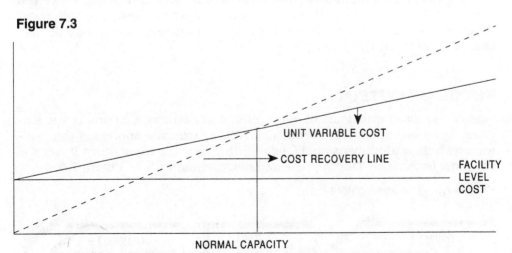

It can be seen from Figure 7.3 that any capacity level less than normal capacity will result in an under-recovery of cost (and conversely an over-recovery). This under- or over-recovery could be treated as a capacity loss or gain and can be measured as shown in Figure 7.4.

Figure 7.4

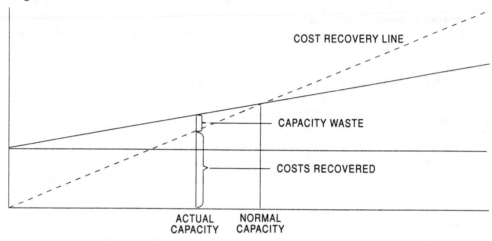

(The capacity waste could, in turn, be analysed between the under-recovered portions of unit variable and facility level costs.)

Output measures should not be identified arbitrarily but should bear a close correlation with the costs of the activity. If such a relationship does not exist, the tracing of cost to the cost object may become meaningless. Various methods could be used for the determination of this relationship such as the conventional high-low cost analysis or a more sophisticated technique such as regression analysis. The high-low method is generally well known and found in most textbooks on cost accounting. Reference will thus only be made to the use of regression analysis later in this chapter. When it is not possible to identify a proper output measure, it may be necessary to re-define the activity.

FOCUS ON OUTPUT

One of the main criticisms of conventional accounting systems is the singular focus on inputs (cost elements). ABC specifically addresses this concern with its multidimensional focus. In this case the input/output focus is the most important. This is presented diagrammatically in Figure 7.5.

Figure 7.5: The input/output focus

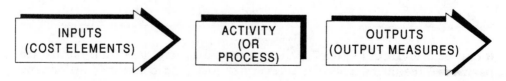

This simple relationship is not only useful in understanding the cost relationship but equally so in planning and restructuring the activities or processes of an organisation. The focus on the output also helps to identify the activities that need to be identified for this purpose. It is believed that this focus on outputs, and specifically on outputs required by the customer, gives sense and direction to the organisation.

NUMBER OF OUTPUT MEASURES (AND ACTIVITIES)

Addressing the issue of the number of output measures that are required for a given organisation, very few specific rules can be dictated. Too few output measures will inevitably result in cost categories being too broadly defined or too aggregated for the results to be meaningful. Too many output measures and activities may cause the accountant to become entangled in so much detail that the real and relevant cost relationships are missed.

IDENTIFICATION OF OUTPUT MEASURES

Various methods exist to find the relevant output measures for a given situation. A distinction must be drawn between those methods that are applied to identify possible cost drivers, and those that validate the relationship of the output measure with the activity or process.

Methods to identify possible cost drivers

Many different factors may have an effect on costs. To identify all possible factors for evaluation the following methods may be applied:

- **Interviewing:** People involved in the activity could be interviewed to identify possible factors. Questions could be structured to determine when more (or less) resources are required in an activity or what causes the workload or idle time.
- **Questionnaires:** The same type of information that can be gathered by interviewing can also be obtained from formal questionnaires. Questionnaires may be used as a time-saving device or when it is impractical to reach all the relevant people.
- **Observation:** Physical observation is often necessary to obtain a thorough understanding of the workings of an activity and also the factors that may be influencing its cost structure.
- **Analytical reviews:** Historical and current information may contain many clues as to the factors which may be influencing cost. It should be realised that this may represent vast quantities of information which would need to be analysed. If this information is available in an electronically accessible format, this task would be much easier.

Methods to validate output measures

One of the most serious criticisms of conventional costing systems is that in many cases they still use labour as a base to allocate overheads to products. Labour, as a percentage of total cost, has become insignificant in many cases but is still used as an output measure, often leading to meaningless information. ABC should guard against falling into the same trap by ensuring that cost drivers and output measures are meaningful and relevant.

As noted earlier the high-low method could be used for this purpose but results could be suspect. A more scientific method to apply is **regression analysis** which is employed in many other disciplines. Reference to the theoretical base of the technique can be found in most statistical textbooks as only the application of the technique is discussed here.

Regression analysis determines the relationship between variables. It supposes that certain costs may be influenced by specific factors. Repairs and maintenance costs may be influenced by the number of operating hours, debtors' collection costs may be influenced by the number of customers or number of invoices. These cost structures usually consist of a fixed and a variable portion. If the cost changes proportionately to the factor influencing it, the relationship may be referred to as linear regression. Changes could also be affected in a non-linear fashion for which specific mathematical formulae must be developed. Costs could be affected by single factors or many factors. This can be depicted as in Table 7.3.

Table 7.3: Regression methods		
Relationship	**Number of factors**	
	One	*Many*
Linear	Simple linear	Multiple linear
Non-linear	Simple non-linear	Multiple non-linear

A linear regression model depicting the cost relationship for collection costs (debtors) could be as follows:

Collection costs = Fixed cost + (number of invoices × coefficient) + (number of customers × coefficient) + error term

where

Fixed costs	=	Infrastructure costs of debtors' department
Invoice coefficient	=	Cost of collecting moneys per invoice
Customer coefficient	=	Cost of collecting moneys per customer
Error term	=	Random element that is unpredictable in model

The availability and applicability of the technique through spreadsheet systems (LOTUS and others) makes the use of regression analysis a practical reality. Reference can be made to single overhead rates or multiple overhead rates that can be calculated.[4]

Single overhead rates

Single overhead rates will be calculated where a satisfactory coefficient of determination (an indicator of correlation) can be found between two sets of variables (simple linear regression). Good correlation could indicate that one factor (the output measure) may be affecting another (the cost of the activity). Logic and common sense must still prevail as good correlation does not automatically indicate a cause and effect relationship.

Suppose that the cost of a customer-related activity (such as collecting customer accounts) is to be analysed to determine the factor which causes the costs to change. Various factors may be suggested, such as the number of customers, the number of invoices or the size of the accounts. All three of these factors may appear to be legitimate output measures. The regression analysis will be performed on the historical data which is available on these various factors and the historical cost pattern.

SIMPLE LINEAR REGRESSION

Suppose that the best possible cost driver must be found for a customer-related activity (say customer collections). Three possible cost drivers have been identified: the number of invoices, the number of accounts and the value of accounts. The following table of observations of these variables has been extracted for the past 12 months:

Table 7.4

Customer collection costs £	Value of accounts £	Number of invoices	Number of customers
310 000	990 000	1 100	100
319 000	1 070 000	1 080	115
341 000	1 100 000	1 120	124
325 000	1 110 000	1 205	102
372 000	1 210 000	1 595	105
268 000	1 170 000	1 104	78
288 000	1 150 000	1 086	84
299 000	1 030 000	1 091	90
360 000	1 120 000	1 298	103
354 000	1 130 000	1 400	105
380 000	1 180 000	1 506	101
402 000	1 200 000	1 689	107

A correlation of the above three factors with the customer collection costs indicates the following relationships (expressed as the coefficient of determination or the square root of the correlation coefficient):

Value of accounts   = 22 %
Invoices   = 79 %
Number of accounts   = 36 %

(Calculations performed with LOTUS 1-2-3.)

From the above percentages it can be deduced that the number of invoices "explains" 79 % of the variation in customer collection costs. This cost could thus be traced to customers on the the basis of the number of invoices per customer. It is further relevant to recognise that the regression analysis performed provides two more significant statistics namely:

> The X coefficient (similar to a variable cost rate)
and
> The Y coefficient (similar to a fixed cost rate),
which in this case are:

> X = £161,48 per invoice
and
> Y = £129 283 per month.

It could thus be deduced that a certain amount of fixed cost (£129 283) exists which is similar to the plant level costs or infrastructure costs referred to above. These two cost structures may be indicators of the existence of two activity levels.

Multiple overhead rates

The above regression "explained" only 79 % of the variation of cost, thus 21 % remained unexplained. This may be attributable to other activity levels influencing cost. The test to be performed to determine whether other factors could help to explain the variation better, is multiple regression analysis.

MULTIPLE LINEAR REGRESSION

Multiple linear regression uses more than one factor (multiple factors) to explain the variation in the dependent variable (collection costs). In the above case it was indicated that invoices explained 79 % of this variation. Multiple regression could ascertain whether any other factor(s) could improve this percentage. Two or three factors could thus be combined to determine whether this can improve the explanation of the variation in cost. This could be done by calculating the multiple correlation coefficient.

Applied to the above case this is as follows:
    Multiple coefficients of determination:

        Invoices and value of accounts   = 83 %
        Invoices and number of customers = 95 %

(Calculations performed with LOTUS 1-2-3.)

A combination of invoices and number of accounts thus explains 95 % of the variation in customer collection costs (which would be more than acceptable in most practical situations). The amount of variation which is attributable to invoices and number of accounts respectively, can be found in the coefficients of the two factors which are as follows:

        Invoice coefficient   = £143,65
and
        Number of accounts coefficient = £1 319,88

while the amount of fixed cost is now only £18 464, which is considerably lower than the £129 283 in the first case.

It could thus be argued that three types of output measures can be found in this one activity, namely:

- Invoices — a volume-related output measure;
- Number of accounts — a batch-related output measure; and
- Infrastructure — a fixed cost or plant level type of output measure.

Similar analyses can thus be made of other activities to determine relevant output measures.

VALIDATION OF OUTPUT MEASURES

It is considered prudent to validate output measures from time to time. It would therefore be good practice to subject costs and output measures to a regression analysis on a regular basis (say every six or twelve months). This will also help to identify changes in cost behaviour which may require changes in the tactics for managing cost.

CONCLUSION

This chapter explained all the various types of cost drivers and their uses. Distinctions were drawn between resource drivers (first-stage cost drivers) and activity drivers (second-stage cost drivers), process drivers and also output measures. Methods of identifying and validating cost drivers were proposed. An understanding of all these concepts is necesary to understand cost behaviour.

SOURCES CONSULTED

1.   Shank, JK. Strategic cost management: New wine or just new bottles? *Journal of Management Accounting Research*, Fall 1989: 47–65.
2.   Ostrenga, MR & Probst, FR. Process value analysis: The missing link in cost management. *Journal of Cost Management*, Fall 1992: 4–13.
3.   Romano, P. Trends in management accounting. *Management Accounting* (US), August 1990: 53–56.
4.   Novin, AM. Applying overhead: How to find the right bases and rates. *Management Accounting* (US), Mar 1992: 40–43.

8

Cost management

INTRODUCTION

In recent times few organisations have escaped the severity of what is said to be a depression worse than that of the 1930s. Dramatically reduced profit announcements (or larger losses), worker and even executive lay-offs and huge surplus capacities are all just symptoms of this traumatic business experience. These developments have necessitated that most businesses come to grips with modern cost management practices.

Postponement of capital expenditure, large percentage reductions in the workforce, early retirement programmes or closing of branches are all indications of stress and the crisis management which prevails in many businesses. The problem with a lot of these measures is that while they remove cost (temporarily), they seldom reduce the work. The end result of this type of shotgun approach is not a sustainable improvement in the bottom line but rather a very negative effect on employee morale. The effect that some of these measures may have on the competitive capability of the business and its future existence, must be questioned. Popular expenses to be cut in some of these archaic cost reduction exercises are research and development cost, marketing and information services costs. Many of these costs may be close to the heart of (future) competitive capability.

Modern cost management techniques focus on the factors which cause the workload and especially on those which identify unnecessary work. This implies a strategic and operational analysis of the organisation to determine the optimal business processes and the amount of value that is added by each of the activities that are performed. A thorough understanding of cost drivers and cost behaviour patterns is required before the cost management process can begin. The approach is generically referred to as activity-based management. The concept requires a fully integrated approach to management issues such as quality, productivity and capacity. It helps the organisation to identify unprofitable products and services, customers, marketing and distribution channels. The identification and elimination of wastage in all its forms whether it be materials, capacity, or manpower is a high priority.

Activity-based management (ABM) is a fundamentally new way of managing an organisation. ABM comprises:

- A strategic analysis of the business to identify unprofitable products, customers, marketing and distribution channels, etc;
- An evaluation of the business from a value chain perspective. Linkages, both internally and externally, are taken into consideration;
- The optimisation of business processes and activities instead of functions, and the evaluation of the effect of both upstream and downstream decisions;
- The implementation of continuous cost improvement programmes instead of comparisons with outdated standard costing approaches;
- The use of performance measurement systems that are early indicators of corporate success in critical areas such as time, quality and cost;
- The improvement in activities that add value while value-destroying activities are identified and eliminated. Particular emphasis is placed on the evaluation of support activities;
- The elimination of capacity and other constraints;
- The integration of quality management programmes with the costing system, not only to identify wastage but also to develop the methods to value and to eradicate it;
- The implementation of productivity management programmes that are supplemented by appropriate benchmarking and service level evaluations;
- Value engineering and value analysis that are used as important tools to restructure product costs;
- Changes in costing and accounting systems to reflect total cost approaches instead of conventional classifications of cost between production, marketing, administration, etc (or only the minimum information that is required by law);
- A thorough understanding by management of the cost behaviour and the underlying cost drivers;
- The introduction of the cost of capital theory as well as residual income theory to cost decision making in order to optimise the use of capital resources;
- Managing costs with a long-term focus. Few costs are considered fixed and therefore non-manageable.

Whether the organisation is striving for excellence or struggling for survival, it must take these new developments into account in the formulation of strategies. This could help to ensure that it survives and is able to compete successfully.

This chapter deals with the aspects necessary to develop a comprehensive cost management strategy.

STRATEGIC ANALYSIS

No cost system will probably ever become a strategic management system but it should support strategic management and change. In this regard an ABM system could help in identifying and evaluating:

— unprofitable products;
— unprofitable customers;
— costly raw materials;
— costly business processes and activities;
— non-value-adding elements of products or services;
— unprofitable or costly marketing channels;
— unprofitable or costly distribution channels.

By continuing the analysis of Example 5.1 set out in Chapter 5, the following insights can be identified to facilitate strategic change:

Raw materials

Three raw materials A, B and C were purchased but the procurement cost of these three materials differed substantially. This can be calculated as follows:

Table 8.1: Differences in procurement cost £

	Raw material		
	A	B	C
Direct cost	410 000	230 000	678 000
Procurement cost	24 609	82 103	84 405
Thus % "add-on"	6 %	36 %	12 %

The above result may be indicative of an abnormal acquisition method for material B or in fact that a replacement material B must be sought. This may entail several strategic changes such as the re-engineering of the product or searches for alternative suppliers or acquisition methods.

The element of raw material waste could also be considered in the evaluation of various materials. The wastage percentages of the three materials are:

Table 8.2: Wastage percentage

	Raw material		
	A	B	C
Procured materials	434 609	312 103	762 405
Wastage	10 865	4 459	15 248
Wastage %	2,5 %	1,4 %	2,0 %

The wastage percentage may be relevant in the evaluation of defects, in particular materials, but also in respect of defects caused in the final product. Various alternative raw materials may be evaluated in order to engineer these deficiencies out of the product cost.

Finished products

Determination of relative profitability of products may be done at various levels such as:

— at manufacturing or operational level;
— at marketing level; or
— at distribution level.

Example 5.1 in Chapter 5 may be analysed as follows:

Table 8.3

	Product 1	Product 2
Selling price	30,00	25,00
Manufacturing cost	23,29	12,61
Operational margin	6,71	12,39
Percentage	22 %	50 %

When marketing costs are taken into consideration this margin changes as follows:

Table 8.4

	Product 1		Product 2	
	Agents	Wholesalers	Agents	Wholesalers
Operational margin	6,71	6,71	12,39	12,39
Marketing cost	5,20	1,04	3,62	1,15
Marketing margin	1,51	5,67	8,77	1,24
% of selling price	5 %	19 %	35 %	45 %
Cost of marketing channel				
% of selling price	17 %	3 %	15 %	5 %

It can clearly be seen from this analysis that the two products are not equally profitable and that the two marketing channels have different cost structures to market the products. In extreme cases products at this level may have an inadequate margin to cover other organisational costs, such as distribution or customer-related costs and serious consideration needs to be given to the possible elimination of the product from the range offered or not marketing it through certain marketing channels. Product elimination may have far-reaching consequences such as:

— further reductions in capacity utilisations and increases in costs of remaining products;
— the organisation losing the status of a "full range" supplier and eventually losing even more business.

All relevant cost considerations need to be taken into account in the formulation of strategies in this regard.

Distribution channels could be similarly evaluated to determine appropriate strategies. From the decision tree in Chapter 5, which determines product profitability after marketing and distribution costs, it is also apparent that diverging deductions can be made.

Table 8.5: Decision tree

	Product 1				Product 2			
Manufacturing cost	23,29				12,61			
Marketing cost	5,20 (Agents)		1,04 (Wholesale)		3,62 (Agents)		1,15 (Wholesale)	
Distribution cost	.28,49		24,33		16,23		13,76	
	7,41 (Road)	0,80 (Rail)	7,41 (Road)	0,80 (Rail)	1,59 (Road)	3,07 (Rail)	1,59 (Road)	3,67 (Rail)
Cost	35,90	29,29	31,74	25,13	17,82	19,30	R15,35	17,43
Price	30,00	30,00	30,00	30,00	25,00	25,00	25,00	25,00
Profit/(loss)	(5,90)	0,71	(1,74)	4,87	7,18	5,70	9,65	7,57
%	-20 %	2 %	-6 %	16 %	29 %	23 %	39 %	30 %

Product 1 is less profitable than Product 2, mainly due to high road distribution costs. This could be the information required to trigger an investigation into alternative distribution methods or methods to cut costs of existing distribution or marketing channels.

The fact that a product is a loss maker at this level does not necessarily imply that it must be eliminated from the product range. Rather, an investigation into the reasons why the product is not rendering a positive contribution should be investigated in an attempt to also make this a profitable product. These could be, *inter alia*:

  — that the product has only recently been launched and its market
    share is still growing;
  — this product is used to sell other products;
  — the product may be an industry loss leader and its price is pitched
    to create a certain perception in the market;
  — the product is unprofitable but yields a positive cash flow;
  — temporary conditions may exist as to why the product is unprofitable.

Customers

Relative customer profitability is as follows:

Table 8.6: Relative customer profitability			
	Customer		
	P	*Q*	*R*
Turnover	1 775 000	1 850 000	560 000
Profit	200 350	275 970	22 720
Profit percentage	11 %	15 %	4 %

All customers are not equally profitable and the ABM model is an excellent
vehicle for determining the reasons why. In the above example it appears
that the larger customers have higher profit margins. This may be an indication that the company ought to focus on this specific segment of the
market where economies of scale would appear to exist.

   Alternatively, the methods of serving smaller customers may be questioned and a unique cost-effective approach could be developed for these
customers. The methods of serving specific customers may also be changed
or re-engineered to achieve acceptable profitability (hence the term "customer engineering").

Strategic and structural cost analysis

It is imperative when analysing the cost structures of an organisation to
also attend to the strategic and structural cost analyses that can be done
with such information. The importance of such an approach was under-
scored by Richard Wilson[1] with the following comment: "If the business is
suffering from intense competitive pressures, is in a declining industry or
is lagging behind in the adoption of current technology, no amount of marginal adjustments to insignificant details will improve its fortunes". Knowing the cost of poor quality, late deliveries, poor product positioning and
relating this to the level of profitability of the organisation, may help management to focus on the strategic direction of the organisation. Wilson went
on to suggest the following categorisation of costs to develop a proactive
strategic approach:

Table 8.7: Cost categorisation by Wilson		
	Strategic	**Operational**
Tangible	Debt charges New plant Product development Market development	Labour Materials Energy Supplies Contract services
Intangible	Poor product positioning Technological obsolescence Poor location of facilities	Poor quality Absenteeism Labour turnover Low morale Lost output Late delivery

The traditional management accounting focus of the top right-hand quadrant has limited scope for identifying strategic issues or developing appropriate strategies. The issues in the matrix must be tailored to each individual business.

Value engineering

Another important development in managing cost is to be found in the value engineering (VE) approaches adopted by Japanese companies. In the VE approach product (and service) attributes are analysed between so-called "hard" and "soft" attributes. *Hard attributes* are considered to be tangible and measurable characteristics of products such as the fuel consumption of a car. A *soft attribute* can be the way the car handles, which is subjective. The cost associated with the provision of each of these attributes is calculated. When the benefits of each of these attributes are evaluated from a customer perspective, a value index can be calculated. Attributes with a low index value could possibly be eliminated and those with high indices could possibly be expanded. Benefits are normally determined by market research where customers' perspectives are sought on the various characteristics of products.

The value index is calculated as follows:

$$\text{Index} = \frac{\text{Degree of importance}}{\text{Percentage of cost}}$$

If the product manufactured is, for instance, an electric kettle, the following attributes could be evaluated:

Table 8.8: Electric kettle attributes £				
	Cost	%	Benefit	Value index
Hard attributes				
Size of kettle	12,00	55 %	25 %	25/55= 0,45
Time to boil water	6,00	27 %	35 %	35/27= 1,30
Soft attributes				
Ease of pouring	3,00	14 %	15 %	15/14= 1,07
Colour(s)	1,00	4 %	25 %	25/4 = 6,25
	22,00	100 %	100 %	

This analysis gives an indication of the relative values of the product costs. Adding colours to the kettle gives a high index value, while increasing the size of the kettle gives a low index value. In this way the cost of the kettle could be managed by adding or reducing cost where the most benefits could be obtained.

Cost variability

A further analysis of the cost could be done to facilitate better understanding of the cost structure by analysing costs according to their behaviour as follows:

Table 8.9: Kettle costs variability £					
	Unit	Batch	Product	Facility	Total
Hard attributes					
Size	8,00	2,00	1,00	1,00	12,00
Time to boil	4,00	1,00	1,00	–	6,00
Soft attributes					
Ease of pouring	1,00	–	2,00	–	3,00
Colour(s)	–	0,50	–	0,50	1,00
	13,00	3,50	4,00	1,50	22,00

Unit variable costs will change in direct proportion to volume changes of the products such as material or assembly time. Batch variable cost will vary with the number of batches. This cost is particularly relevant where batches are of an uneven quantity or significant set-up costs are incurred with each batch. Product variable costs relate to product variations such as redesigns or specification changes of the product. Facility costs are normally considered fairly fixed and can be related to specific capacity settings.

This type of analysis will facilitate decision making, knowing which cost will increase/decrease by volume (unit) or batch changes or which costs are spent to support the product (advertising, etc) or the facilities (premises, etc). This cost analysis is considered more meaningful than the conventional fixed cost/variable cost analysis.

Bromwich[2] used the following table to analyse costs of a fast food product. The principal view is the benefit the consumer derives from the product or service.

Table 8.10: Strategic cost analysis					
Costs	Product/ volume- related costs	Activity- related costs	Capacity- related costs	Decision- related costs	Total
Product benefits					
Texture					
Nutritional value					
Appearance					
Taste					
Consistency of above					
Quality					
Low cost					
Outlet benefits					
Service					
Cleanliness					
Outlet facilities					
Location					
Other benefits					
Product advertising					
Total cost attributable to consumer benefits					
Product costs not attributable to consumer benefits					
Total product cost					

This analysis is a powerful tool to evaluate and manage costs. The benefits to be reported will be determined by the specific business concerned but should be such that the particular strategies it pursues are supported and highlighted. Cost categories indicated above, can be further analysed to suit the particular business. To the extent that competitor information is available, the same analysis can be performed to compare with the above.

It is important to note that in most of these strategic analyses, accuracy is of less importance than the structural view obtained.

Value chain

Any strategic cost analysis would be incomplete without an analysis of the costs associated with the elements of the value chain. The value chain analysis is particularly useful for comparisons with other organisations. Competitors may not be involved in the same elements of the value chain. The value chain costs are obtained from the ABM income statement which appears in Chapter 5. If a competitor's costs can be modelled in the same fashion it will be readily apparent where the firm may have a competitive advantage/disadvantage and where it should focus its attention in managing its costs. Linking the value chain backwards to suppliers and forwards to customers, it may also be apparent whether any sustainable advantage could occur if these links were changed. Shank and Govindarajan[3] stress the need for understanding these linkages. They contrast this approach with conventional management accounting with its narrow organisational focus (a typical value-added focus) which they say "started too late and stopped too early". They imply that the cost accounting process started too late by excluding supplier links and stopped too early by only including manufacturing costs in the process and ignoring all subsequent costs.

The following example may illustrate the benefit of value chain analysis. Company A manufactures wooden pallets and buys the timber from a timber company in the form of logs. The company then cuts the logs into planks of the required thicknesses and sells off any remaining timber to a chipboard manufacturer. Transport cost is one of the significant costs in this business. Both supplier and purchaser could gain from this example if the supplier could trim the logs into squares and only the squares need be transported (assuming the supplier is able to perform this work and that disposing of the remaining timber is not causing any unnecessary expense). This can be illustrated by Figure 8.1:

Figure 8.1

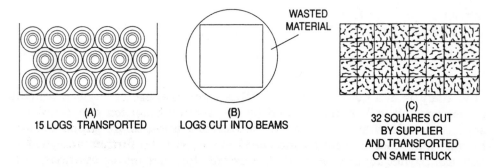

It can clearly be seen that loading space can be used much more efficiently by transporting squares rather than logs.

One of the advantages of breaking costs down into the components of the value chain is that the comparison with other businesses may be limited to selected elements. For example, an organisation could compare its procurement activities with one competitor and its distribution activities with another. In this way it can benchmark the elements of its value chain with the best alternative (which may not even be a direct competitor).

A company could evaluate its procurement activities with the following benchmarks obtained from a company with a similar procurement process:

Cost of issuing a purchase order	£50 per order
Time to place an order	2 days
Percentage of items ordered correctly	98 %

These benchmarks could be used to evaluate the company's procurement performance. Similarly, benchmarks could be obtained for certain distribution activities. Examples of these could be:

Average loading time	2 hours
Delivery cycle time	72 hours
Transport cost per kilometre	93 pence

These benchmarks could be used to evaluate distribution performance.

Advanced manufacturing technologies

The technology employed by a business will influence the cost structures and competitiveness of the business. Advanced manufacturing technologies consist of a variety of methods such as robotics, flexible manufacturing systems and numerically controlled machines. These methodologies generally have the effect of increasing indirect costs (depreciation) by replacing direct costs such as labour. Although this text does not purport to give a specific view on the use of these technologies, cost management cannot be said to be done effectively without the evaluation of the impact of these technologies.

PROCESS AND ACTIVITY ANALYSIS

An increasing number of organisations are realising that the way things get done in organisations can be viewed as business processes which cross organisational boundaries. The cost system should provide a comprehensive view of all business processes and relevant performance information such as cycle times, costs and triggers. These views are useful in evaluating alternative ways of performing processes or in benchmarking processes with other organisations. This may lead to substantial process re-engineering or outsourcing of processes. The technique of process analysis is described in Chapter 6.

In order to improve a process, particular attention is given to analysing activities which are the constituent parts of processes. The aim is to change activities in order to eliminate all unnecessary or overly expensive activities.

The classification of activities into those that add value or those that destroy value and those that are essential or discretionary may highlight the activities that need attention. The cost management strategies to be applied in each case can be categorised as follows:

Table 8.11: Activity management matrix		
	Value-adding	**Non-value-adding**
Essential	Manage for performance	Minimise
Discretionary	Define, when required, how much customer is prepared to pay	Eliminate the cause of the activity

Applying this matrix to a procurement process the following classifications could (arguably) be made:

Table 8.12: Procurement classifications		
	Activity	
	Value-adding	*Non-value-adding*
Essential	Buying	Receiving
Discretionary	Quality control	Storage of excess stock

These activities should be managed by the rules of the activity management matrix.

The expression "non-value-adding" has in practice been found to have behavioural connotations which can adversely affect the implementation process.[6] These issues of implementation are discussed more fully in chapter 11.

Time is an important cost driver in most organisations. Time delays in delivery or manufacturing or any other processes may result in unnecessary work-in-progress or lengthy payment cycles by customers. Excessive time consumed by an activity or process typically causes a lot of cost and should be eliminated or minimised as far as possible. Storage of excess stock consumes time-related cost such as interest or cost of capital. Wastage (of time) in this case is thus directly proportional to the time the excess stock is held in storage.

The procurement process described in Chapter 5 may be analysed as follows:

Procurement process

Buying	33 687
Receiving	19 440
Storage	79 320
Payment	58 686
Cost of process	£ 191 133
Number of orders	1 900
Cost per order	£ 100,58

This analysis may indicate that this cost is extremely high compared with other organisations and a more detailed analysis may indicate that the cause of this ineffectiveness is the relatively high storage cost (£79 320/ 1 900) of £41,72 per order. Specific attention may be given to reorganising the causes of time in storage.

Other examples of changes which impact on the cost of the procurement process are to place standing orders, to move to a just-in-time ordering system or even to use alternative purchasing systems such as credit card purchasing which lessens the administrative work.

One of the prime advantages of the process-focused cost system is that the cost of the total process is evaluated and not only one activity in isolation. In the above example storage costs may be saved by ordering more frequently but this will inevitably have the effect of increasing the ordering and receiving costs. These are sometimes referred to as the upstream or downstream impacts. Process redesign has the objective of lowering the overall process cost.

Cost visibility

One of the important features that needs to be built into ABC systems is to have cost visibility, ie to be able to view the effect that all the support or secondary activities are having on the cost of the cost object. In the case of the procurement process, personnel as well as information technology costs (secondary activities) have been charged to the primary activities. In order to achieve cost visibility it is necessary to indicate the effect these costs may have on the process or the cost object. This can be illustrated for Product 1 as follows:

Table 8.13: Procurement process — product 1

Activities	Primary cost	Secondary activities		Total
		Personnel	IT	
Buying	4 200	158	960	5 318
Receiving	1 986	83	847	2 916
Storage	5 500	63	2 368	7 931
Payment	5 920	67	2 458	8 445
Total	17 606	371	6 633	24 610

In Table 8.13 it can clearly be seen what the added cost is for support activities. The buying activity costs £4 200 without support costs but £5 318 with such costs.

CONTINUOUS COST IMPROVEMENT

The continuous cost improvement philosophy is vastly different from the conventional standard costing philosophy. Under the standard costing philosophy the organisation strives to achieve "standard" at whatever level this is set. Success is determined when standards are met with very little incentive to perform beyond the standard. With the continuous improvement philosophy the objective is to meet the target cost which is continually lowered. A long-term approach is taken to manage costs at all levels down to reach the target.

The operational activities in Example 5.1 discussed in Chapter 5 are reprinted in Table 8.14.

Table 8.14: Bill of activities

Activity	Product 1		Product 2		Total	
	Quantity	Cost	Quantity	Cost	Quantity	Cost
Engineering	200	43 690	150	32 768	350	76 458
Production act. 1	35 000	181 983	70 000	363 965	105 000	545 948
Production act. 2	34 000	177 140	13 000	67 730	47 000	244 870
Production act. 3	75 000	170 636	100 000	227 515	175 000	398 151
Quality control	400	4 554	1 600	18 214	2 000	22 768
Operational admin	100	12 900	180	23 220	280	36 120
Storage	340 000	140 678	140 000	57 926	480 000	198 604
Conversion cost		73 1581		791 338		1 522 919
Units		60 000		115 000		
Conversion cost per product £		12,19		6,88		

This example focuses only on the application of the target cost implications for continuous improvement. The application of the target costing approach would normally start during the design stage of a product and will continue throughout the production phase.

An analysis of the bill of activities indicates that the majority of costs are spent on the production activities. For example, product 1 requires 35 000 units of production activity 1 at a cost of £3,03 (181 983/60 000) per unit. The continuous improvement methodology sets out to lower this (and other) activity costs. This is done by eliminating any unnecessary work associated with this product and also by eliminating any wastage which may occur during the production process. Production methodologies are also subjected to continuous scrutiny to improve throughput per unit of input. For example, an objective may be set to lower the conversion cost of product 1 below £10, which may help in making this a profitable product. Once this is achieved the target cost may become £8, etc.

The continuous improvement philosophy focuses on all costs. In some instances costs may be increased over the short term (for instance by investing in new technology) in order to manage costs down over the long term. All costs are considered variable and manageable over the long term.

PERFORMANCE EVALUATION

Most world class companies realise that managing costs implies that all factors affecting cost such as quality, time and flexibility need to be managed simultaneously. Performance measurement (PM) systems have this specific objective in mind. In the example of the production activity mentioned above, the PM system will measure not only cost but will also determine the necessary quality, time and flexibility criteria for this activity. The following criteria could, for instance, be defined:

- **Quality:** to produce 99,5 % of all units according to quality specifications (ie subject to a defect rate of less than 0,5 %). Quality defects could thus be valued and shown as a cost of non-quality (price of non-conformance — PONC);

- **Time:** allowable time per unit may be 0,1 hour;

- **Flexibility:** this may be defined as the set-up time to change over to alternative products.

The PM system sets out to evaluate the performance of a business by evaluating all the relevant factors which may affect the output of the business.

CAPACITY MANAGEMENT

Capacity management is not new in the production environment but the same principles are now applied to other facets of the organisation such as administration, sales and distribution. In Example 5.1 discussed in Chapter 5, capacity waste was principally calculated for the operational activities, but this could also be done for most other activities.

In the discussion above (Strategic analysis — Finished products) it was noted that product 1 appeared to be unprofitable due to high road transport costs. This could possibly be the result of capacity waste which is included in the cost. Assume, as correct, the information about the road transport activity as in the above case.

Table 8.15: Road distribution cost £		
	Product 1	**Product 2**
Delivery activity	110 000	50 000
Delivery administration	16 000	12 000
Total cost	126 000	62 000

These costs may represent total activity cost inclusive of unit variable cost such as fuel for the delivery vehicles. Capacity waste is calculated by excluding the unit variable cost: £6 000 for product 1 and £2 000 for product 2. If the actual capacity utilisation is 40 %, the costs can be restated as follows:

Table 8.16: Profit impact of capacity waste		
Total cost	126 000	62 000
Less Unit variable cost	6 000	2 000
	120 000	60 000
Capacity waste 60 %	72 000*	36 000
Normative cost	48 000	24 000
Add back Unit variable cost	6 000	2 000
	54 000	26 000
Units delivered	17 000	39 000
Cost per unit	3,17	0,67
Previous cost	7,41	1,59
Surplus capacity cost per unit	4,24	0,92
Profit impact (x units delivered)	72 080*	35 880

(** Difference due to rounding off of costs per unit.*)

If this is related to the above discussion about the profitability of the products, it can be seen that the surplus capacity cost can have a dramatic effect on the unit profitability. The inherent problem therefore does not lie with the product but with the capacity waste which was costed into the product.

Capacity waste should therefore be measured and managed throughout the organisation. Decision making on whether to drop specific products should also be related to the effect on the capacity waste of the whole organisation. In many cases capacity waste will increase because semi-variable costs cannot be eliminated.

Capacity could also be a constraining factor, as is the case in production activity 1 in the example. Required capacity amounts to 105 000 units as opposed to an available capacity of 100 000 units. If capacity cannot be "stretched" by working overtime or some other method to eliminate the constraint or bottleneck, then a cost optimisation technique may have to be applied. This could be done by using the conventional contribution per unit of limiting factor (CULF) approach, that is:

Prioritise products which yield the highest contribution per unit of limiting factor (selling price less marginal cost).

Alternatively, the concepts of throughput accounting may be used.[4] Product prioritisation is based on throughput per factory hour, which is defined as follows:

$$\text{Throughput per factory hour} = \frac{\text{Sale price} - \text{material cost}}{\text{Time on bottleneck resource}}$$

This approach can be strongly criticised since it obviously assumes that all non-material costs are fixed, which may be very difficult to substantiate scientifically.

QUALITY MANAGEMENT

An increased customer focus is required in terms of major factors which influence customer satisfaction such as price, quality or delivery. In many cases the response to customer requirements may have to be "re-engineered" to be able to be performed profitably. A clear understanding of customer requirements may indicate several sources of wastage. A good example is "over-engineered" quality where quality management programmes were driven from the perspective of the engineers instead of from that of the customer. Customer resistance to incessant price increases has reached such a level that in many instances customers are not buying except when absolutely necessary.

World class companies do not tolerate wastage. Most of these companies have introduced quality management systems (QMS) to monitor quality and measure wastage. ABM and QMS have the objectives of measurement and elimination of wastage in common and could be used together. QMS have strong wastage identification capabilities and ABM can use this capability to calculate the cost of quality (price of non-conformance). The success of a QMS is determined by the cost of quality, ie if the cost of appraising and preventing quality defects exceeds the cost of quality failures which are eliminated, the QMS is financially successful. ABC facilitates the measurement of the cost of quality — in some cases the cost of the entire activity is part of the cost of quality, while in other cases part of the cost of an activity will be identified with the cost of quality.[5]

Referring to Example 5.1 in Chapter 5, the quality measurement activity costs £22 768. The potential for the elimination of wastage is enormous considering the wastage which was recorded, namely:

Product defects	12 610
Raw material waste	30 572
Capacity waste	100 877
Manpower waste	143 000
Energy waste	77 000
Time waste	56 000
Other	105 000
Total wastage	£ 525 059

In this case the amount of the wastage is almost equal to the loss incurred. This is extremely important from a management perspective as this can focus management attention on the specific problem areas in the business.

PRODUCTIVITY MANAGEMENT

Productivity management, in its broadest sense, encompasses the effective utilisation of all organisational resources such as people, machines, capital, etc. ABM facilitates productivity management as follows:

- Activity investment analysis;
- Cost of capital management through the residual income model;
- Time and throughput analysis from a process perspective.

Activity investment analysis

Activity costs require the analysis of the asset investment by activity to determine the costs associated with investment such as depreciation, wear and tear and cost of capital. Capital productivity can be evaluated by benchmarking critical capital utilisation ratios within the organisation or within external organisations.

The customer administration activity in Example 5.1 discussed in Chapter 5, can be analysed as follows:

Investment	£
Computer systems	300 000
Premises and other facilities	150 000
Total	450 000

This investment can be benchmarked to other businesses, for instance by using ratios based on the debtors book managed, the number of accounts or the number of invoices. This would respectively be as follows:

Investment per debtors £ (£450 000/3 000 000)   = £0,15
Investment per customers account (£450 000/2 000) = £225
Investment per invoice (£450 000/50 000)   = £9

These figures could give some indication as to the reasonableness or otherwise of the debtors infrastructure investment. Service levels are often a factor of the investment in an activity. If the investment in debtors is indicated by the number of debtors days outstanding, the days outstanding could possibly be improved by investing in better technology to help monitor customer accounts or to speed up the processing of statements or payments. The investment in debtors infrastructure could thus be evaluated by the reduction in the amount invested in debtors itself.

In certain types of activity the capital turnover ratio, if available, may be a useful statistic to evaluate capital productivity. Capital turnover can be expressed as the amount of turnover generated by every £ invested in a particular activity. An investment could, for example, be made in a new machine which could increase turnover by a certain percentage. The percentage increase could thus help in the investment decision.

Residual income model

The combination of residual income theory and ABM provides a useful basis for evaluating which products or customers do not provide an adequate return on capital. Cost of capital, being one of the major costs in most businesses, is charged to activities based on the assets used by the activities (equipment, inventories, debtors, etc). Should a product be able to "break even" on this basis it implies that it in fact provides an acceptable return. Products and customers that require a disproportionate amount of capital are penalised. In order to manage cost of capital down, the use of scarce capital resources has to be constrained.

An important cost driver of cost of capital is of course time. The time that an asset is held (such as the number of months in inventory or the number of days a customer's account remains outstanding) and the amount invested in such assets, determines the amount of cost of capital it will attract. This is an important failure in conventional accounting systems which ignore the time value of money in the treatment of income and expenses. The problem is compounded by treating some of the costs of capital (interest) as period charges but by ignoring the most important "cost", namely the cost of equity.

Many businesses try to overcome this shortcoming by calculating the so-called "value added" to the firm during a period. Value added, as used here, is defined as the amount by which the profit before interest exceeds the cost of capital. The problem with this approach is that it is by nature a macro model and does not indicate specifically where value has been added or lost. ABM, using residual income theory, proposes to indicate at the specific product and customer level where value is added or lost.

PROCESS AND CYCLE TIME

Most organisations realise that time is a costly resource and should be managed effectively. Time, however, hardly ever features in the conventional accounting model (other than the transaction date). Time should be one of the integral elements measured in a performance measurement model. Time is also relevant in an ABM perspective such as in the following instances:

— elapsed time in a process;
— elapsed time for an activity in a process;
— time to conduct an activity;
— time to conduct the tasks within an activity (such as in a material requirements planning system).

For example, the sales process can be broken up into the activities of order taking and sales administration, which can be analysed as follows:

Table 8.17: Analysis of sales process	
Order-taking tasks	
Call on customer	20 minutes
Check stock	5 minutes
Write down order	10 minutes
Phone order to head office	5 minutes
	40 minutes
Sales administration tasks	
Capture order on computer	10 minutes
Check creditworthiness	10 minutes
Process picking slip	5 minutes
Process invoice	3 minutes
	28 minutes

The effective time that the particular order spends in the sales process is thus 68 minutes. This is not a reflection of the cycle time of the process which may be much longer. The cycle started with the customer call and ended with the processing of the invoice. This period may be 24 hours or longer. The cycle efficiency is thus (68 mins/24 hrs) 4,7 %. If this efficiency can be managed up, the customer may get the goods faster and the business may get its money more quickly, which means less cost of capital.

Focusing at the task level (or micro-activity) it may be necessary to determine the relative productivity with which tasks are performed. In the sales administration activity, for example, the statistics may be kept on the computer system where the capturing or processing is done. If the actual statistics are as follows, relative to the standards, an idea may be formed as to why costs have exceeded or were less than budgeted levels:

Table 8.18: Productivity analysis

Sales administration tasks	Standard time	Actual time	Productivity %
Capture order on computer	10 mins	9 mins	+10 %
Check creditworthiness	10 mins	10,5 mins	–5 %
Process picking slip	5 mins	4 mins	+20 %
Process invoice	3 mins	4 mins	–33 %
Activity	28 mins	27,5 mins	+6 %

Low productivity can be an important cost driver. However, the opposite is also true: high productivity can generate profits without any additional input. Productivity improvements are thus attractive areas of attention normally promising high yields on relatively little investment. It is advisable to determine the effect of productivity on organisational performance. Following the Pareto principle, the firm may initially focus its attention on those activities which may render the highest return on productivity improvements.

Although time management focuses very strongly on the people aspect of cost it must be borne in mind that people are still the only source of innovation or creativity in an organisation. Any cost management drive which has as its sole objective the displacement of people must be approached with caution. Unproductive people are often the indicators of weak and unsupportive systems, processes and procedures. The systems should be rectified before an attempt is made to improve productivity.

CONCLUSION

This chapter illustrates some of the techniques used in modern cost management. The particular circumstances of an organisation will dictate the methods and approaches to be used. Logic and common sense as well as good analytical skills must be used in developing a cost management method.

SOURCES CONSULTED

1.   Wilson, R. Strategic cost analysis. *Management Accounting* (UK), Oct 1990: 42–43.
2.   Bromwich, M. *Accounting information for strategic excellence.* Dept of Accounting and Finance, London School of Economics and Political Science, 1990.
3.   Shank, JK & Govindarajan, V. Strategic cost management and the value chain. *Journal of Cost Management,* Winter 1992: 5–21.
5.   Dilton-Hall, K & Glad, E. Activity-based costing empowers quality management. *Accountancy SA,* Jun 1992: 164–168.
6.   Friedman, AL and Lyne SR. *Activity based techniques: the real life consequences. CIMA,* 1995.

9

Activity-based budgeting

INTRODUCTION

The fundamental activity-based costing principles and methodology provide a superb basis for the budgeting process. Activity-based budgeting is therefore a logical progression from activity-based costing and management.

A primary requirement for employing activity-based budgeting (ABB) is a thorough understanding of activity-based costing and management (ABC & M) premises and systems. An ABB system comprises, *mutatis mutandis*, the same principles as ABC & M. This chapter assumes such an underlying comprehension and accordingly only deals with the supplementary aspects pertinent and vital to effective activity-based budgeting. Moreover, all other requirements and principles pertaining to sound budgeting must also be adhered to in ABB, eg management commitment, budget planning, form design, budget manual, communicating budget objectives and procedures, managing and co-ordinating the budgeting process.

Organisations with operational ABC & M systems will be able to implement an ABB system with relative ease. Apart from having the appropriate foundation to base ABB on, such an organisation's management and other staff members concerned will also be familiar with the principles and functioning of their ABM system. However, an existing ABM system is not a precondition for utilising ABB. In fact, a most effective budget can be prepared in such a situation, mainly because proficient managers normally pursue a more clinical course of conduct (a "zero-base" approach) when assessing the effectiveness and necessity of activities, the value chain, the various processes, improvement targets, etc. Prior to launching a "stand-alone" ABB process the necessary groundwork and analyses will necessarily also have to be done (on the same basis as in the event of implementing a new ABC & M system).

STEPS IN THE ABB PROCESS

The ABB process in context with the strategic planning process can be depicted as in Figure 9.1.

Figure 9.1: ABB in context with strategic planning

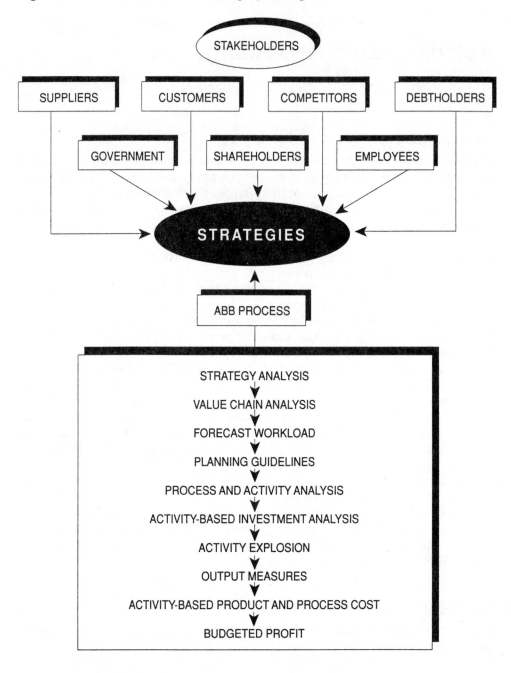

The principal steps can be described as follows:

Strategy analysis

Strategic planning deals with the interpretation of stakeholder requirements and expectations as well as organisational and environmental issues
and the formulation of plans to meet these requirements and address these
issues. Strategy analysis is a very important element of the ABB process as
this provides the link with the strategic planning process and helps to for-
mulate the framework within which the ABB has to be developed.

Like the conventional budget and planning processes, ABB starts with
a review of the critical issues facing the company such as customer dissatisfaction, low productivity, increased competition and other factors addressed in the strategies adopted by the organisation. Critical success
factors need to be developed for each strategy, if not already defined in the
strategic plan.

ABB will focus on the measurement and successful management of
these critical success factors. As an example of a strategy to address customer dissatisfaction, Figure 9.2 shows an analysis of factors impacting on
customer satisfaction:

Figure 9.2: Customer satisfaction factors

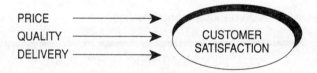

Market research supports the notion that customer satisfaction is primarily
influenced by the factors price, quality and timeous delivery. These factors
could be evaluated, weighed and expressed as a customer satisfaction
index. For each of these factors a specific strategy could be launched to address the issue. Figure 9.3 is an example.

Figure 9.3: Customer satisfaction factors and strategies

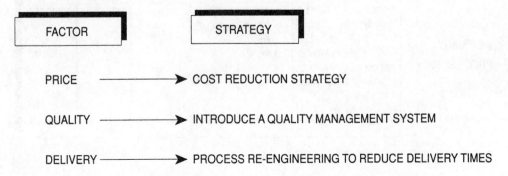

For each of these strategies critical success factors (CSFs) could be developed such as percentage reduction for the cost reduction strategy, a reduction in the number of rejects measured by the quality management system and a specific reduction in the number of late deliveries to customers. The ABB should then specifically focus on integrating these CSFs into the budget.

Value chain analysis

This element of ABM can serve as an extremely powerful tool to set effective budgets. An examination of the value chain will clearly indicate which processes and activities fit in with the proposed strategies and which do not. This affords management the opportunity to eliminate the non-strategic (ie non-value adding and non-essential) activities and processes as far as possible. Hence, the business may be restructured or significantly simplified by virtue of an analysis of its value chain. A value chain analysis also permits a useful comparison of particular information with that of competitors (insofar as comparable information is obtainable).

A typical question addressed during these analyses is which processes and activities could be outsourced. For example, the value chain of a manufacturing business can be depicted as in Figure 9.4.

Figure 9.4: Value chain of manufacturing business

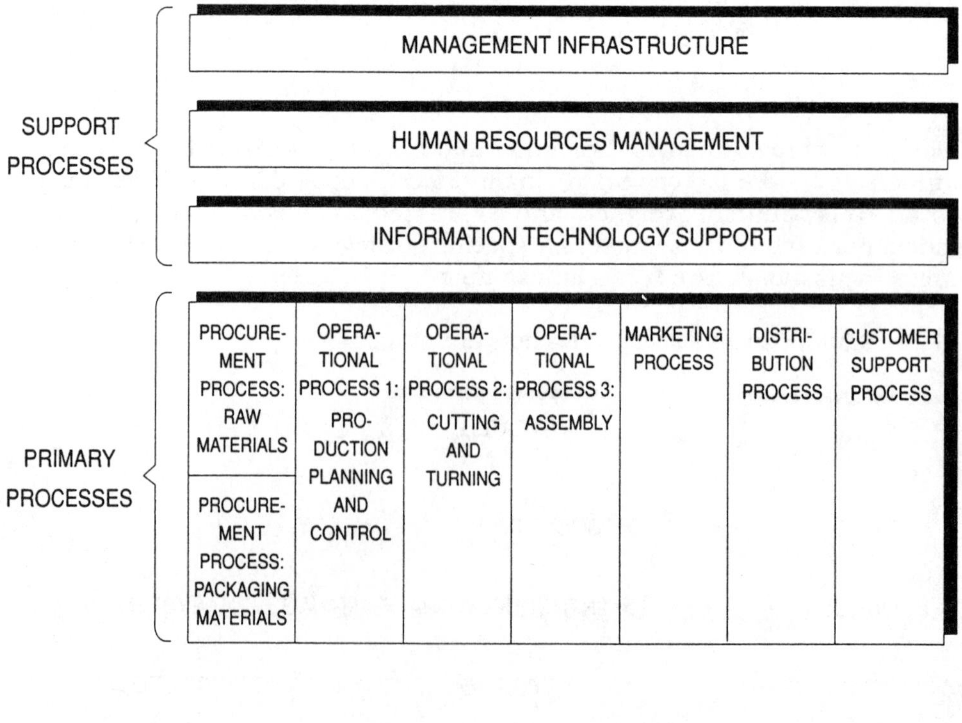

Forecast workload

Workload forecasting entails determining product quantities that will probably be required by customers, taking the strategic direction and value chain analysis into consideration. This is commonly known as the organisation's sales plan. The plan can be translated into workloads for the various processes of the organisation, taking into account inventory policies and other organisational constraints.

The sales plan is translated into specifics such as:

— specific quantities which must be produced at a specific cost;
— a certain percentage of deliveries which must be made within specified delivery schedules;
— the maximum number of rejects that will be tolerated in the quality management system.

In another way this specifies the outputs of the various components or processes of the organisation.

For example, it may be deduced that the company plans to do the following to give effect to its strategies:

Sell products	17 000 units
Selling price	£ 365 per unit
Delivery time	72 hours
Product conformance to quality specification	95 %
Inventory reduction	2 000 units
Net profit required	£ 800 000

The projected sales and inventory reduction indicates that 15 000 (17 000 – 2 000) units must be manufactured which conform to quality specifications. This implies that 15 790 (15 000/95 %) units must be manufactured. Manufacturing process and resource planning will be done accordingly. Distribution resources must be planned to give effect to the delivery requirement of 72 hours. These are some examples of the type of criteria, or outputs, that may be specified for the individual processes in the organisation.

Planning guidelines

Planning guidelines consist of macro- and micro-economic guidelines provided by the board of directors or other authoritative body. These may include factors such as guidelines in respect of assumed inflation and interest rates, required growth rates, dividend policies, gearing ratios and any other exogenous factors which planners should take into consideration in the planning process. These factors are no different from those for a conventional budget.

Process and activity analysis

This entails the analysis and definition of the required processes and concomitant activities which will yield the outputs defined above. Processes may be redefined or restructured by eliminating, *inter alia*, non-value adding activities. Management can endeavour to simplify the indispensable activities and have them performed in the most cost-effective way (ie determining whether there is a less costly alternative). This approach is set out in Chapter 6.

The process for procuring raw materials (referred to in the above value chain) may be analysed into the activities shown in Figure 9.5.

Figure 9.5: Raw materials procurement process

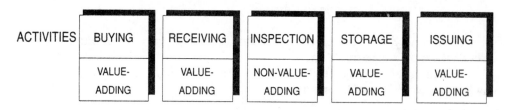

The process consists of four (business) value-adding activities and one non-value-adding activity. The company could possibly eliminate the non-value-adding activity (inspection) by negotiating with reliable suppliers to deliver raw materials that meet specifications. In this way, the inspection activity may not be necessary and can be eliminated, in which case the process will be reconfigured as in Figure 9.6.

Figure 9.6: Reconfigured raw materials procurement process

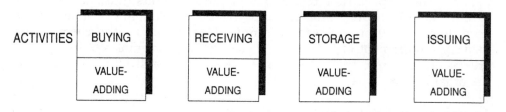

Activity investment analysis

The investment in activities to a large extent determines their cost structures (level of technology, age of assets). The impact of new investment should specifically be evaluated to determine the impact on future (long-term) cost structures.

An example of such an activity investment analysis of the assembly process in the above value chain can be depicted as in Figure 9.7.

Figure 9.7: Manual assembly process

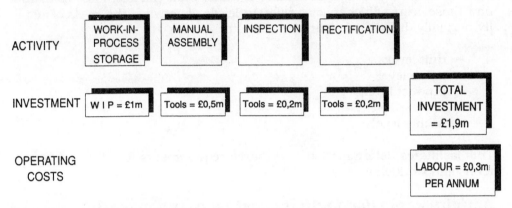

As can be seen from Figure 9.7, the total investment in the process amounts to £1,9m with operational costs of £0,3m per annum. This can be contrasted with a robotised assembly process and the application of just-in-time manufacturing principles, which could yield the process depicted in Figure 9.8.

Figure 9.8: Robotised assembly process

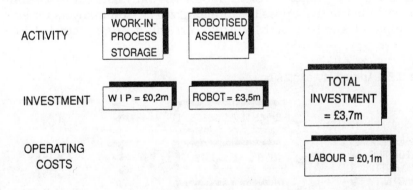

These two proposals illustrate the value an activity investment analysis should have for the budget preparer in providing the necessary insight into issues such as capital availability, operational expense, capacity constraints and possible human resource implications. Based on this type of analysis an improved budget should be possible.

Activity level analysis

An activity-based budget system clearly exposes costs, what drives costs and how costs will behave under different circumstances. This will afford management a better understanding of costs, what causes those costs, and how those costs will change at different levels of activity. The levels of activity normally distinguished are (see Chapter 7):

— unit level;
— batch level;
— product level;
— process level;
— facility level.

This facilitates determination of resource requirements for all the different levels and workloads.

Activity explosion (activity cost by cost element)

Assuming the required activity structure could be defined in terms of the aforegoing, costs will be budgeted per cost element per activity, taking into consideration the appropriate activity levels. The level of understanding required of the business makes this a valuable exercise in itself.

One of the specific cost elements which may be included in the ABB is cost of capital, which dynamically addresses the issue of the effective utilisation of funds.

Should an ABC & M system be in operation, the analysis of historical activity costs and resource consumption should make an explosion of resource costs per activity possible (utilising regression analysis for example). An example of such an activity explosion could be as depicted in Figure 9.9.

Figure 9.9: An activity explosion

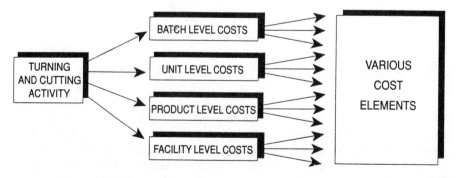

This projection of cost could then be used by process managers to evaluate reasonability of the budgeted figures. Historical trends and cost patterns should be reflected in these projections and they can be adjusted with known changes in factors such as inflation and interest rates or expected wage increases. This predictive capability of ABC & M systems may well, in future, become one of the prominent features of the activity approach as management becomes more concerned with future costs than with an analysis of historical cost.

These attributes provide management with an excellent opportunity to streamline all aspects of the enterprise, do suitable modelling and prepare an effective budget.

Output measures

Output measures need to be determined for all activities in order to calculate activity rates for product costing purposes.

The following outputs may be projected for the anticipated workload to manufacture 15 790 units (based on past experience and future expectations) of activities in the production planning and control process:

Material requirements plans: 27 plans
Scheduling of batches: 250 batches
Shop floor control (per batch): 250 batches
Expediting: 75 times

The determination of the above type of outputs facilitates calculation of budgeted activity cost rates. If the scheduling budget amounts to £62 165 and 250 batches must be scheduled, the applicable rate is £280,30 per batch. Cost rates will be determined for all activities in accordance with the steps set out in the activity-based costing exercise in Chapter 5.

Activity-based process and product costs

The activity-based budgeting exercise culminates in the calculation of budgeted process, activity and product costs. All the normal process and product bills of activities need to be defined as for a properly installed ABC system. In fact, all the actions will be performed except that measurement of actual cost will not have taken place. All decisions emanating from the ABB must thus take into consideration that a degree of risk exists as far as the accuracy of information is concerned. These calculations will be done in accordance with the method set out in Chapter 5.

Many important business decisions can normally be taken based on the information that is made available. Costly processes or activities can be re-engineered, unprofitable products can be eliminated, marketing or distribution channels could be changed, etc.

Budgeted profit

With the above information available, a budgeted profit figure can be determined with relative ease. Table 9.1 is a summary of such a budget.

Table 9.1: Summary of an activity-based budget		
	Schedule	**£**
BUDGETED SALES (17 000 units @ £365)		6 205 000
LESS: BUDGETED COST OF SALES		
PHASE 1: PROCUREMENT		2 606 427
Direct cost of materials (15 790 units @ £150)		2 368 500
Procurement process 1 (raw materials)	1	361 140
		2 729 640
Less: Material wastage (15 790 − 15 000)/15 790 ×		
£2 729 640		136 568
Material cost for 15 000 units		2 593 072
Procurement process 2 (packing materials)		
15 000 units		13 355
PROCUREMENT MARGIN		3 598 573
PHASE 2: OPERATIONS		1 164 890
Operational process 1 (production planning		
and control)	2	227 720
Operational process 2 (cutting and turning)		583 693
Operational process 3 (assembling)		414 828
		1 226 241
Less: Operational wastage 790/15 790 × £1 226 241		61 351
Operational cost for 15 000 units		1 164 890
OPERATIONAL MARGIN		2 433 683
PHASE 3: MARKETING AND SALES		
Marketing process		830 655
MARKETING MARGIN		1 603 028
PHASE 4: DISTRIBUTION		
Distribution process		598 105
DISTRIBUTION MARGIN		1 004 923
PHASE 5: SERVICES		
Customer processes		103 400
		901 523
UNTRACEABLE COST AND WASTAGE		284 060
Material wastage		136 568
Operational wastage		61 351
Untraceable cost		86 141
BUDGETED NET INCOME		617 463

All itemised processes will be supported by accompanying schedules detailing the activities that the relevant processes consist of, for example:

Table 9.2: Schedule 1: Procurement process 1 — Raw materials				
Activity	Output measure	No of units	Rate per unit (£)	Total cost (£)
Buying	No of purchase orders	1 456	62,35	90 782
Receiving	No of goods received notes	1 600	50,70	81 120
Storage	Mass (kg)	106 900	0,72	76 968
Issuing	No of requisitions	5 150	21,80	112 270
				361 140

Table 9.3: Schedule 2: Operational process 3 — Production planning and control				
Activity	Output measure	No of units	Rate per unit (£)	Total cost (£)
Requirement planning	No of product lines	27	2 307,00	62 289
Scheduling	No of batches	250	248,66	62 165
Shop floor control	No of batches	250	280,30	70 075
Expediting	No of time-overruns	75	442,55	33 191
				227 720

The budgeted profit figure of £617 463 reveals a shortfall against the desired profit of £800 000. An analysis of the budget will indicate that this approximately reflects the wastage which is forecast in the budget (material and operational wastage = £197 919). Management attention should thus first be focused on the elimination of this wastage in order to achieve the profit objective. Similar analyses could indicate that better utilisation of capacities, further restructuring of processes, more effective utilisation of resources and outputs, etc could help to futher increase profitability.

The budget should also be constructed in such a way that the usual "what if" analysis can be easily performed. The structure of an ABB makes this eminently suitable as most cost behaviour patterns should have been addressed and built into the budget.

DIFFERENCES BETWEEN ABB AND CONVENTIONAL BUDGETING

Although ABB and conventional budgeting have a lot in common, certain important differences exist which may be emphasised. The majority of these differences also highlight the advantages of ABB over conventional budgeting:

1. ABB focuses on the appropriate value chain necessary for the organisation to meet its strategic needs. The appropriate value chain is fundamentally questioned during the budgeting process. This may not be as specifically emphasised in conventional budgeting.

2. The forecasted workload is specifically determined from a customer's perspective rather than from an organisational constraint perspective. The emphasis is thus what the customer requirements are rather than what the organisation can and wants to deliver.

3. ABB differs fundamentally from conventional budgeting in the approach to process and activity analysis. Conventional budgeting normally follows the convention of budgeting for cost elements (expense items) within cost centres or departments and "rolling" these up (or consolidating them) into organisational budgets. This is one of the principal reasons why conventional budgets normally go through many iterations before being finalised. ABB questions the existence of each process and each activity in requiring it to be classified as value-adding or not. The ABB may be the trigger to start business process redesign.

4. Activity investment analysis must be seen as a more specific, and thus comprehensive, evaluation of the investment of funds in activities and also considers the impact this may have on current and future cost structures. The cost of investing in the form of the cost of capital is also specifically taken into consideration.

5. Conventional budgets classify costs primarily between fixed and variable costs. The classification of cost into the activity levels of unit, batch, product, process or facility variable costs provides a new insight into cost behaviour. These relationships may be used in the budget process to "explode" activity costs into the resources required at each level.

6. Conventional budgeting would most probably have classified costs between material costs, labour, fixed and variable overheads as far as production costs are concerned while all other costs would have been broadly classified as selling or administrative overheads. ABB, as in ABC & M, extends the cost calculation (and thus budgeting) horizon as far as possible to the day that the cheque from the customer is finally banked.

7. ABB requires the same detailed level of understanding of the process and product structures through the definition of the appropriate bills of activities that a proper ABC & M system would require. This necessitates a full understanding of the complexities, not only of manufacturing the product, but also of making it available through the distribution and marketing channels to the customer. Conventional budgets usually do not require this type of detailed or far-reaching analysis.

8. ABB specifically focuses on the customer, marketing and distribution channels as cost objects. These objects are related to their outputs and not merely budgeted as cost elements within a marketing budget. Cost information can be attached not simply to the product as the cost object but also to the customer. This feature can therefore also be incorporated into the budgeting system in order to afford management the opportunity of assessing and, where necessary, upgrading the profitability of individual trading relationships.

9. Benchmarking is normally an integral part of ABB. So is the focus on those elements of the business which may give it a competitive advantage or disadvantage.

10. ABB specifically focuses on support costs and their relationship to primary activities. Support costs in many companies form a major proportion of cost and also need to be related to the outputs produced and the relevance in the organisational value chain.

11. One of the strongest advantages of an ABC system is its preoccupation with non-financial information. From a budgeting point of view this attribute presents a totally different perspective to the budget preparer. Contrary to the traditional approach, ABB focuses primarily on the requisite *activities* to operate an effective organisation. Furthermore, the organisation's performance measurement system will also provide the budget preparers with non-financial norms and targets to be observed and incorporated into the various budgets. Such norms and targets will also create a better understanding of the activity levels and the resources required to operate at these levels.

12. Another important function of budgets, namely cost control, will also improve because a major shortcoming of conventional costing, ie cost distortion, is eliminated. Reported actual costs will therefore be reliable and meaningful analyses and comparisons with budgeted figures can be done.

13. When an ABB system is linked to a quality management system, a specific focus on wastage can be incorporated into the budgeting process. The ABB helps to determine the value of wastage at the point where it occurs.

CONTROLLING THROUGH ACTIVITIES

As with conventional budgets, annual ABBs are also analysed into shorter (eg monthly) periods for control purposes. This dissection is based on the expected activity levels for such periods. Actual cost and non-financial data are then recorded in the normal way by the ABC system: Costs are charged to the various activity cost pools, the respective output measure units for the period are totalled, and the actual unit cost per output measure is determined. The actual ABC data are then compared to the ABB data: Actual cost per output measure unit to its budgeted cost, actual activities to the budgeted number of activities, and both cost *and* activity variances are analysed. The required corrective action can then be taken.

Actual resource consumption is managed by controlling activities. Excess use of activities predominantly implies wastage. An analysis of actual activity cost versus budgeted activity cost may reveal the elements of wastage such as:

— resource waste (manpower, electricity, etc);
— capacity waste;
— output waste.

Reasons for excess activities are determined, eg late deliveries by suppliers, short deliveries by suppliers and returns to suppliers indicate problems with some suppliers (who are to be identified) which are to be solved/eliminated without delay. The clear picture that ABC & M presents of costs and what causes costs offers management a favourable opportunity to not only identify deficiencies in operational performance, but also to continuously improve performance. Contrary to the budget overruns that are common in a traditional budgeting environment, organisations operating ABBs may be improving all the time and may thus show even better results in the end than those initially budgeted. An ABB is much more accurate from the outset and lends itself extremely well to continuous improvement.

CONCLUSION

The very nature of ABC & M makes it an ideal concept on which to found a budgeting system. From a budgeting point of view an ABC & M system is much more supportive for planning and budgeting than a conventional system. ABC & M provides a clear insight into costs (cost visibility), what causes costs and how costs will behave. These attributes "simplify" an organisation's operations and thus make planning and budgeting less complicated and more reliable than under traditional systems which report *(doubtful) historical* costs.

SOURCES CONSULTED

1. Biggs, JR, Long, EJ & Fraedrich, KE. Integrating accounting, planning, and control. *Journal of Cost Management*, Spring 1991:11–21.
2. Brimson, J & Fraser, R. The key features of ABB. *Management Accounting* (UK), Jan 1991:42–43.
3. Gietzman, MB. *The development and design of an activity-based budgeting system: Initial experiences*. London School of Economics and Political Science, 1992.
4. Morrow, M & Connolly, T. The emergence of activity-based budgeting. *Management Accounting* (UK), Feb 1991:38–41.
5. Harvey, M. Activity-based budgeting. *Certified Accountant*, Jul 1991:27–30.
6. Johnson, HT. Activity-based information: A blue-print for world-class management. *Management Accounting* (US), Jun 1988:23–30.

10

Performance measurement

EFFECTUAL MEASURES

Traditionally, the bottom line and ratios emanating therefrom have been the acceptable norms for evaluating organisations — both internal and external reporting have focused on net profits, return on investment and earnings per share as measures of organisations' performance. This approach can be severely criticised in the following respects:

- The attention of management and other users is mainly directed at a single, aggregated figure.
- It provides historical statistics and is therefore not indicative of future performance.
- It only stresses one of many important measures, namely financial performance. Some authors appropriately compare the concept of performance measures to a game of sport: The scoreboard (ie net profit) reflects the results, but to be successful the various elements of the game are to be mastered and performed effectively. Also, a player only applying his mind to the scoreboard and not focusing on his function on the field, is unlikely to win the game. The causal factors that lead to the given final result and the strategies and actions that need to be executed to achieve overall excellence and improve profitability, remain concealed.
- Because it fundamentally focuses on measuring and reporting to shareholders it ignores the interests of other stakeholders such as employees, suppliers, government, debtholders and the community at large.
- Financial performance measures are micro-performance criteria and ignore the macro environment within which the organisation operates. To evaluate the organisation properly it needs to be compared with its competitors, the industry within which it operates as well as the broad economic environment.
- It ignores the role and the performance of the organisation within the physical environment in which it operates. This could be indicative of its future capability to do business (if, for example, it destroys its environment or natural resources).

- Even with generally accepted accounting practice (GAAP) organisations still find it possible to manoeuvre and manipulate financial statements in such a way as to conceal important trends and events.

The global increase in competition has necessitated a substantial move towards the identification of all the important factors that would ensure success, as well as the implementation, evaluation and continuous improvement of strategies. In this process performance measures other than financial criteria have emerged to such an extent that purely financial measures are no longer predominant. In essence, non-financial performance measures are of primary importance for the overall success of organisations. Such was the focus on external financial reporting over the last two decades, that reporting of internal financial and operational performance has been severely neglected. This does not imply that financial results are less important. Rather, properly implemented non-financial controls will vastly improve financial returns. The use of non-financial measures confirms the importance of the underlying operations and activities of an organisation, which will lead to the ultimate success of an organisation, if properly controlled and improved.

ROLE OF ACTIVITY-BASED MANAGEMENT WITHIN A PERFORMANCE MEASUREMENT SYSTEM

Activity-based costing and management (ABC & M) systems tend to be much closer to a proper performance measurement system than a traditional accounting system. However, several features of a comprehensive performance measurement system (PMS) are not found in an ABC & M system, such as:

- The macro focus on the broad environment such as competitors, industry, economy, etc. Benchmarking partially fulfils this focus, but remains a micro focus on specific organisational matters;
- The focus on physical environmental factors such as air pollution, destruction of natural resources, etc;
- The measurement of organisational flexibility in terms of meeting future market changes;
- The focus on expectations of the various stakeholders in the organisation. ABC & M narrowly focuses on the organisational factors influencing profitability.

Notwithstanding the above, ABC & M can play a significant role in supporting a PMS through:

- — excellent cost measurement and management methodologies;
- — the specific focus on measurement and reporting of quality and non-quality in the organisation;

— the focus on all forms of productivity measurement;
— the measurement and reporting of capacity issues;
— striving to link the cost management system with (internally focused) strategies and the measurement and reporting of critical (or key) success factors;
— measurement of non-financial factors and their integration into the reporting process;
— the process versus functional perspective on the organisation, focusing on the outputs to be delivered by the process and not merely on reporting of the resources consumed by functions.

In summary, it can be said that a PMS measures comprehensively **all** factors influencing organisational health while the ABC & M system mostly focuses on internal factors.

THE DESIGN OF A PERFORMANCE MEASUREMENT SYSTEM

The design of a performance measurement system (PMS) basically involves the following steps:

1. Identify the factors (internal and external) that are essential for the organisation's successful survival and long-term growth, ie the critical success factors. This may be the result of a strategic planning exercise evaluating, *inter alia*, the strengths, weaknesses, opportunities and threats of the organisation and the formulation of strategies to address these issues.
2. Determine the measures that will provide objective indicators regarding the state of the respective critical success factors and the relative improvements thereof. These can normally be analysed between short- and long-term factors.
3. Set the *goals and objectives* to be achieved in respect of the performance measures. This is a specific focus on the outputs that are to be delivered by different processes in the organisation.
4. Cascade the goals and objectives (or required outputs) down the organisation to define relative responsibilities at all levels.[1]
5. Implement an appropriate PMS that will measure and report the relevant measurements.

Critical success factors

Identifying the critical factors that are imperative for an organisation's success is a primary and crucial prerequisite for formulating strategies and determining suitable performance measures. The present-day market place is characterised by constant change, intense competition, and greater responsiveness to customer demands. Enterprises are compelled to provide customer satisfaction and improve business performance. Initiatives such as expanding product differentiation, improving customer service, introducing total quality and pursuing continuous improvement have become the cornerstones of corporate strategy.[2]

Since the ultimate success of most enterprises depends on the extent to which customers' demands can be satisfied, a logical point of departure is to determine the factors that will ensure the success of the enterprise's products in the market place. Thereafter the factors that will satisfy those market requirements are determined, eg manufacturing excellence; in turn, the factors determining manufacturing excellence are ascertained, and so forth until the total spectrum of critical success factors has been established.

Apart from the holistic approach, all critical success factors and, consequently, the performance measures relating thereto will be linked if the above procedures are followed.

The following are examples of critical success factors:

— responsiveness to customers;
— customer satisfaction;
— reliability;
— innovation;
— technological leadership;
— manufacturing excellence;
— flexibility;
— quality;
— resource management;
— cost;
— cash flow;
— profitability.

Some of the above examples may be overlapping and conflicting; however, every organisation should determine its own key success factors, define each once precisely and clearly outline the elements that each factor comprises. For example, reliability (about promised delivery times, after-sales service, etc) can also be incorporated with responsiveness to customers which, in turn, can be classified under customer satisfaction. Hence, the number of groupings can vary while the same end result can be achieved. However, if relatively few groupings are used, care should be exercised that such an approach does not cause important aspects to be overlooked. For this reason it may be more effective to apply narrower definitions to the respective critical success factors and therefore work with more factors which will ensure that all the indicators to be measured by the particular enterprise are covered.

After having determined and defined its critical success factors, the organisation's next goal would be to measure them properly in order to manage them better, which would improve the overall performance of the organisation.

Determining performance measures

In general terms, performance measures are measures that indicate how well an enterprise is doing in the things that really matter. These measures are, like ABC & M, focused on outputs and not only inputs; on measuring results or performance and not merely on spending. After having established the critical or key success factors, the measures to gauge the performance efficiency in regard to those factors can be determined.

The following aspects are to be taken into consideration when developing performance measures:

- More than one measure will normally be required to monitor and measure the performance in respect of a critical success factor.
- Measures will have different meanings at different levels in the organisation;
- Measures should be easy to track and preferably be quantifiable. Quality should, for example, be expressed as "number of perfect products per 1 000";
- An appropriate reporting cycle should be defined to ensure that adequate opportunity exists for rectifying problem areas (ie timeliness of reporting concept);
- The measures must focus on the business processes and not on the conventional functional divisions;
- The measures must effect pro-active problem identification and promote the continuous improvement process;
- All measures must relate to key success factors; those that cannot be linked to key success factors do not play a part in executing strategies and should be disposed of;
- Measures must be clearly understood by the employees concerned and should, where possible, always be stated in positive terms, eg report productive machine time instead of machine down time, on-time deliveries instead of late deliveries, etc. This approach will have a positive psychological effect on personnel — pursuing goals instead of recognising failures.

Table 10.1 shows examples of performance measures in respect of some key success factors:

Table 10.1: Examples	
Critical success factor	**Performance measures**
Customer satisfaction	Delivery cycle
	Completeness of orders
	Service cycle
	Service quality
	Customer complaints
	Customer returns
	Warranty claims
	Market share
	Repeat orders
Manufacturing excellence	Manufacturing lead time
	Manufacturing interval
	Set-up times
	Schedule changes
	Line disruptions
	Scheduled machine down time
	Unscheduled machine down time
	Production cycle time
	Product yields
	Cost of scrap
	Throughput (No of units)
	Head count productivity
	Times product handled
	Rework quantities
	Product redesign
	Improvement ideas
	Space utilised
Quality	First pass percentage
	Number of defective units
	Outgoing quality rate
	Customer complaints
	Customer returns
	Warranty claims
Profitability	Sales – unit
	Sales – value
	Gross profit
	Product profitability
	Customer profitability
	Net profit
	Return on investment
	Earnings per share
	Residual income

Performance measures will differ from enterprise to enterprise; each organisation and each division within an organisation should develop its own set of performance measures.

GOALS AND OBJECTIVES IN RESPECT OF PERFORMANCE MEASURES

Once the respective performance criteria have been defined, relative values need to be determined in order to be able to evaluate performance or ascertain acceptable performance. Measurement normally takes place by way of time, number, percentage or money value. Although this forms part of the broader definition of the concept of performance evaluation and management, an example to illustrate it is as follows:

Taking the critical success factor of customer satisfaction described in a previous paragraph into account, the following goals and objectives can, for example, be set for the performance measures:

Table 10.2: Example: Performance evaluation and management		
Critical success factor	**Performance measures**	**Goals and objectives**
Customer satisfaction	Delivery cycle	48 hours
	Completeness of order	99 %
	Service cycle	Weekly
	Service quality	Mean time between failures
	Customer complaints	100 per month
	Customer returns	Less than 3 per 1 000 transactions
	Warranty claims	Less than 1 % of turnover
	Market share	25 %
	Repeat orders	85 % of customers

The advantage of defining the goals and objectives as specifically as above, implies that they are measurable and manageable or that an improvement in these ratios should lead to an improvement in customer satisfaction. This notion needs to be supported by market research. These factors can sometimes be combined or weighted to form a single (customer satisfaction) index.

Cascading the performance goals down the organisation

Organisation levels and linkages

Normally measures are fairly detailed and require quick responses at the lower levels of an organisation. Conversely, the higher the level the broader the measures tend to become. This aspect and the linkage of measures at the different management levels are aptly illustrated by the following example with regard to the critical success factor, resource management, which can be defined as optimising outputs to inputs in people, inventory and capital employed[1]:

Figure 10.1: Linkage of measures at different management levels

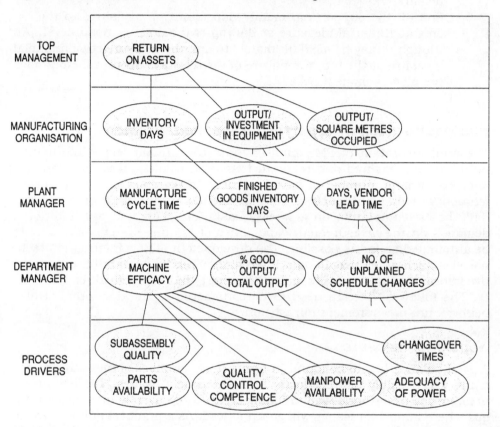

In the example the measures for a critical success factor for resource management, namely return on assets, were determined as inventory days, value of output yielded by the investment in equipment and value of output per square metre.

In turn, inventory days are linked to manufacturing cycle time, which is linked to machine efficacy, which can ultimately be linked to several manufacturing process drivers.

Explicit arrangements such as the one depicted in Figure 10.1:

— clearly indicate individual managers' responsibilities;
— enable each manager at each level to control his measures;

— acquaint each manager with the measures at the level above his and how his measures support those on the upper level;

— enable each manager to perceive the source of problems and/or poor performance at the lower level that affect his performance negatively;

— link all the supporting, mainly non-financial, measures to the aggregate financial measure at the top of the organisational level. (Although it may be ideal ultimately to link the measures to a financial measure at the top, the nature of most critical success factors does not always make it possible.)

Implementation of a performance measurement system

The implementation of PMS implies that substantially more information needs to be measured and reported than in a traditional accounting system. Also a large number of measures need to be reported with increased frequency, such as productivity and production or output information on a daily basis, complaints on a weekly basis, etc. This will put additional demands on the measurement capabilities of existing systems and should be automated as far as possible. The development of new information technologies such as electronic data interchange, relational data bases, executive information systems, etc makes this more than a practical reality.

The following factors need to be considered in the development of a performance measurement infrastructure[3]:

Number of measures

A good balance has to be found in terms of the number of measures as too many will possibly distract focus from the crucial issues. Too few measures, on the other hand, will probably create a too narrow management focus where important issues will go unnoticed. As a practical guide, three to six critical success factors are normally relevant at any time and the PMS should be structured around these.

Bases of comparison

Comparisons of performance can be made within the organisation or outside the organisation. Internal comparisons are feasible if the organisation, for example, has several branches or manufacturing sites, etc. This is normally referred to as *best practice* comparisons. Alternatively, external comparisons can be made and these can take several forms such as *formal inter-organisation comparative surveys* or informal comparisons with competitors or other organisations. *Benchmarking* has become a popular method for continuously improving the organisation and the requirements for benchmarking need to be specifically designed into the PMS.

Time horizon

The short- or long-term impact of critical success factors needs to be embodied in the PMS in terms of the measurement horizon. Certain factors, for example, need to be monitored with long-term trends while others only need to be kept track of for the very short term. These issues are thus relevent in determining how and when to collect performance measures and also the period for which storage needs to be provided.

Reporting frequency

The nature of the performance measure will determine how often reporting will be necessary. For some factors, such as labour productivity, or other operational issues such as quality, hourly or at least daily reporting will be necessary. On other issues such as sales or physical production, weekly reporting may suffice. The choice of the reporting frequency may require a reporting dynamism which is unknown in most organisations (with traditional accounting systems). The requirement that accuracy, integrity and timeliness are equally important with more frequent reports must also be understood. World class companies will most probably strive to report most critical aspects in a real-time mode.

Presentation methods

Because of the large volumes of data that need to be manipulated and presented, conventional reporting methods may lead to a perspective of information overload among users. Instead, information must be presented in imaginative ways such as in bar charts, graphs, pie charts and other methods which the new media make so spectacularly appealing. The real test for successful presentation is whether the feedback creates action.

CHARACTERISTICS OF PERFORMANCE MEASURES

In order to be able to establish the individual performance measures it is essential to have a clear sense of the general attributes of performance measures and a fit performance measurement system. Moreover, the success of the performance management system will depend on how well these attributes are incorporated into the system. Therefore, due consideration should be paid to the following attributes[4]:

Comprehensibility

The achievement of an organisation's goals and objectives depends to a major extent on the success of its continuous improvement programme which, in turn, hinges on employee motivation and behaviour. To influence the latter positively and to ensure that the system operates effectively it is imperative that there be no ambiguity about the meaning and interpretation of any performance measure — the relationship between the objectives measured and the indicators used to establish performance in that regard, ie the performance measures, must be clearly understood by all involved in the process. Furthermore, there must be no misconception about the exact levels of performance for each measure.

Management commitment

As with any other system or execution of strategies, management at all levels must clearly comprehend, accept and demonstrate their support of and commitment to the performance measures to ensure the efficient and successful functioning thereof. The use of performance measures as a management tool must become an integral part of the day-to-day control and decision-making process.

Limited in number

The time and attention that will be devoted to individual performance measures will bear a direct relationship to the number of measures that have to be attended to. Therefore, the number of performance measures must be limited to those that are crucial to the success of the organisation. Too many measures may diffuse the attention that should be paid to distinct measures, thereby weakening the impact of important measures.

Timely reporting

To be most efficient, reporting has to be punctual and at suitable intervals. Such attributes will enable the officials concerned to take the required corrective action promptly.

The frequency of reporting will depend on the specific situation relating to the respective performance measures, eg the reporting intervals on the factory floor will be considerably shorter than those at top management level; also, ideal reporting intervals will differ from product to product and from production process to production process. However, caution should be exercised that short-term fluctuations do not distort or obscure the interpretation of the measure. Progressive companies are moving closer to real-time reporting and costing rather than periodic (typically monthly) reporting.

Visible results

To induce constant motivation and positive behaviour the results of performance measures have to be clearly communicated, not only to those directly concerned, but in a generally visible way to everybody by, for example, displaying the information prominently in the relevant work areas.

Linkage to employee evaluation system

The explicit linking of the employee evaluation process to the prevailing performance measures will reinforce the importance of the latter. Employee performance should only be rated positively to the extent that the organisation's goals and objectives could be achieved which, in turn, would depend on the commitment to the performance measures.

THE BALANCED SCORECARD

Kaplan and Norton[14] suggest that an organisation's measurement system powerfully influences the behaviour of its managers and workforce. They propose a "balanced scorecard" which combines financial measures with operational, organisational innovation and improvement measures. The balanced scorecard becomes the manager's instrument panel for managing the complexity of the organisation.

Each organisation needs to develop its own set of measures upon which senior managers should focus their attention. It is important that the balanced scorecard contains sufficient information for informed decisions, without swamping managers in trivia. It should not become a "wish-list" of information which might conceivably be of use. Table 10.3 gives an example balanced scorecard, adapted from various sources,[14,2] which indicates the type of measures which might be considered:

Table 10.3: Example Balanced Scorecard	
Financial Outlook	
Goals	**Measures**
Survive	*Cashflow
Succeed	* Sales growth by strategic business unit * Operating income by strategic business unit
Prosper	* Return on market value of capital invested by strategic business unit
Customer Outlook	
Goals	**Measures**
Delight	* Quality/zero defects * On-time delivery * Level of satisfaction
Improve market penetration	* Market share by strategic business unit

Table 10.3: Example Balanced Scorecard *continued*	
Operational Outlook	
Goals	**Measures**
Manufacturing excellence	* Cycle time
	* Yield
	* Defects
Supplier partnership	* Share of key account purchases
	* Level of information sharing
Innovation and Organisational Outlook	
Goals	**Measures**
Learning organisation	* Annual attitude survey
Motivated workforce	* Staff turnover
	* Annual attitude survey
	* Summary of appraisal interviews
New product introduction	* Percentage of sales from new products
	* Diffusion rates of new products
Technological leadership	* Time to develop next generation products

As a general principle, each measure should be capable of expression quantitatively and of being compared against a pre-set standard. Where possible, these standards should be developed in a rigorous way making full use of customer perceptions and competitive benchmarking.

The difficulties of implementing a balanced scorecard approach should not be under estimated, involving much more than just the resource implications of data acquisition. As part of the introduction of an ABC & M system, the balanced scorecard will require managers to alter their focus from traditional functions and departments towards customers and activities[14]. While such a change of perspective is to be encouraged, managers may find the re-orientation threatening. Unlike traditional measurement systems which were often introduced exclusively by the finance function, the balanced scorecard requires the involvement of senior managers to provide a holistic picture of the firm's objectives and priorities. This will not only provide useful information, but also produce powerful champions for the introduction of an ABC & M system.

CONCLUSION

Activity-based costing and management contain a subset of the measures that will be used in a comprehensive performance measurement system. It is therefore relevant to understand the areas of commonality and the objectives of both approaches.

SOURCES CONSULTED

1. Beischel, ME & Smith, KR. Linking the shop floor to the top floor. *Management Accounting* (US), Oct 1991: 25–29.
2. Maisel, LS. Performance measurement: The balanced scorecard approach. *Journal of Cost Management*, Summer 1992: 47–52.
3. Glad, E & Dilton-Hill, K. Performance measurement. *Accountancy SA*, Aug 1992: 232–236 (Part 1) and Sept 1992: 279–282 (Part 2).
4. Greene, AH & Flentov, P. Managing performance: Maximizing the benefit of activity-based costing. *Journal of Cost Management*, Summer 1990: 51–59.
5. Allen, D. Out of Africa. *Management Accounting* (UK), May 1991: 19.
6. Eccles, R. The performance measurement manifesto. *Harvard Business Review*, Jan-Feb 1991: 131–137.
7. Fisher, J. Use of nonfinancial performance measures. *Journal of Cost Management*, Spring 1992: 31–38.
8. Green, FB, Amenkhienan, F & Johnson, G. Performance measures and JIT. *Management Accounting* (US), Feb 1991: 50–53.
9. Kaplan, RS. Measures for manufacturing excellence: A summary. *Journal of Cost Management*, Fall 1990: 22–29.
10. Le Saint-Grant, F. Performance evaluation: All the answers. *Management Accounting* (UK) Apr 1992: 42–46.
11. Nanni, AJ, Dixon, JR & Vollmann, TE. Strategic control and performance measurement. *Journal of Cost Management*, Summer 1990: 33–42.
12. Sellenheim, MR. JI Case company performance measurement. *Management Accounting* (US), Sep 1991: 50–53.
13. Stalk, G. Time — the next source of competitive advantage. *Harvard Business Review*, Jul-Aug 1988: 41–51.
14. Kaplan, RS & Norton, DP. The balanced scorecard — measures that drive performance. *Harvard Business Review*, Jan-Feb 1992: 71–79.

11

Implementation

INTRODUCTION

Implementation of an ABC & M system has much more to it than the theory may suggest. Implementation is complicated, not because of the design characteristics but because the system must handle both financial and non-financial data and because of the large volumes of data that are typically required. Integrity of data, especially non-financial data, is a concern in most systems. None of these problems are insurmountable when the necessary care is taken in the implementation of the system. Fortunately the development of new data base technologies, electronic data interchange and other modern information handling capabilities, makes even the most complete ABC & M system a practical reality.

This chapter sets out the implementation steps for an ABC & M system as well as a number of ancillary aspects such as design structures, computerisation issues and the role of consultants. An overview of the steps is provided in Figure 11.1.

STEPS TO IMPLEMENT ABC & M

1. FEASIBILITY STUDY AND REVIEW

It is important to define the objectives of such a system before embarking on actual implementation. Implementation of the system will require considerable effort and expense and it should be questioned whether or not it will add value to the business. Information overload as well as the capability of the management team to absorb the contents of the system, certainly will be factors to consider in this respect.

Costs

The feasibility study should look at the normal cost considerations which can be summarised as follows:

- Development cost:
  - outside assistance;

Figure 11.1: Steps to implement an ABC & M system

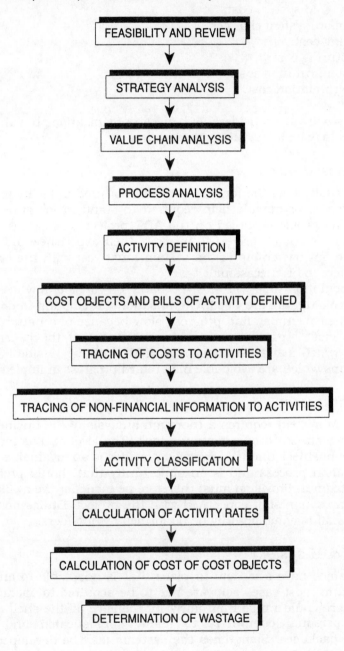

- — internal staff costs;
- — ABC & M system cost;
- — support system changes.
- • Operating cost:
- — capturing cost;
- — system running cost;
- — interpretation cost.

These costs will vary considerably between organisations but the following short notes may be taken into consideration.

Outside assistance

This will usually take the form of consultants hired to facilitate the development process or outside help required to stand in for duties normally performed by people occupied on the ABC project team. Consultants can certainly add to such a project in terms of their experience and knowledge of the topic but ownership of the system must vest with the organisation for the system to be successful.

Implementation time will most probably be considerably less when experienced consultants are used. Organisations attempting to do an installation on their own may find progress slow because of a natural inertia to change in most organisations and also because of the general lack of knowledge which may exist about ABC & M. Without outside help, pitfalls and problems which are avoidable may retard progress in implementation.

Internal staff cost

An ABC & M system requires a thorough analysis of the business and its processes which is a time-consuming task. The level of understanding regarding the business that this analysis provides is an invaluable part of the implementation process and is an opportunity that should preferably not be contracted out. Provision must therefore be made for the availability and cost of organisation staff concerned with the project. Duties normally performed by staff may temporarily be performed by outsiders.

The ABC & M system

Few companies have a system in place that is adaptable to an ABC & M system and in most cases software has to be acquired to operate the system. Software could range from fairly inexpensive off-the-shelf ABC packages for personal computers to highly sophisticated and expensive integrated packages. Sometimes the systems may be developed in-house but this could be expensive. Packaged software does not always meet the organisational requirements and there is then little choice but to develop own systems.

Support systems

ABC & M systems usually acquire their data from various support systems such as production control systems, general ledger systems, debtors or inventory systems. These systems may not, at the outset, provide information in an activity format and may have to be adapted to do so. Interface programs may also be required to integrate the support systems with the ABC & M system.

Most complete ABC & M systems draw information, and specifically non-financial data, from organisational data bases. If such a data base does not exist, consideration must be given to the cost of installing and maintaining one.

Capturing cost

The design of the ABC & M system is quite important as more information needs to be captured than was previously the case. If the existing data capture process could be extended to incorporate additional fields, the costs are normally minimal. However, in some cases, information may have to be recaptured (where data is not electronically available) or re-analysed which may add considerably to costs. One of the main problems in this regard is the general ledger system which may still be structured on a functional (departmental) basis, which normally implies a total analysis of all source documents to attain an activity structure and, in the long run, a re-design of the general ledger system.

System running cost

Running cost mostly amounts to increased storage capacity that needs to be created for information. Output measures and cost drivers may, for instance, be stored for 36 months or more to facilitate trend analyses or validation of cost drivers.

Other system running costs should not amount to much unless new networks and communication channels are set up for this purpose. Use is typically made of existing facilities. Companies that set up activity structures in their general ledgers may find an escalation of work because of an increase in the number of transactions and ledger accounts that are kept.

Consideration should be given to the automatic integration of financial and non-financial data into the ABC & M system. Manual collection and processing of non-financial data in one installation led to the results from the system being significantly delayed.

Interpretation cost

This is referred to as a specific cost as it can be expected to be considerably more than in a conventional system. Much more information about the organisation can be made available and in order to obtain the foreseen benefits, time and effort must be spent interpreting information.

Benefits

Although numerous benefits can result from an ABC & M implementation, it will be hard to quantify such benefits upfront. Cost of developing such a system should possibly be treated as a sunk cost but continued operation should be evaluated from time to time. In this regard information that has been provided to restructure the organisation should be taken into consideration. It may be relevant to question the level of detail that is required from the system. This may either be raised or lowered from time to time. Pilot studies may also reveal the type of advantages that may be realised in a particular organisation.

Initially, it may be more appropriate to identify the information that the system is required to develop, ie which decisions will be better made with the new information.

Reasons

Reasons for developing systems must be properly evaluated. Some of the specific reasons that have been found for the development of ABC & M systems are:

- to be able to improve product costing;
- to be able to increase the accuracy of costs of a number of cost objects such as customers, products, processes, etc;
- to get a process and activity perspective of the organisation as opposed to a functional perspective;
- to understand better the occurrence and treatment of overheads in the organisation;
- to determine the viability of distribution or marketing channels;
- to ascertain customer profitability or to facilitate customer re-engineering;
- to integrate the total quality management (TQM) system with the accounting system;
- to integrate time and other productivity systems into the accounting system;
- to improve management of cost of capital;
- to identify capacity and other constraints that may exist;
- to manage activity levels or to be able to perform better cost modelling;
- to obtain a better basis for future cost prediction or budgeting.

Many more reasons could be considered but care should be taken not to develop a system just for the sake of having such a system or because "everybody else" is developing such systems. Competitor actions could be monitored to anticipate changing price strategies which may be the result of such a system.

The feasibility study should carefully consider all the relevant aspects in order to give management the opportunity of making an informed decision. Should a decision be taken to proceed with an implementation, the following steps must be considered:

2. STRATEGY ANALYSIS

Cost systems should fulfil a twofold role in strategy support:

- They should be able to provide information and analytical support for the deployment of existing strategies.
- They should provide an impetus for the development of new or revised strategies.

Existing strategies

Existing strategies can usually be classified between internally and externally focused strategies. Examples of internal strategies may be the reduction of cost or improvement of quality or reduction in delivery times, etc. The cost system must find the linking mechanism, through the critical success factors, between these strategies and the measurements or key performance indicators. Many of these measures are non-financial measures which may be accessible by the system and which could be provided as a valuable by-product.

The progress and ultimate success of a particular strategy could also be monitored in many instances. An organisation may want to improve customer service by improving delivery times, percentage of order fulfilment and elimination of complaints. These factors may be included in a customer satisfaction index, which could be calculated to evaluate progress with this strategy. Many of these issues are frequently recorded for the ABC & M system and could thus also be used to determine whether the particular strategy is having the desired effect, ie to improve customer service.

New strategies

The cost system should indicate areas of concern or facets of the business which require specific management attention in the form of new or revised strategies. Unprofitable products or product groups or customers or marketing and distribution channels may all be areas which may necessitate strategy revision. The purpose of the cost system is thus one of attention focusing or directing.

Strategic focus is a particular focus that needs to be designed into the cost system and requires a certain amount of skill and experience on the part of the system designer.

3. VALUE CHAIN ANALYSIS

The value chain focus does not only permit the definition of the various accounting phases as described in Chapter 5, but also provides a particular strategic perspective for comparing the business with competitors and other firms (benchmarking).

The identification of the various value chain processes should focus on the organisation from the customer's perspective, ie what needs to be done by the organisation to meet customer requirements. Certain facets of the value chain, such as distribution, may be considered non-strategic and therefore candidates for outsourcing. A gas manufacturing company supplying industrial gas to a variety of businesses may have developed a reliable customer inventory management system which makes supply and distribution of gas almost a formality. It is therefore not critical for the company to undertake its own deliveries (to ensure good customer service) and this process can comfortably be contracted out if the contractor can guarantee delivery cycles and times which meet the company's requirements.

This analysis is the fundamental base from which the components of the ABC & M system should be developed.

4. PROCESS ANALYSIS

The main value chain processes (such as inbound logistics or operations) should be analysed into the business processes that they comprise. This should also be the first level of cost analysis to be performed for a business. From this perspective, processes which should be subjected to re-engineering, can be identified. Processes for re-engineering include those that:

— are costly compared to those of other organisations (benchmarking);
— present pertinent quality problems (as indicated by the TQM system);
— create bottlenecks in the organisation (capacity focus);
— are not conforming to time requirements (delivery, etc).

Processes should be evaluated from an output perspective. Required outputs or customer requirements (even internal customers) must be used as the basis for determining process descriptions. Processes yield homogenous outputs and this could facilitate the identification of the activities which help to produce these outputs. Process and activity analysis are described in more detail in Chapter 6.

Particular emphasis needs to be placed on the integration of other management systems into the ABC & M system. Examples are productivity management systems, capacity management systems, quality management systems, cost of capital management systems, etc. These systems may have specific requirements which need to be taken into consideration in the design of the system. Most of these needs are pertinent at the process definition stage.

5. ACTIVITY DEFINITION

Activities form the basis of measurement of all relevant information in an ABC & M system. It is therefore imperative to define the activity at the right level of detail. Too much detail will cause an information overload and too little detail may lead to insufficient information being available for analysis. Various sources of information are accumulated at the activity level, notably:

— cost;
— output measures;
— capacity;
— quality;
— productivity;
— activity investment (balance sheet analysis).

This information should present a useful view as to whether or not the activity is performed satisfactorily (a performance measurement perspective).

6. COST OBJECTS AND BILLS OF ACTIVITY

An ABC & M system should be able to provide costs for a multiplicity of cost objects. A major part of the analytical work in the practical implementation revolves around the determination of cost objects. It is important, from a design perspective, to clarify cost objects at the outset to ensure that the system will provide these cost views.

Many different cost objects usually exist in an organisation. The ones more frequently found are products, services, customers, materials, processes, activities, distribution channels, marketing channels, geographical regions and functions. The designer of the cost system must ensure that these views are built into the cost structures. Different levels in the organisation may also have different demands for information. In many cases it may be a demand solely for non-financial information, such as time to deliver a product or number of quality defects.

Each cost object will require a bill of activities (BOA). The BOA specifies the "routing" or series of activities and the quantities of each activity that are consumed by the particular cost object.

7. TRACING OF COST TO ACTIVITIES

Once activities are defined costs or resources must be traced to activities. This could be done in one of two ways:

- Define the activity structure at the source of the transaction and capture the activity code as part of the transaction code. The transaction could then be routed through the general ledger system into appropriate cost accounts which are structured for the ABC system. Alternatively, transaction data could be loaded into a data base structure which is structured for ABC. Integrity of the data is a prime concern. This may involve more work initially to get transactions processed but should give the most accurate results.
- Obtain the information from the general ledger which is not normally structured in an activity format and reprocess or analyse the data into the ABC structure. This may involve a re-analysis of all accounting transactions which may require a disproportionate amount of work. Unless costs fluctuate substantially, a once-off analysis will suffice to determine the profile of costs. In the case of an *ad hoc* investigation into the cost structures this may be the only possibility.

8. TRACING OF NON-FINANCIAL INFORMATION TO ACTIVITIES

Tracing of non-financial information poses a more serious practical problem than tracing financial information. Non-financial information is usually extracted from a variety of support systems such as inventory, production control, debtors and invoicing. The availability and integrity of information poses the single biggest stumbling block in this area.

Data is often not available and special efforts must be made to collect such information. This may add to the cost of the system. Another problem is that non-financial information may not be electronically accessible which may make it cumbersome to obtain and manipulate. The non-financial information is mostly used for the cost drivers and output measures. In many cases no certainty exists as to what the best possible cost driver is. Several possibilities may have to be evaluated before an appropriate cost driver is identified. It is advisable in this respect, for companies wishing to introduce ABC & M systems in future, to start building a data base of non-financial information.

Integrity is often another serious problem with non-financial information. Financial systems have been concerned with data integrity for hundreds of years (debits balance to credits, control accounts, etc) and integrity is therefore part of the system. With support systems it is not always easy to ensure integrity as an external measure of control is often not available. The lack of integrity in this information could result in incorrect cost rates and other results. Incorrect decisions could be made.

9. ACTIVITY CLASSIFICATION

Activities need to be classified for various purposes during the implementation process. Some of these classifications and their reasons are as follows:

Primary/secondary classification

This classification indicates which activities are traceable to cost objects. Primary activities are traceable to "external" cost objects such as products or customers. Secondary activities support internal "customers" and their costs must be borne by these internal customers or activities. Personnel activities such as screening and evaluation of staff are performed for the various primary activities and the cost must therefore be traced to the primary activities based on their "consumption" of the support activity.

Value-adding/non-value-adding

This classification is essential for an understanding of the relative value of the activity. Value-added is viewed from a customer perspective, ie what the customer is prepared to pay for a particular activity. A customer may be prepared to pay for the privilege of buying stock over the counter. However, the customer will not be prepared to pay for the storekeeper keeping unnecessary stock in his store room. Activities that do not add value must be questioned to determine their future existence.

Discretionary/essential

Activities could be further classified into those executed at the discretion of management and those which are essential for specific reasons. Operating a library may be "nice to have" but represents an activity that can be terminated at the discretion of management. On the other hand an activity such as movement of stock may be considered essential from the perspective of bringing the stock closer to the manufacturing unit (this may, however, not add any value). Often it is the combined perspective which helps the decision making or cost management in relation to activities. An activity which is both discretionary and non-value-adding may be eliminated, while an activity which is non-value-adding but still essential, may only be minimised.

Statutory

Some activities, such as the provision of annual financial statements, are considered statutory and therefore almost "not negotiable". The cost of these activities will preferably be kept to a minimum.

Repetitive/non-repetitive

This indicator may focus attention on activities which are or are not performed regularly and where the opportunity may or may not exist to reconfigure the cost. Activities which are typically performed once only, such as once-off design of processes and products, may not provide the opportunity for continuous improvement and cost management.

Inventoriable/non-inventoriable

The objective of an ABC & M system is to determine the cost of bringing cost objects such as products or raw materials to their current status. The costs incurred in this process may typically include costs which are not considered to be "product costs" from an external inventory valuation point of view. These costs are therefore identified for elimination from the ABC cost calculation to arrive at the inventory valuation in terms of generally accepted accounting practice (GAAP).

Quality activities

If the ABC & M system is integrated with a quality management system it may be advisable to create quality activities for the measurement of quality assurance and prevention of failure. In many cases it is useful to measure wastage as a specific activity in a process.

10. CALCULATION OF ACTIVITY RATES

Once cost of activities has been determined and output volumes collected, activity rates could be calculated (activity rate = cost of activity/volume of output). Two rates are normally calculated, namely:

- **Primary rate.** This is the cost which has been traced directly to the activity (utilising the resource driver) divided by the appropriate output quantity.
- **Combined rate.** The combined rate is the primary rate as calculated above, plus the cost of secondary activities which have been traced to the primary activities.

For a detailed explanation of the calculation, see Chapters 3 and 5.

11. CALCULATION OF THE COST OF COST OBJECTS

At this stage costs can be calculated for all cost objects utilising the cost rates defined in stage 10 and the relevant bills of activity of the particular cost objects. Calculation of the cost of cost objects is explained in Chapter 5.

Consideration should also be given to the calculation of the ABC income statement as set out in Chapter 5.

12. DETERMINATION OF WASTAGE

Where an ABC & M system has been developed in conjunction with a total quality management system, wastage is normally well defined and can be integrated easily into the ABC system. This is achieved by highlighting wastage as a specific and manageable cost in the income statement.

In the event of wastage not being defined specifically by way of a TQM system, an effort should be made in the ABC & M system to evaluate wastage. Wastage measurement could focus on inputs (resources) or outputs. Input waste occurs where resources are wasted before being consumed in the operational processes, eg unutilised manpower or payment for goods or services which are never consumed. Output waste occurs where products and materials are wasted in or at the end of the operational processes. Output waste should be valued at the cost of bringing the wasted product to the point where the wastage occurred. Furthermore, should potential sales be lost because of the wasted product, it could be argued that the opportunity cost of the lost sale should also be taken into account.

Wastage should not be included in the valuation of the product for external reporting purposes or in the calculation of any transfer prices, even though this may be permissible in a conventional inventory valuation utilising the net realisable value concept. Such costs should be normative costs only, otherwise wastage is "absorbed" by inventories and carried forward to future periods. Another specific example of such wastage is capacity waste which will most probably never be recovered.

SYSTEMS DESIGN AND COMPUTERISATION ISSUES

ABC & M systems could be designed in many forms such as:

- manual systems;
- spreadsheet-based systems;
- package systems;
- data base systems.

Schnoebelen[1] distinguishes between the following levels of integration in advanced cost systems:

- systems connected manually and through human intervention;
- partially automated integration;
- automated integration through the use of interfaces;
- automated integration of systems residing in the same software environment.

The following practical suggestions can be made in respect of the different forms:

Manual systems

ABC & M systems need not necessarily be computerised systems. Smaller organisations may be able to perform calculations manually. A manual system is, however, only recommended where the organisation has relatively few cost objects, the general ledger systems are computerised, and activity structures could be integrated easily into the general ledger. Thereafter cost calculations are done manually.

Spreadsheet-based systems

These systems are normally useful for first-time users of ABC applications and should be used only where the system is not too complicated. A spreadsheet application is not considered to be a long-term solution as the upkeep and data integrity are normally linked to the designer of the system. Should this person leave, design knowledge and the structure of the system may also be lost.

Spreadsheet systems may be practical for organisations wishing to experiment with ABC before investing in permanent systems. Organisations with complex file and organisational structures would be well advised to rather use an inexpensive package for this purpose.

Packaged software

Several packaged systems are already commercially available. Some of these systems are relatively inexpensive and may be the ideal solution for the first-time user. These systems will contain system and file structures for a typical ABC system which will create an awareness within the user of the requirements of such systems. However, structures are fairly rigid and may not suit the conditions of a specific company.

Packaged software may be the ideal solution to experiment with ABC in a prototype or experimental environment as existing systems need not necessarily be adapted or changed. In most cases the package provides for the importation of information (financial and non-financial) from other support systems, which should make the running of the system fairly easy. Export of information in graphic form is usually a standard feature as is the form of the standard output reports (process reports, activity reports, cost object reports, etc).

Data base systems

Data base systems seem to be the logical direction in which ABC & M systems will go. They facilitate the collection of financial and non-financial information from a variety of other systems such as production control systems, inventory systems, debtors systems, creditors systems. It is normally fairly inexpensive to extract the information required from these support systems via an interface program, for input into the ABC system. The data base system should contain all the relevant structures and controls to ensure data integrity. Information and reports can usually be extracted via the use of report writers which could be used on the data base. Reports are typically user-defined and provide much more flexibility than packaged systems. An example of such a system structure is set out in Figure 11.2.

Figure 11.2: ABC & M system architecture

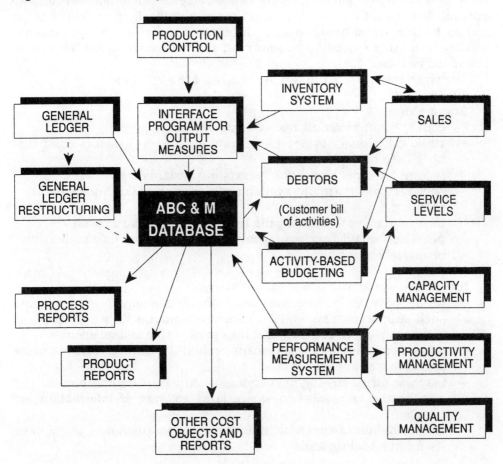

Ultimately a new breed of system may evolve in which all organisational information is stored on a central data base. This data base should contain financial and non-financial information which will be ideal for an ABC application.

STAND-ALONE OR INTEGRATED SYSTEMS

The issue is often debated whether the ABC & M system should be integrated into existing systems or whether it should be operated as a stand-alone system. Stand-alone systems can be used without interfering with existing systems although the support systems typically provide the information for the stand-alone system. Integrated systems are run simultaneously with other systems and information is received and fed back in an automatic fashion.

The characteristics of the two approaches are as follows:

- **Stand-alone:**
  — could be run as an *ad hoc* system, ie when required;
  — could take longer to provide results as support systems must first be "closed off";
  — is ideal for experimentation as existing systems are not affected;
  — packages are normally available which may make implementation cheaper;
  — uses actual costs and outputs (no need for standard costs);
  — provides limited cost management capabilities as information may be available too late.

- **Integrated system:**
  — would have to be implemented with other support systems, and such support systems must be able to support ABC principles;
  — is normally more complex and may take longer to implement;
  — offers excellent cost management capabilities if information is made available fast (real-time);
  — may use target costing to encourage continuous improvement;
  — may be the only solution where large volumes of information are handled;
  — allows the use of electronic data interchange which may prove to be useful in handling large volumes of data.

The chosen solution may also be determined by the need for ABC information. The information may be used only for strategy review sessions which are held once a year or for pricing purposes half-yearly. On the other hand, if costs need to be managed on a continual basis, an integrated system may be the only solution.

Some organisations are already moving in the direction of measuring costs and performance in a real-time mode. This is quite feasible where organisations already have real-time production control, inventory management and accounting systems.

LEVEL OF CONFIDENCE IN COSTS

The level of confidence in traditional cost systems was often not very high. These systems ignored some of the most important and biggest costs for costing cost objects. Marketing, finance and administrative costs were usually not taken into consideration in the determination of cost. Furthermore, the tracing of indirect costs (factory overheads) to products or other cost objects was questionable because of the single overhead driver that was most often used.

Although the accuracy of a cost system can never be 100 %, an attempt must be made in an ABC system to obtain a high level of accuracy. In practice, approximately 85 % to 95 % of costs can be traced to cost objects, which should give a high level of confidence in the cost system. In Chapter 5 it is explained that costs are classified between primary and secondary activity costs and that certain costs may be untraceable. If the untraceable portion amounts to say 10 %, the complement (90 %) gives an indication of the level of confidence in the accuracy of the system. Some other traceable costs may also have been traced in an arbitrary manner. These factors should be taken into consideration by the system designer in forming an opinion about the accuracy of the costs provided.

Accuracy of cost is a relative concept and should be related to the margin the organisation makes on its products. The smaller the margin, the higher the desired accuracy of cost. If the organisation makes a 5 % margin then 80 % accuracy of cost may not be acceptable, but if the organisation had a 30 % margin then 80 % accuracy may be quite acceptable.

APPLICABILITY OF ACTIVITY-BASED COST AND MANAGEMENT SYSTEMS

ABC & M systems are appropriate in a wide variety of organisations and applications. A review of the literature as well as empirical evidence suggests that few organisations will not benefit from the introduction of ABC & M concepts.

Historically, cost systems are classified as either job costing or process costing systems. *Job costing* systems apply to heterogenous jobs or projects, where the specifications relating to the job are typically not known until the order is received. *Process costing* on the other hand, refers to continuous manufacturing of either discrete units or continuous streams or volumes. The product in this case adheres to fairly rigid specifications which are normally known in advance of the receipt of the order.

Process applications pose few problems with the implementation of an ABC & M system as the logic fits well with the process logic in ABC. Most service-related businesses such as banks, insurance companies and medical aid societies can also be classified as process cost systems. These organisations usually produce several homogenous "products" or services on a continuous basis. A bank may process cheques and deposits and an insurance company a number of insurance policies. The medical aid society processes medical claims. The main difference between manufacturing companies and service companies is that the latter cannot keep an inventory of its products. Inventory valuation is therefore not such an important issue.

Job costing systems deal with products which are unique and may change from customer to customer. Product costing can thus not be done in the conventional sense. Instead, the "product" becomes the job or project undertaken. In a "jobbing" or works order environment the opportunities for managing job costs are less than in a repetitive process. Activities can still be defined in a jobbing environment but they are not necessarily executed in the same way every time. The activity methodology can also be used to trace costs to the jobs. Some service businesses can also be classified as jobbing environments. Examples are accounting and consulting services, architects and some engineering services.

LINKS WITH OTHER MANAGEMENT SYSTEMS

Activity-based management systems must be seen as a holistic approach to solving business problems. For this purpose they must remain linked to and integrated with other systems such as quality management systems, productivity management systems or capacity management systems.

Quality management systems (QMS)

The increased focus on customer satisfaction has necessarily brought the specific requirements of the customer to the forefront. These requirements usually form the base for a QMS and any deviations are classified as quality defects and their costs are referred to as the "price of non-conformance" or PONC. The cost of quality defects can be measured and evaluated outside or inside the cost system. If evaluated outside the cost system, the implication is that the cost of non-quality is included in the cost of the product or other cost object. In order to determine normative costs for cost objects, it is preferred that cost of non-quality is determined and eliminated from the product cost. The intention is that such cost be accounted for as wastage in the accounting system and reported to management as a separate and manageable cost.

Accounting for quality is normally classified under the following headings:

— prevention;
— appraisal costs;
— internal failure costs;
— external failure costs.

Prevention costs are incurred to prevent defects and failures in products and services. *Appraisal costs* are incurred to measure, inspect or evaluate processes, products or services to ensure conformance to requirements. Quality control or quality inspection costs are usually included in this category.

Internal failure costs relate to defects that are identified prior to delivery to the customer. *External failure* costs result from the discovery of defects after delivery to the customer.

Prevention and appraisal costs are usually incurred in identifiable activities. These could be classified as separate activities in the ABC & M system. Each process should contain at least one such activity, although multiple quality activities at various stages are quite possible. Many examples of such costs exist in businesses and an extract of such costs can be found in Table 11.1.

Table 11.1: Examples of quality costs[2]	
Examples of prevention costs	**Examples of internal failure costs**
Part and tool design reviews	Some engineering changes and tool enhancement after sampling
Control plan preparation	
Quality planning and procedure design	Redesign costs due to deficient planning
Supplier qualification and quality assessments	Purchase reject reporting and related repurchasing efforts
Supplier purchase order review and control	Cost of processing claims on suppliers
Capability study and review	Rework
Preventative maintenance	Scrap and some stock shrinkage
In-line statistical process review	Quality downgrading losses
Design expenses for inspection equipment	Quality downtime
Cost of inspection equipment	Plant and equipment downtime
Operator and management training	Specification changes
Some quality control administration	Excess material purchasing costs
Joint planning with suppliers	Cost of safety stock to cushion for quality problems
Some prototype trial costs	
Customer trial costs	Administration cost to investigate and follow up failures
	(Continued on next page)

Table 11.1: Continued	
Examples of appraisal costs	**Examples of external failure costs**
Sample preparation	Some engineering changes and tool
Inspection of sample parts and initiation of	improvements
tool design changes after sampling	Warranty claims on suppliers for field failures
Most testing costs	Scrap and inventory shrinkage
Supplier product testing	Rework on returned goods
Incoming inspection of materials and	Reinspection and retest
components	Pricing errors — lost margin
In-process and final inspection test	Downgrading loss
Spot inspections	Customer return processing and transport
Quality audits	Discounts and allowances
Maintenance and calibration of inspection	Warranty and liability costs
equipment	Investigation of failures
Field audit of product usage	Administrative time spent on follow-up
Administrative appraisal costs	with customers
Some production process/environment	Loss of existing and future customers
testing and monitoring	Loss of goodwill
Configuration and reliability engineering	Loss of reputation
on prevention projects	
Some information systems costs	

Table 11.1 also shows examples of failure costs — activities which are more difficult to define. However, it may be important to define these as activities for specific reasons such as :

— to be able to measure trends (up or down);
— to be able to manage the cost driver (a negative cost driver in this case);
— to relate the measurement of defects or failure to the spending on prevention and appraisal. This could help to determine the net cost of quality.

Table 11.2 could be used as a method to report on quality costs by comparing the resultant changes between years.

Table 11.2: Quality cost report			
	19.3	19.4	Change
Prevention cost			
Quality systems	£10 000	£ 15 000	+£5 000
Training	20 000	30 000	+10 000
Appraisal cost			
Inspection cost	6 000	9 000	+3 000
Laboratory testing	5 000	7 000	+2 000
Internal failure cost			
Scrap and rework	30 000	20 000	-10 000
Downtime	25 000	5 000	-20 000
External failure cost			
Returns	9 000	6 000	-3 000
Warranty claims	17 000	8 000	-9 000
Total quality cost	£122 000	£100 000	-£22 000

The change in cost indicates the result of the quality effort in a particular period and it is from this notion that the advocates of TQM proclaim that "quality is free". What it really implies is that the effort and cost incurred (mostly prevention and appraisal cost) are more than offset by the savings on failure cost.

ABC & M and the quality movement have the intention of identifying and reporting all forms of wastage which may occur in the organisation. Wastage can be defined on inputs (resources) or outputs (products or services) or partially produced products and services, ie in the process. An indication of wastage can also be found in the classification of activities, whether they add value or not. Benchmarking activity rates may also indicate whether resources are wasted.

Porter[3] suggests that organisations reconfigure their value chain with the minimum number of activities and eliminate those activities that do not add value. Any activity that the customer is not prepared to pay for does not add value.

Capacity management

Capacity management is an important factor in the management process in most organisations. The cost treatment of surplus capacity may have far-reaching implications as it may drastically affect the cost price of many products and consequently marketing strategies. The view the organisation holds of its surplus capacity costs may also affect the strategies the organisation pursues to utilise and fill capacity.

Capacity has traditionally been a key factor in manufacturing organisations and only recently have service organisations started to focus on capacity issues. Capacity management impacts on the organisation at large. All functions and processes may be affected and capacity may not be the homogenous (manufacturing) concept that previously existed. Capacity constraints and surpluses may appear anywhere in the organisation and capacity should thus be viewed from a value chain perspective. This is depicted in Figure 11.3. This figure reflects the extent to which capacity in each element of the value chain has been utilised.

Figure 11.3: Capacity utilisation[4]

0	CAPACITY				100%	
SUPPORT PROCESSES	FIRM INFRASTRUCTURE					
	HUMAN RESOURCE MANAGEMENT					*MARGIN*
	TECHNOLOGY DEVELOPMENT					
	PROCUREMENT					
100% **CAPACITY** 0	INBOUND LOGISTICS	OPERATIONS	OUTBOUND LOGISTICS	MARKETING AND SALES	SERVICE	*MARGIN*
	PRIMARY PROCESES					

Capacity could thus be viewed from a value chain element perspective to determine specific under- or over-utilisation of capacities. The individual elements in the value chain could, in turn, be analysed to indicate the capacity utilisation at activity level within processes. This is shown in Figure 11.4, which highlights the capacity bottlenecks in the process.

Figure 11.4: Capacity bottlenecks[4]

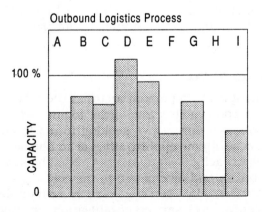

Outbound Logistics Process

Management of capacity could be facilitated by an ABC & M system, by providing the above views and by providing insights into the treatment of costs in the product. A useful technique in evaluating capacity issues is capacity modelling, where the consumption of capacity by various cost objects is modelled as is shown in Figure 11.5. This capacity model could be programmed to search for the optimal combination of products and services to yield the highest profit.

Figure 11.5: Model of consumption of capacity by cost objects[4]

	PRODUCTION				MARKETING				ADMINISTRATION				
	A1	A2	A3	A4	A1	A2	A3	A4	A1	A2	A3	A4	A5
Product A	10	40	30			2	1		3				5
Product B		20	60	60	5			10		1		4	
Product n	nn	nn	nn	nn	nn	nn	nn	nn	nn	nn	nn	nn	nn
Req. Cap.	45	120	120	100	10	15	7	60	11	9	7	10	20
Avail. Cap.	50	100	200	100	30	20	10	50	10	10	9	15	19
Surplus/ Shortfall	5	-20	80	0	20	5	3	-10	-1	1	2	5	-1

Treatment of surplus capacity cost in the product is an important principle which management must decide on. Idle capacity cost could be absorbed by the product, usually resulting in the so-called death spiral of costs. Idle capacity pushes cost prices up which management may try to recover in the market in the form of higher sales prices. The result is invariably lower sales volumes and more idle capacity with even higher costs and selling prices in the next round of price fixing, which may ultimately be the death knell of the organisation. Idle capacity costs should rather be treated as a wastage cost which must be eliminated from the cost of the cost object. This wastage should be reflected with other wastage factors for management attention.

Managing surplus or shortage of capacity, and their cost treatment, could be summarised using the following suggested principles:

1. **True surplus capacity.** The usual approach is to downsize the capacity by selling excess equipment, etc in order to cut costs. The opposite may be a more profitable approach — seeking to utilise the excess capacity and flexibility to seek new opportunities or to add value to existing customers.

   Capacity costs should be charged to the cost objects based on a realistic or practical capacity. Surplus capacity cost should be reported as wastage.

2. **Surplus capacity caused by policy decisions.** If the surplus capacity has been created because of a strategic decision (eg back-up facilities on a computer system), then the cost of surplus capacity should not be removed from the activity or process. The definition of practical capacity could be amended to exclude that portion of practical capacity which is impossible to use.

3. **Surplus capacity in areas that are not bottlenecks.** The capacity in non-bottleneck areas will always reflect a surplus, unless the business is restructured to utilise this surplus capacity. The cost of the products should thus include the cost of this idle capacity. Cost management of activity cost will be concentrated in the efforts to reduce product costs.

4. **Surplus capacity established in advance of needs.** Practical capacity in this case would be revised to exclude that portion of capacity that is impossible to use. The cost of surplus capacity would be reported separately. If this capacity could be utilised in a future period, by working overtime for example, it could be argued that such capacity costs could even be capitalised for future use.

Productivity management

Productivity management has been receiving tremendous attention in the past two decades with the result that huge gains in productivity have been recorded by most industrialised nations. This can clearly be seen in Figure 11.6.

Figure 11.6: Multifactor productivity in the private economy, 1979–1990

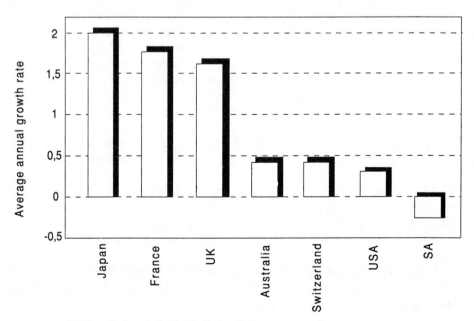

Source: National Productivity Institute

However, the same increases have not been experienced all round with the result that certain countries and, in effect, certain enterprises are realising competitive advantages because of the productivity factor. The productivity factor also has a direct bearing on relative product costs and companies therefore see productivity management as a useful and specific mechanism to drive costs down.

Productivity management firstly implies that productivity is measureable. It secondly implies that input factors can be monitored to determine their influence on the outputs of the organisation. Productivity management therefore refers to multifactor productivity and not the narrow definition of manpower productivity. This ties in well with ABC & M which endorses output-focused accounting.

The more important inputs or resources affecting outputs are manpower (both employees and management), material and capital. Productivity ratios could be expressed for each of the important inputs or resources but a method must also be found to express the sum of all productivity efforts. This is referred to as the multifactor productivity index.

Productivity is simplistically expressed as:

$$P = \frac{\text{Outputs}}{\text{Inputs}}$$

This ratio should preferably be measured in non-financial terms to eliminate any pricing or inflationary distortions. Where financial information is used in the evaluation, this should be done at constant prices in order not to distort the ratio. The following examples illustrate the principles:

Example 11.1 – Raw material productivity (constant prices)

A company produces a certain product P (price £10) from a certain raw material A (cost £2). For a particular year it consumed 500 units of material A in order to produce 1 000 products P. The productivity ratio, or yield of raw material A, can therefore be expressed as 2 (1 000/500). If, in a following year, the company manufactures 1 500 products P and uses 800 units of material A, the productivity of the raw material could again be evaluated by using the output/input ratio. (It is assumed in this case that changes in the output ratio are attributable to the usage of the material.) In this year the ratio is 1,87 (1 500/800) which is lower than in the previous year. This may be an indication of inefficient use of the raw material or non-productivity in the use of this particular resource. The loss attributable to the reduction in productivity is determinable, namely:

	Units	£
Expected output (800 input units x 2)	1 600	16 000
Actual output	1 500	15 000
Productivity loss	100	1 000

If the reduced output is solely attributable to inefficiency in the use of the raw material, then the productivity loss is equal to the value of 100 units of output, ie 100 x £10 = £1 000. In monetary terms a £1 spending on the input (material = £1 600) should yield £10 (output £16 000) of output. It actually yielded £15 000. (Output/input ratio £15 000/£1 600 = 9,3.)

The effect of price changes or inflation has therefore not influenced this situation.

Example 11.2 – Raw material productivity with changing prices

The distortion of the above productivity ratio can be illustrated by assuming that the price of the product in Example 11.1 changes to £9 and the cost of the raw material increases to £2,50. The output/input ratio is thus:

Output (1 500 x £9)	£ 13 500
Input (800 x £2,50)	£ 2 000
Ratio	6,75

The output/input ratio has fallen from the standard of 10 to 9,3 and with changing price levels to 6,75. The "loss" attributable to changing prices can thus be calculated as follows:

	£
Sales price loss	
Actual output at constant prices (1 500 x £10)	15 000
Actual output	13 500
Sales price loss	1 500
Material price loss	
Actual material consumption	2 000
Material consumption at constant prices	1 600
Material price loss	400

The total loss for the period is thus £1 000 + £1 500 + £400 = £2 900. This indicates the accentuating effect that price changes can have on the productivity calculation.

Multifactor productivity

As indicated above productivity can be affected by many factors and organisations normally prefer to calculate a productivity profit or loss which includes the effect of all the input factors. Ideally the effect of each factor should be isolated, but this may be rather difficult in practice. The multifactor productivity profit or loss is calculated as in Examples 11.1 and 11.2 except that inputs will be combined inputs (materials, labour and capital).

Service level management

In contrast to the objective in quality management systems of zero defects, many organisations realise that the delivery of 100 % service may be impractical and sometimes very costly. Service levels may be applied to delivery of goods and services to customers within prescribed times or the availability of inventories for internal consumption. The reaction or occurence of cost at cumulatively increased service levels is illustrated in Figure 11.7. From the figure we note that costs increase disproportionately as service levels increase.

Figure 11.7: Service level costs

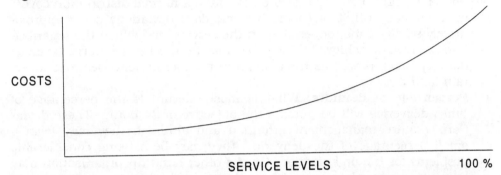

Organisations that want to perform service level management should commence with the measurement of service levels. A service level in a distribution business can, for instance, be the time it takes to deliver the product to its customer. The organisation may have as an objective delivery within 24 hours and an actual measurement of delivery times may be illustrated by the distribution of actual deliveries (see Figure 11.8).

Figure 11.8: Distribution of actual deliveries

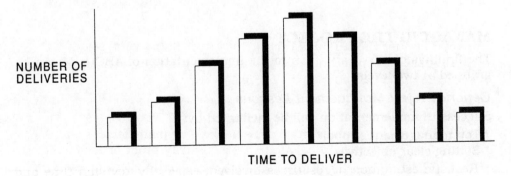

As the deliveries are depicted as a statistical distribution, various statistical calculations can be performed on this data such as:

- **Average or mean delivery times.** This merely describes what delivery times were on average. An average delivery time of 18 hours does not mean that customers will be satisfied as a significant number of them may be serviced outside the set 24-hour service level.
- **Standard deviation.** The standard deviation gives a significant indication of the dispersion of services around the mean. A standard deviation of 7 hours indicates that customers will receive their goods 68 % of the time within 18 hours (the mean), plus or minus the standard deviation of 7 hours. (One standard deviation in a normal distribution covers approximately 68 % of cases; two standard deviations cover approximately 95 %.) Thus, depending on the service level which the organisation wishes to achieve, it may be able to specify the norm (average delivery time) as well as the maximum number of deliveries over a certain limit.
- **Percentage of defaults.** What is most relevant is the percentage of times deliveries will be outside the objective of 24 hours. These deviations require management attention and although they may form a small percentage of the deliveries, they may be causing considerable problems for the organisation. On the other hand the organisation may be quite prepared to live with a service level of 95 % as the cost to achieve 100 % service may be exorbitant.

The ABC & M system can greatly assist service level management by accumulating information for service level analysis. This could be in the form of statistics which are accumulated to calculate the statistical distributions. Time, which is normally an important service level factor, could be measured in the ABC & M system as well as cost for activities at various service levels. In this way, informed service level management will be made possible.

MANAGING THE PROJECT

The findings of surveys[9,10,11] into the implementation of ABC & M can be grouped at two levels:

Generic Project Management Lessons

Successful implementation will be facilitated by:

* Top management support.
* Setting clear objectives.
* Realistic estimation of resources involved, especially key staff time and computer capacity.
* Clearly identified project champion.
* Staff involvement.
* Consultants as advisors, not implementors.
* Sufficient staff training.

Specific ABC & M Project Management Lessons

Successful implementation will be facilitated by:

* High front-end investment in activity analysis and identification.
* Realistic levels of accuracy in the allocation of costs to activities, especially while existing general ledger systems are still in operation.
* A pragmatic approach to the selection of cost drivers realising that a perfect causal linkage between activities and cost objects is probably impossible and that cost driver volumes must be practically measurable.
* Avoidance of "non-value-adding" terminology, which may cause resistance to or possible manipulation of the project.
* Incorporating the ability to filter out those costs which are not relevant for stock valuations under SSAP 9.
* Avoidance of massive complexity in an attempt to achieve great precision (many activities and multiple cost drivers).
* An incremental, "toe-in-the-water" approach, rather than a total replacement of existing systems.

CONCLUSION

This chapter illustrates some of the practical implementation considerations which need to be taken into account during the design of an ABC & M system. It must be stressed that not necessarily all organisations will apply all facets of ABC & M as mentioned in this text. Each organisation will select those facets or elements which it may find suitable and applicable to its own circumstances.

SOURCES CONSULTED

1. Schnoebelen, SC. Integrating an advanced cost management system into operating systems (part 1). *Journal of Cost Management,* Winter 1993: 50–54.
2. Atkinson, JH, Hohner, G, Mundt, B, Troxel RB & Winchell, W. *Current trends in quality: Linking the cost of quality and continuous improvement.* Institute of Management Accountants: Montvale, New Jersey, 1991.
3. Porter, ME. *Competitive Advantage.* New York: Free Press, 1985.
4. Dilton-Hill, KG & Glad, EJ. Managing capacity. *Journal of Cost Management,* Spring 1994: 32–39.
5. Cooper, R. Implementing an activity-based cost system. *Journal of Cost Management,* Spring 1990: 33–42.
6. Cooper, R. A structured approach to implementing ABC. *Accountancy,* Jun 1991: 78–80.
7. Miller, JA. Designing and implementing a new cost management system. *Journal of Cost Management,* Winter 1992: 41–53.
8. Turney, PBB. Ten myths about implementing an activity-based cost system. *Journal of Cost Management,* Spring 1990: 24–32.
9. Friedman, AL and Lyne, SR. *Activity based techniques: the real life consequences.* CIMA, 1995.
10. Cobb, I, Innes, J and Mitchell, F. *Activity based costing: problems in practice.* CIMA, 1992.
11. Player, RS and Keys, DE. Lessons from the ABM Battlefield: Getting off to the right start. *Journal of Cost Management.* Spring 1995: 26–37. Developing the pilot. Summer 1995: 20–35.

12

Strategy support

INTERACTIVE RELATIONSHIP

Strategic planning is one of management's most important functions. Without it no enterprise is able to survive in a competitive and continually changing environment. To be successful an organisation needs to have and maintain a competitive advantage over its competitors which, in turn, can only be achieved through proper analysis, planning and control.

Many organisations have strategic planning systems and accounting systems which operate in compartments with very little, if any, formal links. Strategic planning in many organisations tends to be a once-off exercise performed every three to five years, with possibly some annual updating. Strategies in many cases are nothing more than general inclinations for the organisation to move in certain directions. Traditional accounting systems seem to have little in common with strategic planning. The effects of strategies do not seem to be measured or evaluated and the feedback loop between traditional accounting systems and strategic planning systems appears to be very weak.

Activity-based costing and management systems are strategy support systems par excellence. Various elements and attributes of activity-based costing and management (ABC & M) are extremely well suited to assist management in the strategic planning process (including strategy formulation) and the accomplishment of set strategies. Most of these elements are described in preceding chapters. An ABC & M system in itself would normally reveal aspects that need to be addressed strategically. Hence, there is a link and interplay between strategic planning and ABC & M:

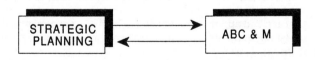

The objective of this chapter is not to address the broad subject of strategic planning or how every fitting element of ABC & M can interact with strategies, but to create an awareness of the usefulness of ABC & M in this context. The approach is therefore to illustrate the opportunities presented by ABC & M by focusing on a number of relevant aspects. All the other features of ABC & M should accordingly be borne in mind with regard to setting and accomplishing strategies.

ABC & M supports the strategic planning process as follows:

- Strategy formulation is supported by the reports on several matters which may require strategic decision making such as unprofitable products, customers, market segments, costly processes or areas in which the organisation does not meet the benchmarking criteria of a world class company.
- Strategy implementation is supported by the measurement and evaluation of critical success factors and the specific reporting of strategy deployment.

BENEFICIAL CHARACTERISTICS OF ABC & M

The ABC & M discipline comprises specific attributes that make it extremely suitable for and effective in business strategies, notably:

Reliable information

A fundamental requirement for the competent management of an organisation is to ensure that strategic decisions are based on hard facts, not only intuition.[1] The true costs and other accurate information provided by an ABC & M system put management in a position to make decisions with confidence and reliably evaluate the effect of strategies.

Visibility of costs

The visibility of costs brought about by an ABC system lead to a better comprehension of and insight into an organisation's cost structure. Apart from understanding the organisation to a greater degree, such cost visibility also highlights where the respective costs lie and what they consist of. This, *inter alia*, facilitates the identification of areas to be attended to and the comparison of alternatives. The pertinent focus on secondary or support costs extends proper cost management into all facets of the organisation. Costs are no longer seen as overheads about which little can be done.

Distinct cost determinants

The concept of cost drivers is at the heart of an ABC system. Cost drivers as such are most useful in strategic management — to be *au fait* with the factors that cause and drive the various costs of an organisation is inevitably very valuable when determining strategies.

Comprehensive cost measurement

The tracing of all costs to cost objects (and not only production costs to products) affords a clear overall picture of the various elements of a business and their respective total costs. Cost objects such as customers, marketing and distribution channels and market segments relate very closely to elements of the strategic focus.

Modelling facility

The basis of an ABC system, the principles on which it operates and the data it generates, are such that the outcome of manifold suppositions can be projected with relative ease. Furthermore, the system can be applied to competitor modelling as well. These features obviously constitute powerful tools in regard to budgeting and strategic planning.

Life-cycle accounting

The incorporation of life-cycle accounting into the system ensures that all costs relating to a product are assigned to the product during its economic life. Accordingly, cost of activities that occur before manufacturing of the product begins are included.[2] This technique, together with the accurate cost allocation under an ABC system, provides a proper perspective of the product's profitability and promotes better strategic decision making with regard to the product. It becomes more important when products have short life cycles, as is the current trend.

Process, activity and value analyses

These analyses place a new perspective of the business at management's disposal by, *inter alia*, providing a clear picture of the business processes, concomitant activities, linkages, and whether activities are adding value or not. This perception puts management in an outstanding position to streamline and re-engineer its operations. The system also lends itself to value engineering, ie the elimination or downsizing of characteristics that customers are not prepared to pay for. In general, information is furnished which enables management to accomplish the necessary competitive advantage.

Non-financial information

Another powerful strategic role of ABC & M emanates from the great emphasis that is placed on the generation of non-financial information. Performance with regard to most critical success factors (eg various facets of quality and customer service) can and should mainly be measured in non-financial terms. The vital importance of complying with these factors to ensure the survival and success of an organisation inevitably requires that the strategies relating to such aspects be effective. The information produced by a properly designed and implemented performance measurement system is exceptionally well-suited to this purpose. On the other hand, such information will more often than not also reveal areas that require strategies for improvement.

STRATEGIC APPLICATIONS

Strategic plans and goals will normally differ from organisation to organisation, as will the usefulness of the various facets of ABC & M with regard to different strategies. Nonetheless, the following fields of application of ABC & M in the strategic process serve as examples of its usefulness:

Customer satisfaction

As has been emphasised throughout this text, the main goal of all organisations, if they wish to achieve their overall objectives, should be customer satisfaction. In turn, to satisfy customers, a number of requirements will have to be fulfilled (established by market research, etc), for example affordable price, differentiated products, quality of products, reliable deliveries and prompt, efficient after-sales service. ABC & M can help with the management and measurement of these elements as follows:

Low cost

Business is about interpreting customer requirements and fulfilling these profitably. By running an efficient operation and managing costs effectively products/services can be supplied to customers at the best prices. Under an ABC & M system costs are reduced by managing the activities that consume resources — accordingly, activities instead of product costs are managed. This is facilitated by the clear understanding of physical activities presented by an ABC system. Consequently, cost reductions can be effected by, *inter alia*, eliminating non-value-adding activities, eliminating inefficient activities (for example, by altering product design) and replacing inefficient activities with more efficient ones.[3]

ABC & M focuses on the total customer value chain and identifies elements which are not conducted profitably. With its calculation of market channel or market segment profitability and customer profitability, it is relatively easy to determine whether customer requirements are not met profitably. If not, this can prompt strategies to re-engineer customer requirements or the way these requirements are met.

Product differentiation

This term refers to products being different from their ordinary, everyday counterparts by virtue of added attractiveness and/or features. The primary focus of a differentiation strategy is therefore to create something that customers perceive as being unique.[4]

Although differentiated products normally carry a premium price because of their additional attributes, they are often sold at a loss without management realising it. This problem is consequent upon the inability of conventional costing systems to produce accurate product costs. The accurate costing brought about by an ABC system not only puts management in a position to steer clear of this pitfall, but also enables it to identify the viable areas of product differentiation. An ABC system allows management to accurately determine the costs of benefits or attributes which are additional to those provided by competitors, and thereby affords it the opportunity to make the right strategic decisions in this regard — identifying profitable differentiation possibilities and putting these products on the market to satisfy customer demand.

Quality

Total quality management (TQM) is an important constituent of a proper ABC & M system. Cost of quality (the cost of maintaining and improving quality, eg supervision, inspection, reworking and wastage) is measured and analysed for management to take appropriate action. Various performance measures are installed to monitor quality and a continuous improvement programme should ensure ongoing quality enhancement. An ABC & M system thus offers a variety of tools to assist management in quality control and improvement, should this be a strategy.

ABC & M systems fundamentally accept the norm that any form of wastage must be measured, evaluated and reported upon. Because of the process approach that is adopted, quality costs can be identified in specifically earmarked activities. Equally, wastage such as rework and output which does not meet specifications, is specifically reported on. On the other hand, the system will also indicate where strategies are needed, ie where quality issues are out of line with pre-set norms.

Customer service, delivery and after-sales service

Strategies and goals to ensure prompt and high-quality service in these respects can be exceptionally well monitored by an ABC & M system. Conversely, the ABC & M system will also indicate where strategies are needed (ie where performance is not up to standard to be competitive). Performance criteria such as service levels, benchmarking and best practice analysis can be integrated into the ABC & M system, to properly evaluate and continuously improve all elements of customer service.

Functional and organisational structures

These aspects will normally always be included in an organisation's strategic planning. Organisations continually reshape themselves to meet customer requirements or ward off competition better. Downsizing or rightsizing are particular buzzwords frequently used in this context, ie finding the appropriate organisational structure to meet current challenges. One of the more important methods used to reshape organisations is process re-engineering, which requires the organisation to steer away from a functional view of the organisation and to adopt a process perspective. Once again, the features of an ABC & M system make it exceptionally well suited to assist management in fulfilling strategies with regard to process re-engineering. The insight into and thorough understanding of processes and activities brought about by process and activity analysis (discussed in Chapter 6) are unequalled in this context.

The accomplishment of continuous improvement strategies, which usually include steps to eliminate wastage, reduce response time, simplify product design and improve quality[5], are likewise facilitated to a major extent by an ABC & M system. Most of these criteria are critically evaluated during process analysis.

Product pricing

Accurate product prices, as produced by an ABC system, are extremely important in strategic decision making with regard to products and markets, especially as to which products should be promoted and which not. (Also see Differentiated Products above.) The proven insight into costs facilitates the necessary strategies with regard to loss-making products, eg discontinue those products, reprice them, or reduce the cost of producing them (for instance by redesigning the product or the manufacturing process).[5] Strategies can accordingly be implemented to shift resources towards activities that produce meaningful outputs[6] or to outsource products and services that the organisation cannot render profitably.

Through life-cycle accounting a better understanding can be had of the impacts of product life cycle and the ultimate decision to discontinue, to substitute or to persevere with a particular product.

Competitor evaluation

The ultimate strength of a strategy lies in intelligence. This is particularly relevant in a competitive environment — the information on competitors available to decision makers in the organisation is invaluable for strategic planning purposes. Data on competitors and their activities can normally be acquired from various sources, eg from the sales and marketing areas, financial sources (annual reports, prospectuses, professional talks, financial analysts' reports, etc), industry contacts and, most importantly, the organisation's own staff, who will normally have a lot of information on competitors' activities.[7] Sifting this information to make it comparable with the organisation's own and applying benchmarking to these competitor activities will greatly enhance effective strategy formulation.

Supplier evaluation

Suppliers form an integral part of the organisational value chain. Focusing and costing this value chain helps the organisation to identify suppliers who add unnecessary cost such as excessive inspection and quality control, rework and production defects. Conversely, supplier value chain analysis can also help to identify cost reductions which can lead to increased profitability to both the organisation and its suppliers. For instance, a manufacturer of mining equipment used to stock all its sheet metal requirements. It cut its own profiles and also had to dispose of all its off-cuts. A supplier value chain analysis revealed that several suppliers could provide the sheet metal cut into the appropriate profiles at a much lower cost. In this way the company saved on the direct cost, but it also liquidated its investment in unnecessary inventories and in underutilised profile cutters. An added bonus was the renting out of its sheet metal warehouse.

Cost planning and projection

Due to the detailed analysis of the organisation that needs to be done in order to understand cost relationships, this knowledge can be applied usefully to cost planning and projection. It is foreseen that in future this role of ABC & M could be one of the dominant reasons for the development and implementation of such systems. Already companies are experimenting with real-time accounting systems, ie the measurement of costs and revenues on a continuous basis rather than on an interval or periodic basis (normally monthly). Real-time cost measurement also necessitates the continuous prediction of interval type costs (rent, salaries, etc) as well as the impact of current expenditure on future cost structures and income earning potential.

CONCLUSION

As a guide for planning, and to choose among alternatives, organisations need information about the financial consequences of intended actions. They especially need reliable cost information, which serves in many planning and decision support roles[8]. An ABC & M system can generate this quality information and interrelate superbly with strategic planning to, *inter alia*, produce products of a higher quality cost-effectively and achieve overall customer satisfaction.

Both the financial and non-financial insights that an ABC & M system provides can facilitate and support strategic decision making and execution extremely well. The system also serves as an indicator of problem areas needing strategic action.

SOURCES CONSULTED

1. Freeman, A. Understanding costs. *Australian Accountant*, Feb 1993: 28–30.
2. Shields, MD & Young, SM. Effective long-term cost reduction: A strategic perspective. *Journal of Cost Management*, Spring 1992: 16–29.
3. Beaujon, GJ & Singhal, VR. Understanding the activity costs in an activity-based cost system. *Journal of Cost Management*, Spring 1990: 51–72.
4. Shank, JK & Govindarajan, V. Strategic cost management and the value chain. *Journal of Cost Management*, Winter 1992: 5–21.
5. Reeve, JM. The impact of continuous improvement on the design of activity-based cost systems. *Journal of Cost Management*, Summer 1990: 43–50.
6. Anderson, BM. Using activity-based costing for efficiency and quality. *Government Finance Review*, Jun 1993: 7–9.
7. Tricker, RI. The management accountant as strategist. *Management Accounting* (UK), Dec 1989: 26–28.
8. Johnson, HT. Activity-based management: Past, present and future. *Engineering Economist*, Spring 1991: 219–238.

Bibliography

Books

Brimson, J. *Activity accounting: An activity based costing approach*, New York: Wiley, 1991.

Bromwich, M & Bhimani, A. *Management accounting: Evolution not revolution*. Research Studies, The Chartered Institute of Management Accountants, 1989.

Bromwich M and Bhimani A. *Management Accounting: Pathways to Progress*. The Chartered Institute of Management Accountants, 1994.

Cobb I, Innes J and Mitchell F. *Activity based costing: problems in practice*. The Chartered Institute of Management Accountants, 1992.

Cooper, R & Kaplan, RS. *The design of cost management systems*. New Jersey: Prentice Hall, 1991.

Friedman AL and Lyne SR. *Activity based techniques: the real life consequences*. The Chartered Institute of Management Accountants, 1995.

Johnson, HT & Kaplan, RS. *Relevance lost: The rise and fall of management accounting*. Boston, Mass: Harvard, 1987.

Monden, Y & Sakurai, M. *Japanese management accounting*. Massachusetts: Productivity Press, 1989.

O'Guin, MC. *The complete guide to activity based costing*. New Jersey: Prentice Hall, 1991.

Porter, ME. *Competitive advantage*. NJ Free Press 1985.

Rumble, G. *Activity costing in mixed-mode institutions: A report based on a study of Deakin University*. Deakin University, 1986.

Shank, JK. & Govindarajan, V. *Strategic cost analysis: The evolution from managerial to strategic accounting*. Boston: Irwin, 1989.

Soutar, D. *Activity based costing: A solution to product cost distortions caused by traditional cost accounting*. Cape Town: Graduate School of Business, University of Cape Town, 1989.

Staubus, G. *Activity costing and input-output accounting*. Homewood: Irwin, 1991.

Tanaka M, Yoshikawa T, Innes J and Mitchell F. *Contemporary Cost Management*. Chapman and Hall, 1993.

Turney, PBB. Common cents: The ABC performance breakthrough. *Cost Technology*, Portland, Ore, 1992.

Ward, K. *Strategic management accounting*. Oxford: Butterworth–Heinemann, 1992.

Articles

Aitken, A. How ABC is cutting cost in US companies. *Management Accounting* (UK), Nov 1991.

Aiyathurai, G, Cooper, WW & Sinha, KK. Note on activity accounting. *Accounting Horizons*, Dec 1991.

Alexander, G, Gienger, G, Harwoord, M & Santori, P. The new revolution in cost management. *Financial Executive*, Nov/Dec 1991.

Allen, D. Out of Africa. *Management Accounting* (UK), May 1991.

Anderson, BM. Using activity-based costing for efficiency and quality. *Government Finance Review*, Jun 1993.

Antos, J. Activity-based management for service, not-for-profit, and government organizations. *Journal of Cost Management*, Summer 1992.

Atkinson, AA. Diagnosing costing problems. *CMA Magazine*, Apr 1989.

Atkinson, AA. Life-cycle costing. *CMA Magazine*, Jul/Aug 1990.

Ayres, JB. Understanding your cost drivers — the key to disciplined planning. *Journal of Cost Management*, Fall 1988.

Bailey, J. Implementation of ABC systems by UK companies. *Management Accounting* (UK), Feb 1991.

Banker, RD & Johnston, HH. *Cost driver analysis in the service sector: An empirical study of US airlines*. Carnegie-Mellon University working paper, 1988.

Barton, MF, Agrawal, R, Surendra P & Mason, L (Jr). Meeting the challenge of Japanese management concepts. *Management Accounting* (US), Sep 1988.

Bayou, ME. & Nachtman, JB. Costing for manufacturing wastes. *Journal of Cost Management*, Summer 1992.

Beaujon, GJ & Singhal, VR. Understanding the activity costs in an activity-based cost system. *Journal of Cost Management*, Spring 1990.

Becker, H. Understanding customer profitability. *Accountancy SA*, Oct 1993.

Beischel, ME & Smith, KR. Linking the shop floor to the top floor. *Management Accounting* (US), Oct 1991.

Beischel, ME. Improving production with process value analysis. *Journal of Accountancy*, Sep 1990.

Bellis-Jones, R. Activity based cost management: The overhead revolution. London: Develin & Partners, March 1990.

Bellis-Jones, R. Customer profitability analysis. *Management Accounting* (UK), Feb 1989.

Bellis-Jones, R & Hand, M. Seeking out the profit dissipators. *Management Accounting* (UK), Sep 1989.

Berliner, C & Brimson, JA. Cost management for today's advanced manufacturing. *Harvard Business School Press*, 1989.

Beynon, R. Change management as a platform for activity-based management. *Journal of Cost Management*, Summer 1992.

Bhimani, A & Pigott, D. ABC in a pharmaceutical company: A remedy. *Management Accounting* (UK), Dec 1992.

Biggs, JR, Long, EJ & Fraedrich, KE. Integrating accounting, planning and control. *Journal of Cost Management*, Spring 1991.

Blommaert, AMM, Eimers, PWA & Groot, TLCM. De betekenis van ABC voor de Nederlandse bedrijfseconomie. *Maandblad Bedrijfsadm. en Bedrijfsorg*, 96 (1992) nr 1142.

Bonsack, RA. Does activity-based costing replace standard costing? *Journal of Cost Management*, Winter 1991.

Booth, R. Activity analysis and cost leadership. *Management Accounting* (UK), Jun 1992.

Borden, JP. Software for activity-based management. *Journal of Cost Management*, Fall 1991.

Borden, JP. Review of literature on activity-based costing. *Journal of Cost Management*, Spring 1990.

Brimson, JA. Technology accounting. *Management Accounting* (US), Mar 1991.

Brimson, J & Fraser, R. The key features of ABB. *Management Accounting* (UK), Jan 1991.

Bromwich, M. *Accounting information for strategic excellence*. Department of Accounting and Finance, London School of Economics and Political Science, London, 1990.

Bromwich, M. Managerial accounting definition and scope — from a managerial view. *Management Accounting* (UK), Sep 1988.

Brunton, NM. Evaluation of overhead allocations. *Management Accounting* (US), Jul 1988.

Callan, JP, Tredup, WN & Wissinger, RS. Journey towards cost management. *Management Accounting* (US), Jul 1991.

Campbell, RJ, Janson, M & Bush, J. Developing strategic cost standards in a machine-paced environment. *Journal of Cost Management*, Winter 1991.

Campi, JP. How to put activity-based cost management to work in a manufacturing environment. *Journal of Cost Management*, Summer 1992.

Carlson, DA. & Young, SM. Activity-based total quality management at American Express. *Journal of Cost Management*, Winter 1993.

Carr, LP & Ponemon, LA. Managers' perception about quality costs. *Journal of Cost Management*, Spring 1992.

Chaffman, BM & Talbott, J. Activity-based costing in a service organization. *CMA Magazine*, Dec–Jan 1991.

CIMA. The many faces of ABC. *Management Accounting* (UK), Sep 1992.

Clark, A & Baxter, A. ABC + ABM = Action: Let's get down to business. *Management Accounting* (UK), Jun 1992.

Clemens, JD. How we changed our accounting system. *Management Accounting* (US), Feb 1991.

Committe, BE & Grinnell, DJ. Predatory pricing, the price-cost test, and activity-based costing. *Journal of Cost Management*, Fall 1992.

Convey, S. Eliminating unproductive activities and processes. *CMA Magazine*, Nov 1991.

Cooper, R. A structured approach to implementing ABC. *Accountancy*, Jun 1991.

Cooper, R. Explicating the logic of ABC. *Management Accounting* (UK), Nov 1990.

Cooper R. & Kaplan, RS. How cost accounting distorts product costs. *Management Accounting* (US), Apr 1988.

Cooper, R, Kaplan, RS, Maisel, LS, Morrissey, E & Oehm, RM. From ABC to ABM. *Management Accounting* (US), Nov 1992.

Cooper, R. ABC: The right approach for you? *Accountancy*, 1991.

Cooper, R. Cost classification in unit-based and activity-based manufacturing cost systems. *Journal of Cost Management*, Fall 1990.

Cooper, R. ABC: A need, not an option. *Accountancy*, Sep 1990.

Cooper, R. The rise of activity based costing — Part one: What is an activity-based cost system? *Journal of Cost Management*, Summer 1988.

Cooper, R. The rise of activity-based costing — Part two: When do you need an activity-based cost system? *Journal of Cost Management*, Fall 1988.

Cooper, R. The rise of activity based costing — Part three: How many cost drivers do you need and how do you select them? *Journal of Cost Management*, Winter 1989.

Cooper, R. The rise of activity based costing – Part four: What do activity based cost systems look like? *Journal of Cost Management*, Spring 1989.

Cooper, R. You need a new cost system when... *Harvard Business Review*, Jan–Feb 1989.

Cooper, R. Five steps to ABC system design. *Accountancy*, Nov 1990.

Cooper, R. Implementing an activity-based cost system. *Journal of Cost Management*, Spring 1990.

Cooper, R & Kaplan, RS. Measure costs right: Make the right decisions. *Harvard Business Review*, Sep–Oct 1988.

Cyr, J. Building success through process improvement. *CA Magazine*, March 1992.

Czyzewski, AB & Hull, RP. Improving profitability with life cycle costing. *Journal of Cost Management*, Summer 1991.

Dale, D. Activity-based cost management. *Australian Accountant*, Mar 1991.

Dale, D. ABCM: Challenging tradition. *Australian Accountant*, Apr 1991.

Dhavale, DG. Activity-based costing in cellular manufacturing systems. *Journal of Cost Management*, Winter 1993.

Dilton-Hill, K & Glad, E. Activity based costing empowers quality management. *Accountancy SA*, Jun 1992.

Dilton-Hill, K & Glad, E. Business process management. *Accountancy SA*, Part 1 — Oct 1992; Part 2 — Nov/Dec 1992.

Dilts, DM & Grabski, SV. Advanced manufacturing technologies: What they can offer management accountants. *Management Accounting*, Feb 1990.

Dolinsky, LR & Vollmann, TE. Transaction-based overhead consideration for product design. *Journal of Cost Management*, Summer 1991.

Drucker, PE. The emerging theory of manufacturing. *Harvard Business Review*, May–Jun 1990.

Drury, C. Activity-based costing. *Management Accounting* (UK), Sep 1989.

Dugdale, D. Costing systems in transition. *Management Accounting* (UK), Jan 1990.

Dugdale, D. The uses of activity-based costing. *Management Accounting* (UK), Oct 1990.

Eccles, R. The performance measurement manifesto. *Harvard Business Review*, Jan–Feb 1991.

Edersheim, EH & Vandenbosch, B. How to make accounting count: Causal-based accounting. *Journal of Cost Management*, Winter 1991.

Eiler, R, Goletz, W & Keegan, D. Is your cost accounting up to date? *Harvard Business Review*, Jul–Aug 1982.

Eiler, RG & Campi, JP. Implementing activity-based costing at a process company. *Journal of Cost Management*, Spring 1990.

Emore, JR & Ness, JA. The slow pace of meaningful change in cost systems. *Journal of Cost Management*, Winter 1991.

Engwall, RL. Planning is critical to investment justification. *Journal of Cost Management*, Summer 1990.

Ezzamel, M, Hoskin, K & Macve, R. Managing it all by numbers: A review of Johnson & Kaplan's "Relevance lost". *Accounting and Business Research*, vol 20, no 78, 1990.

Ferrara, WL. The new cost-management accounting: More questions than answers. *Management Accounting* (US), Oct 1990.

Fisher, J. Use of nonfinancial performance measures. *Journal of Cost Management*, Spring 1992.

Flatt, JG. Intelligent cost cutting. *CA Magazine*, Nov 1992.

Fox, R. ABC: A comment about the logic. *Management Accounting* (UK), Oct 1991.

Frank, GB, Fisher, SA & Wilkie, AR. Linking cost to price and profit. *Management Accounting* (US), Jun 1989.

Freeman, A. Understanding costs. *Australian Accountant*, Feb 1993.

Galloway, D & Waldron, D. Throughput accounting: The need for a new language for manufacturing. *Management Accounting* (UK), Nov 1988.

Gardner, MJ & Lammers, LE. Cost accounting in large banks. *Management Accounting* (US), Apr 1988.

Gietzmann, MB. *The development and design of an activity based budgeting system.* London School of Economics and Political Science, London, 1992.

Glad, E & Dilton-Hill, K. Activity based costing — an overview. *Accountancy SA*, May 1992.

Glad, E & Dilton-Hill, K. Cost management in world class companies. *Accountancy SA*, May 1993.

Glad, E. Implementation considerations for an ABC system. *Management Accounting* (UK), Jul/Aug 1993.

Green, FB & Amenkhienan, FE. Accounting innovations: A cross-sectional survey of manufacturing firms. *Journal of Cost Management*, Spring 1992.

Green, FB, Amenkhienan, F & Johnson, G. Performance measures and JTT. *Management Accounting* (US), Feb 1991.

Greene, AH & Flentov, P. Managing performance: Maximizing the benefit of activity-based costing. *Journal of Cost Management*, Summer 1990.

Greenwood, TG & Reeve, JM. Activity-based cost management for continuous improvement: A process design framework. *Journal of Cost Management*, Winter 1992.

Gupta, YP. Advanced manufacturing systems: Analysis of trends. *Management Decision*, vol 27, no 5.

Haedicke, J & Feil, D. In a DOD environment Hughes Aircraft sets the standard for ABC. *Management Accounting*, Feb 1991.

Harr, DJ. How activity accounting works in government. *Management Accounting* (US), Sep 1990.

Harvey, M. Activity based budgeting. *Certified Accountant*, Jul 1991.

Hayde, D. Activity based costing — putting relevance back into cost accounting. *Accountants' Journal*, Feb 1990.

Hazell, M & Morrow, M. Performance measurement and benchmarking. *Management Accounting* (UK), Dec 1992.

Hendricks, JA. Applying cost accounting to factory automation. *Management Accounting* (US), Dec 1988.

Hill, RA. Activity accounting: An application of input output analysis. *Certified Accountants Students Newsletter*, Mar 1989.

Hiromoto, T. Another hidden edge Japanese management accounting. *Harvard Business Review*, Jul–Aug 1988.

Hirsch, ML (Jr) & Nibbelin, MC. Incremental, separable, sunk, and common costs in activity-based costing. *Journal of Cost Management*, Spring 1992.

Holford, D & McAuley, L. Activity based accounting in the national health service. *Management Accounting* (UK), Oct 1987.

Howell, RA & Soucy, SR. Cost accounting in the new manufacturing environment. *Management Accounting* (US), Aug 1987.

Howell, RA & Soucy, SR. The new manufacturing environment: Major trends for management accountants. *Management Accounting* (US), Jul 1987.

Howell, RA & Stephen, RS. Customer profitability as critical as product profitability. *Management Accounting* (US), Oct 1990.

Innes, J. & Mitchell, F. Activity based cost management: A case study of development and implementation. *CIMA*.

Innes, J & Mitchell, F. Activity based costing research. *Management Accounting* (UK), May 1990.

Isenberg, DJ. The tactics of strategic opportunism. *Harvard Business Review*, Mar–Apr 1987.

James, D. Clock-watching becomes a mark of efficiency. *BRW International*, Aug 1991.

Jeans, M & Morrow, M. The practicalities of using activity-based costing. *Management Accounting* (UK), Nov 1989.

Johnson, HT. Activity-based management: Past, present and future. *Engineering Economist*, Spring 1991.

Johnson, HT. Beyond product costing: A challenge to cost management's conventional wisdom. *Journal of Cost Management*, Fall 1990.

Johnson, HT. Activity-based information: A blueprint for world-class management accounting. *Management Accounting (US)*, Jun 1988.

Johnson, HT. It's time to stop overselling activity based concepts. *Management Accounting* (US), Sep 1992.

Johnson, HT & Kaplan, RS. The rise and fall of management accounting. *Management Accounting* (US), Jan 1987.

Jones, LF. Product costing at Caterpillar. *Management Accounting* (US), Feb 1991.

Kaplan, RS. The four-stage model of cost systems design. *Management Accounting* (US), Feb 1990.

Johnson, HT. It's time to stop overselling activity based concepts. *Management Accounting* (US), Sep 1992.

Kaplan, RS. Accounting lag: The obsolescence of cost accounting systems. *California Management Review*, Winter 1986.

Kaplan, RS. In defence of activity-based cost management. *Management Accounting* (US), Nov 1992.

Kaplan, RS. One cost system isn't enough. *Harvard Business Review*, Jan–Feb 1988.

Kaplan, RS. Measures for manufacturing excellence: A summary. *Journal of Cost Management*, Fall 1990.

Keys, DE & Reding, KF. What management accountants need to know. *Management Accounting* (US), Jan 1992.

King, AM, Lee, RA, Piper, JA & Whiter, J. Information technology's impact on management accounting. *Management Accounting* (UK), Jun 1987.

King, AM. The current status of activity-based costing. *Management Accounting* (UK), Sep 1991.

Kingscott, T. Opportunity based accounting: Better than ABC. *Management Accounting* (UK), Oct 1991.

Koehler, RW. Triple-threat strategy. *Management Accounting* (US), Oct 1991.

Lamond, S. Activity-based management: An Australian perspective. *Journal of Cost Management*, Summer 1992.

Lee, JY. Activity-based costing at CAL Electronic Circuits. *Management Accounting*, Oct 1990.

Le Saint-Grant, F. Performance evaluation: All the answers. *Management Accounting* (UK), Apr 1992.

Lewis, RJ. Activity-based costing for marketing. *Management Accounting* (UK), Nov 1991.

Lippa, V. Measuring performance with synchronous management. *Management Accounting* (US), Feb 1990.

Lovell, A. Management accounting under challenge. *Management Accounting* (UK), Dec 1988.

MacArthur, John B. Activity-based costing: How many cost drivers do you want? *Journal of Cost Management*, Fall 1992.

MacArthur, JB. The ABC/JIT costing continuum. *Journal of Cost Management*, Winter 1992.

MacArthur, JB. Zero-base activity based costing. *Journal of Cost Management*, Winter 1993.

MacErlean, N. A new dawn for western management? *Accountancy*, Jun 1993.

Macintyre, DK. Marketing costs: A new look. *Management Accounting* (US), Mar 1983.

Maira, A. Rebuilding US manufacturing industries for sustainable performance acceleeration. *Journal of Cost Management*, Spring 1993.

Maisel, LS. Performance measurement: The balanced scorecard approach. *Journal of Cost Management*, Summer 1992.

Malcom, RE. Overhead control implications of activity costing. *Accounting Horizons, Dec 1991.*

Mateer, RW. The Byrd amendment's "anti-influence" rules on defense consultants. *Journal of Cost Management*, Fall 1990.

McNair, CJ Interdependence and control: Traditional vs. activity-based responsibility accounting. *Journal of Cost Management*, Summer 1990.

McNair, CJ & Carr, L. Toward value-added management accounting. *CMA Magazine*, Apr 1991.

Mecimore, CD. Product costing in a high tech environment. *Journal of Cost Management*, Winter 1988.

Menzano, RJ. Activity based costing for information systems. *Journal of Cost Management*, Spring, 1991.

Miller, JA. Designing and implementing a new cost management system. *Journal of Cost Management*, Winter 1992.

Mills, R & Cave, M. Overhead cost allocation in service organisations. *Management Accounting* (UK), Jun 1990.

Moravec, RD & Yoemans, MS. Using ABC to support business re-engineering in the Department of Defense. *Journal of Cost Management*, Summer 1992.

Morrow, M & Connolly, T. The emergence of activity based budgeting. *Management Accounting* (UK), Feb 1991.

Morrow, M & Hazell, M. Activity mapping for business process redesign. *Management Accounting* (UK), Feb 1992.

Morrow, M & Scott, P. Easy as ABC. *Accountancy Age*, Sep 1989.

Morse, WJ. A handle on quality cost. *CMA Magazine*, Feb 1993.

Nanni, AJ, Dixon, JR & Vollmann, TE. Strategic control and performance measurement. *Journal of Cost Management*, Summer 1990.

Northey, P. Cut total costs with cycle time reduction. *CMA Magazine*, Feb 1991.

Novin, AM. Applying overhead: How to find the right bases and rates. *Management Accounting* (US), Mar 1992.

O'Guin, M. Focus the factory with activity-based costing. *Management Accounting* (US), Feb 1990.

Ostrenga, MR. Activities: The focal point of total cost management. *Management Accounting* (US), Feb 1990.

Ostrenga, MR & Probst, FR. Process value analysis: The missing link in cost management. *Journal of Cost Management*, Fall 1992.

Pasewark, WR. The evolution of quality control costs in U.S. manufacturing. *Journal of Cost Management*, Spring 1991.

Peavey, DE. Battle at the GAAP? It's time for a change. *Management Accounting* (US), Feb 1990.

Pinnnock, A. Direct product profitability. *Management Accounting* (UK), Oct 1989.

Piper, JA & Walley, P. ABC relevance not found. *Management Accounting* (UK), Mar 1991.

Piper, JA & Walley, P. Testing ABC logic. *Management Accounting* (UK), Sep 1990.

Ponemon, LA. Accounting for quality costs. *Journal of Cost Management*, Fall 1990.

Primrose, PL. Is anything really wrong with cost management? *Journal of Cost Management*, Spring 1992.

Pryor, TE. Activity accounting: The key to waste elimination. *Corporate Controller*, Sep/Oct 1988.

Raffish, N. How much does that product really cost? *Management Accounting* (US), Mar 1991.

Raffish, N. & Turney, PBB. Glossary of activity-based management. *Journal of Cost Management*, Fall 1991.

Ray, MR & Schlie, TW. Activity based management of innovation and R & D operations. *Journal of Cost Management*, Winter 1993.

Reeve, JM. The impact of continuous improvement on the design of activity-based cost systems. *Journal of Cost Management*, Summer 1990.

Rezaee, Z. Synchronous manufacturing: The measure of excellence. *CMA Magazine*, Sep 1992.

Romano, PL. Where is cost management going? *Management Accounting* (US), Aug 1990.

Romano, P. Trends in management accounting. *Management Accounting* (US), Aug 1990.

Romano, PL. Activity accounting — An update — Part 1. *Management Accounting* (US), May 1989.

Romano, PL. Activity accounting — An update — Part 2. *Management Accounting* (US), Jun 1989.

Roth, HP & Borthick, AF. Getting closer to real product costs. *Management Accounting* (US), May 1989.

Roth, HP & Borthick, AF. Are you distorting costs by violating ABC assumptions? *Management Accounting* (US), Nov 1991.

Roth, HP & Morse, WJ. What are your client's quality costs? *CPA Journal*, Apr 1988.

Roth, HP & Sims, LT. Costing for warehousing and distribution. *Management Accounting* (US), Aug 1991.

Scapens, R. Research into management accounting practice. *Management Accounting*, Dec 1988.

Schiff, JB & Schiff, AI. High-tech cost accounting for the F-16. *Management Accounting*, Sep 1988.

Schnoebelen, SC. Integrating an advanced cost management system into operating systems (Part 1). *Journal of Cost Management*, Winter 1993.

Scott, P & Morrow, M. Activity-based costing and make-or-buy decision. *Journal of Cost Management*, Winter 1991.

Seed, AH. Improving cost management. *Management Accounting* (US), Feb 1990.

Sellenheim, MR, JI Case company performance measurement. *Management Accounting* (US), Sep 1991.

Sephton, M. & Ward, T. ABC In retail financial services. *Management Accounting* (UK), Apr 1990.

Shank, JK & Govindarajan, V. Strategic cost management and the value chain. *Journal of Cost Management*, Winter 1992.

Shank, JK. Strategic cost management: New wine or just new bottles? *Journal of Management Accounting Research*, Fall 1989.

Sharman, P. A practical look at activity-based costing. *CMA Magazine*, Feb 1990.

Sharman, P. Winning techniques for productivity: The activity link. *CMA Magazine*, Feb 1991.

Sharman, P. Activity-based costing: A practitioner's update. *CMA Magazine*, Jul–Aug 1991.

Sharman, P. The cost management innovators. *CMA Magazine*, Jun 1991.

Sharman, PA. Activity-based management: A growing practice. *CMA Magazine*, Mar 1993.

Sharp, D & Christensen, LF. A new view of activity-based costing. *Management Accounting*, Sep 1991.

Sheridan, T. Don't count your costs — manage them. *Management Accounting* (UK), Feb 1989.

Shields, MD & Young, SM. Effective long-term cost reduction: A strategic perspective. *Journal of Cost Management*, Spring 1992.

Shields, MD & Young, SM. Managing product life cycle costs: An organizational model. *Journal of Cost Management*, Fall 1991.

Smith, KV & Leksan, MP. A manufacturing case study on activity based costing. *Journal of Cost Management*, Summer 1991.

Soloway, LJ. Using activity based management systems in aerospace and defence companies. *Journal of Cost Management*, Winter 1993.

Sourwine, DA. Does your system need repair? *Management Accounting* (US), Feb 1989.

Stalk, G. Time — the next source of competitive advantage. *Harvard Business Review*, Jul–Aug 1988.

Steedle, LF. Has productivity measurement outgrown infancy? *Management Accounting* (US), Aug 1990.

Steimer, TE. Activity-based accounting for total quality. *Management Accounting*, Oct 1990.

Thilmony, H. Product costing: One set of books or two? *Journal of Cost Management*, Winter 1993.

Tricker, RI. The management accountant as strategist. *Management Accountant, (UK)*, Dec 1989.

Troxel, RB & Weber, MG. The evolution of activity-based costing. *Journal of Cost Management*, Spring 1990.

Troxler, JW. Estimating the cost impact of flexible manufacturing. *Journal of Cost Management*, Summer 1990.

Turney, PBB. Activity-based management: ABM puts ABC information to work. *Management Accounting* (US), Jan 1992.

Turney, PBB. How activity-based costing helps reduce cost. *Journal of Cost Management*, Winter 1991.

Turney, PBB & Reeve, JM. The impact of continuous improvement on the design of activity based cost systems. *Journal of Cost Management*, Summer 1990.

Turney, PBB. Ten myths about implementing an activity-based cost system. *Journal of Cost Management*, Spring 1990.

Turney, PBB. Using activity based costing to achieve manufacturing excellence. *Journal of Cost Management*, Summer 1989.

Turney, PBB. What is the scope of activity based costing? *Journal of Cost Management*, Winter 1990.

Turney, PBB. What an activity-based cost model looks like. *Journal of Cost Management*, Winter 1992.

Tyson, T, Weisenfeld, L & Stout, D. Running actual costs vs standard costs. *Management Accounting*, Aug 1989.

Tyson, T. The use of bar coding in activity-based costing. *Journal of Cost Management*, Winter 1991.

Walker, M. ABC using product attributes. *Management Accounting* (UK), Oct 1991.

Walker, M. Attribute based costing. *Australian Accountant*, Mar 1992.

Ward, T. & Ketan, P. ABC — A framework for improving shareholder value. *Management Accounting* (UK), Jul–Aug 1990.

Weisman, DL. How cost allocation system can lead managers astray. *Journal of Cost Management*, Spring 1991.

Wilson, R. Strategic cost analysis. *Management Accounting* (UK), Oct 1990.

Woods, MD. Economic choices with ABC. *Management Accounting* (USA), Dec 1992.

Youde, RK. Cost-of-quality reporting: How we see it. *Management Accounting* (US), Jan 1992.

Index